Bring Down the Walls

Bring Down the Walls

Lebanon's Postwar Challenge

Carole H. Dagher

palgrave

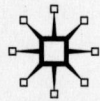

BRING DOWN THE WALLS
Copyright © Carole H. Dagher, 2000. All rights reserved. No part of this book may be used or reproduced in any manner whatsoever without written permission except in the case of brief quotations embodied in critical articles or reviews.

First published in hardcover in 2000 by Palgrave
First PALGRAVE™ paperback edition: December 2001
175 Fifth Avenue, New York, N.Y. 10010 and
Houndmills, Basingstoke, England RG21 6XS
Companies and representatives throughout the world.

PALGRAVE is the new global publishing imprint of St. Martin's Press LLC Scholarly and Reference Division and Palgrave Publishers Ltd (formerly Macmillan Press Ltd).

ISBN 0-312-22920-8 (hardback)
ISBN 0-312-29336-4 (paperback)

Library of Congress Cataloging-in-Publication Data
Dagher, Carole
Bring down the walls : Lebanon's post-war challenge / Carole H. Dagher.
    p. cm.
  Includes bibliographical references and index.
  ISBN 0-312-22920-8 (cloth)
  ISBN 0-312-29336-4 (paperback)
  1. Lebanon—Politics and government—1990- 2. Religion and politics—Lebanon. 3. Political culture—Lebanon. I. Title.

DS87.54D34 2000
956.9204'4—dc21   99–41936
                                                                     CIP

Design by Letra Libre, Inc.

First paperback edition: December 2001
10 9 8 7 6 5 4 3 2 1

A catalogue record for this book is available from the British Library.

Printed in the United States of America

To my brothers,
Nagib and Nabil,
who, like millions before them,
have "chosen" to plant in the West the seeds
of their Lebanese and Maronite
heritage, talents, and hope

Dear young, . . . you are the treasure of Lebanon. . . . Bring down the walls erected in the painful past, don't raise new barricades in your country. Build new bridges of communication among people, families and communities. Make gestures of reconciliation that will turn distrust into trust. The changes you are aspiring for in your country start with a transformation of the hearts. Don't forget your Christian identity. It is your glory, it is your hope, it is your mission.

> —Pope John Paul II in his message to the youth of Lebanon,
> at Notre-Dame of Harissa, May 10, 1997.

You're probably the only country in the world where civilization is born and is still bearing fruits. A country where Christians of all confessions are assembled in such a tiny space, and where the great non-Christian religions are also present. . . . Because of your diversity, you can achieve what is impossible to do elsewhere in Europe where the Eastern and the Western lungs of the Church are choking one another instead of breathing together. Because you are a people who has never ceased to pray and to believe, you can advance the unity of the Christians much easier than in Paris, Geneva, Moscow or New York. . . . You are probably the only ones in the world to be in a situation one might describe as ambiguous, because you belong to two cultures at the same time. But this is why it is also the only place in the world, here in the Middle East, where a true dialogue can take place and where Christianity, Islam and Judaism can meet in mutual respect and freedom. You are ascribed to be the bridge between these worlds originating from the same trunk. If you cannot make it, the world won't be able to make it.

> —Cardinal Jean-Marie Lustiger, Archbishop of Paris,
> at Notre-Dame of Harissa, Lebanon, October 1995.

If Lebanese are put in the difficult situation of having to choose between conviviality and freedom, Lebanese people, and the Christians first, will not hesitate: they will choose freedom.

> —Maronite Patriarch Nasrallah Sfeir, at the inauguration of the meeting of the
> Assembly of Catholic Patriarchs and Bishops, November 30, 1992.

Lebanese Muslims cannot exist as Lebanese without the Christians, and Christian Lebanese cannot exist as Lebanese without the Muslims. Lebanon is not Lebanon without the Christians.

> —Sheikh Mohammed Mehdi Shamseddine,
> head of the Islamic Shi'a Supreme Council

In Lebanon, we have too much sectarianism and too little of religion. If we want to suppress confessionalism, we have to deepen real Christian and Muslim values.

—Sheikh Mohammed Hussein Fadlallah,
spiritual mentor of Hezbollah

Some Islamist groups have a tendency to eyeball Arab Christians with suspicions, and to view them as the bulwark of the West (or the cat's paw for western influence). They are not. Nor are they the fifth column of colonialism. . . . Christianity is not an ideology imported from the West.

—Mohammad Sammak,
in Introduction to the Muslim-Christian Dialogue

Eastern Christians are a bridge between Arab and Western civilizations. Their demise and exodus from the Arab countries will provide an excuse for those who are publicizing the image of an intolerant Islam that is unable to live and interact with another religion or another culture and that does not respect freedom of religion and belief.

—Michel Sabbah, Latin Patriarch of Jerusalem

Contents

Acknowledgments — xi
Foreword   John L. Esposito — xiii

Introduction — 1

Part I
Cognitive Coexistence

Chapter 1   Christian Soul-Searching — 15
Chapter 2   Muslim Self-Assertion — 33
Chapter 3   Dialogue: A Necessity or a Burden? — 49

Part II
Coexistence in Facts and Figures

Chapter 4   Sharing Exile — 67
Chapter 5   Broken and Forfeited Bonds to the Land — 79
Chapter 6   A Synod for Lebanon — 91
Chapter 7   Three Weeks in Rome — 107
Chapter 8   Cloaked in Coexistence — 123
Chapter 9   The Swings of the Pendulum — 137
Chapter 10   Coexistence in Uniform — 159

Part III
The Leaven in the Dough

Chapter 11   The Democracy of the National Pact — 167
Chapter 12   John Paul II in Lebanon — 183
Chapter 13   Peace without Eastern Christians? — 201

Conclusion — 217
Notes — 221
Selected Bibliography — 241
Index — 245

Acknowledgments

This book could not have been written without the help and support of numerous individuals. My thanks go first to John L. Esposito, whose incisive comments and welcome advice have helped me keep my analysis on track. From the beginning, he believed this project was meaningful and provided me with the proper environment to work and write, at the Center for Muslim-Christian Understanding at Georgetown University. There I was able to interact professionally and privately with the faculty and the staff and with my colleague research associates, in a busy and cordial atmosphere. Professor John O. Voll kindly gave me the benefit of his scholarly and friendly counsel. Professors Yvonne Haddad and Diane Apostolos-Cappadona deserve a special mention too, for their patience and wit, as they put up with their angst-ridden colleague next door who had taken on an unmerciful publishing deadline and who kept interrupting them with her inquiries.

I am also grateful to Father Drew Christiansen, S.J., at the Woodstock Theological Center (WTC) at Georgetown University, who has been instrumental in enabling me to pursue my work as a visiting fellow at WTC. I owe him the completion of this book that has been on my mind for a couple of years, as I owe to the whole family of the Woodstock Theological Center the invaluable moments I have shared with my five fellow colleagues at the Center, Izu, Sekhar, Cristina, Budi, and Terence. The strong support, friendship, and commitment to work of all the staff and colleagues at the Woodstock Theological Center as well as our "brown bag lunch" presentations have been an inspiration to me and stimulated my thinking. I would like to thank particularly Father James Connors, S.J., director of the Center, for his warm and discreet presence, his strong sense of humor and continuous encouragement.

I would also like to express my appreciation to Richard N. Haass from the Brookings Institution, and to Father John J. Donohue, S. J., from St-Joseph University, Beirut, for taking the time to read my manuscript and to make useful suggestions. Equally, I would like to thank S. Enders Wimbush for his professional advice, guidance, and enthusiasm.

Finally, I want to mention some individuals who were inspirational figures to me as I tackled this delicate topic of Christian-Muslim relations in the Middle East: Father Michel Hayek, for the long-distance conversations I engaged him in while I wrote the manuscript, his contagious spirituality, and the insightful remarks he shared with me; former Papal Nuncio in Lebanon Pablo Puente, for having fulfilled with deep conviction and personal commitment a most difficult task during the crucial years and gruesome moments of his mission in Lebanon; and the late Father Yoakim Moubarac, who relentlessly called for an aggiornamento of the Lebanese Maronite Church in the postwar era.

I have been gifted with admirable parents, Henry and Renée Dagher. Their unfailing support and affection have been, throughout the years, indispensable assets in my life and career. In the era of global communications, my dad even converted to the Internet to follow up on my work via email and to keep dispensing to me his subtle humor and much needed wisdom. I would like to thank them for their patience and love and thank the Lord for having them.

I also would like to extend my special thanks to the team of St. Martin's Press, and especially to senior editor Karen Wolny for her judicious decisions, to my production editor Ruth Mannes, and to Brook Partner, who has done a wonderful proofreading job.

Last, but certainly not least, I want to thank my friends: Lydia Borland for having been there all the time; Nassib Ziadé, for his genuine kindness; and Mark Gage. Their warm and supportive presence made it a lot easier for me to go through the whole writing process without arriving breathless to the finish!

Foreword

John L. Esposito

"The Lebanon That Was, Is No More." These words were chosen by a good friend, who had spent much of his life in Lebanon, as the title for an article on the situation in Lebanon during its long, bloody civil war. Like Iran, Lebanon had been regarded as among the most stable, developed and prosperous Middle East countries. Beirut, its capital, often was referred to as the Paris of the Middle East, a center of commerce, banking, and education. Lebanon was also multireligious as well as multilingual country celebrated as a land where Christians, Muslims, and Druze lived side-by-side. The article's title reflected the transition that had taken place as the Lebanese mosaic was shattered by a civil war that exacerbated and reflected sectarian differences.

Many factors contributed to the Lebanese civil war. Among the more important were demographic changes (Sunni and Shi'i Muslims had grown and now outnumbered Christians); Palestinian emigration to Lebanon after being driven out of Jordan and PLO military actions against Israel; Israel's invasion of Lebanon, the march to Beirut to drive the PLO out of Lebanon, and Israeli occupation of southern Lebanon; the Iranian revolution, in particular Iran's training and support for Hizbollah and Islamic Jihad. In the aftermath of the Iranian revolution, it became the site of a major theater of Shi'i political activism where Shi'i militias struggled with other Lebanese militias, Israeli troops, Western presence and intervention, in particular American military, government and civilian personnel.

Despite the positive aspects of the Lebanese mosaic, religious sectarianism or communalism had grown out of a history not just of cooperation but of conflict. Mutual cooperation was accompanied by mutual suspicion and distrust, the maintenance of militias, competition and, at times, conflict. The system of proportional representation, based on the 1932 census, ostensibly to represent an equitable distribution of power among Maronite Christians, Sunni, Shi'i, and Druze in government, the bureaucracy, and the military became a means to safeguard the status quo in a Christian-, more precisely a Maronite-, dominated state. Despite, or rather because of, the growth of the Muslim population, no new census was conducted, fueling Muslim charges, especially from the Shi'i community, of inequity and calls for a more equitable distribution of power and wealth. Musa Sadr, a charismatic Shi'i religious leader, who had emigrated from Iran and studied at Qom, emerged as symbol and effective mobilizer of a social movement, the Movement for the Dispossessed, and later its militia and party AMAL (acronym for the Lebanese Resistance Battalions). Hizbollah (the Party of God), seemed to erupt on the scene, a result of the Israeli invasion of Lebanon and the Iranian revolution. With training and support from Iran, it would become a feared and effective militia. The more secular nationalist objectives of AMAL were rejected by a Hizbollah that called for the imposition of an Islamic state.

While Lebanon's civil war resulted from multiple political, economic, and social factors, religion (religious leaders/actors, symbols, and ideologies) did play a role in reinforcing community identity and loyalties, mobilizing popular support and legitimating claims, agendas, and actions. The war not only pitted Muslims against Christians but it also fueled intercommunal rivalries and warfare. AMAL fought Hizbollah and troops (the Lebanese Army's Christian units) loyal to General Aoun (a Maronite Catholic) who engaged the Lebanese Forces of his Christian rival, Samir Geagea as well as Syrian-backed Muslim army units and militias. While some religious leaders called for moderation, others contributed to and legitimated the violence and bloodshed, and with it, a legacy of suspicion and hatred. Many questioned whether Lebanon could ever "come back," could ever recover. The political, economic, and social (human) devastation of the war seemed to be symbolized by the many villages and neighborhoods of cities that were destroyed. The rebuilding of post-civil-war Lebanon has not been without major political, financial, and ecological problems. Lebanon is reemerging from the ravages of war; however, it is a process that occurs in an environment of cynicism and distrust as much as hope. Rebuilding Lebanon as a nation is as much about people as it is about institutions. The physical rebuilding of the country has been easier than the human/spiritual healing that interreligious/communal warfare requires.

In *Bring Down the Walls*, Carol Dagher, a Lebanese journalist and writer, offers a perceptive and at times provocative picture, and analysis of the realties and challenges of reconciliation in Lebanon today. She provides a rare insight into religiopolitical issues and the human dimensions of the struggle to restore the soul of Lebanon. As Dagher notes, while many have been cynical about the real possibility and the value of dialogue, dubbing it "mutual deceit" or "reciprocal trickery," there is no other real alternative. Yet the challenges are many. They reflect the changing demographic realities of Lebanon and of the Arab world, where the numbers of Christians and their political and economic status have diminished as well as the need for Arab-Christians and Muslims to redefine and broaden the pluralism and tolerance of their confessional communities and societies. Dagher chronicles the struggle of the Christians of Lebanon, in particular Maronite Christians, as they grapple with a loss of the privileged position, their growing fear of marginalization, and the response of Muslim leaders. *Bring Down the Walls* reveals the fears and hopes, the debates and conflicts, which have attended the rebuilding or perhaps more accurately recasting of Lebanese national identity. While it focuses on the plight and struggle of Christians, Lebanon's religious and political leaders as well as the Vatican, *Bring Down the Walls* highlights the multireligious dimension of this process as Lebanese Christians and Muslims seek to rebuild Lebanon. The Lebanon that was may be no more. However, as Dagher persuasively argues, the hope and task for Lebanon's Christians and Muslims is to acknowledge that national unity must be rebuilt upon a process of national reconciliation. Acknowledgment of past history and mutual grievances must be transformed by the recognition of their mutual interests and common religious heritage, as they seek to build the bridges of mutual understanding and respect necessary for the reemergence and renaissance of an independent and prosperous Lebanon once again.

Introduction

This book intends to warn against a radical metamorphosis occurring in Middle Eastern societies and culture that would probably condemn them to a long-lasting decay in the age of globalization, equal only to the state of dormancy experienced during the four hundred years under Ottoman rule, before the Arab renaissance of the late nineteenth century shook up the dust of obsolescence from Arab minds, literature, and societies. Only this time there would be no renaissance, since the cosmopolitan forces who initiated it a century ago might not be there anymore. A capital trait of Arab civilization, that was once its main asset, is indeed about to disappear at the turn of the third millennium: the thriving force of diversity, also known as pluralism.

It is mainly through its various religious and ethnic groups, primarily the Eastern Christians, that the Arab world breathed the oxygen of modernity and drew its ingenuity. But Eastern Christians are emigrating in throngs from the region that saw the birth of Christianity and was once overwhelmingly Christian. Christian presence in the Middle East is in rapid decline, even on the verge of extinction, if one is to believe some demographers and sociologists who consider that the slow but steady emigration flow to the West (Europe, the Americas, Canada, as well as Australia) along with the "brain drain" of intelligentsia will spell the extinction of Christian presence in the region in fifty years or so. As Eastern Christians are dissolving in Western societies through an inevitable process called "integration," their Christian siblings remaining in their fatherland with their political leaders and their religious authorities, with great anxiety are seeing themselves turn into feeble minorities. This means they will continue getting pushed to the sidelines of power, seeing their specificity threatened, their right to be different denied, their cultural overtures to the outside world criticized, and their way of life contested. But the fate of Eastern Christians could have—as it has already—dire implications for the whole region.

The marginalization of Christian minorities in an increasingly Islamic-oriented environment translates into an absence of democracy detrimental to all groups. Meanwhile, the Arab world, caught in the quagmire of a long and complicated peace process, is slipping into an economic recession and is witnessing an Islamic revival that puts religious extremists at odds with secularists in their community, and even Muslim fundamentalists at odds with the reformists within the Islamic trend. The outcome of this intellectual and political strife inside Muslim societies will have, no doubt, important consequences for all religious minorities in the Middle East.

Only in the last few years of the twentieth century has the West manifested a little bit more interest in the fate of minorities living in the Middle East, among them Eastern Christians. Books, conferences, seminars, and, in the United States, legislation destined to thwart religious persecution in various corners of the globe have sprung up almost overnight, reminding the larger public of the existence of these descendants of Jesus' disciples who, in early first-century Antioch, were called Christians for the first time.

This sudden interest has been triggered partly by the saliency of ethno-religious conflicts after the end of the Cold War, and mostly by doctrines depicting Islam as the major threat to the West. Soon, "Islam and the West" became the diptych of a new era epitomized by what Samuel Huntington called the "Clash of Civilizations." This bombshell theory of his exploded in the academic and political circles, leaving the impact of a nuclear mushroom. It basically accredited the notion that Islam cannot live with any other religion or culture. Yet under Khatami's Iran, almost twenty years after the Iranian revolution, the "dialogue of civilizations" Khatami called for in his famed CNN interview became also the "counter-balance" notion that many a scholar, in the West as well as in "the Rest" (the rest of the world, in Huntington's words), found attractive and worth exploring.

But in their post–Cold War theories, Western scholars have overlooked the fact that "civilizational dialogue" between Islam and the West starts between Christians and Muslims of the Middle East. By their culture, Christian communities in that region belong to the Arab civilization. By their religion, they share the values and the heritage of the West. They are a bridge between Islam and the West and in that regard they are geographically and culturally at the cutting edge of civilizational dialogue.

Only a few intellectuals in Lebanon and Egypt are aware of the dangers deriving from the eventual breakup of the historical Christian-Muslim association in the Middle East. The disappearance of Christianity from its birthplace would confirm Huntington's theory; it would also deprive Islam from its centennial partner in the making of the Arab civilization and from a useful intermediary in its clashing dialogue with the West. Furthermore, it would leave Islam isolated in the travails of a hypothetical peace in the Middle East.

In most of the region, Christian voices have become echoes from the past or are not heard anymore. An irreversible process of dilution and emigration has already cast its spell over coexistence. Lebanon, by reason of its relatively large Christian population, is the last bastion of such coexistence. In its fifteen-year-long internal and internationalized war, Lebanon was the precursor of the ethno-religious conflicts that are dismembering so many countries today. But it emerged from its ordeal still unified, with one central government, one Parliament for one people, and all the formal attributes of a sovereign (yet non-independent) State on an undivided (although occupied) territory. Most important of all, Lebanon still stands today (and maybe more than ever) as the geographical and national platform of Christian-Muslim relations in the Middle East. Those relations are ultimately expressed in the communal representation and power-sharing formula established by the founding fathers of independent Lebanon and kept alive despite the war. This unique concept of Christian-Muslim power-sharing that singularized Lebanon is nonetheless challenged today by the waning powers of the Christians in the Ta'if accords that redesigned the Lebanese formula dating back to the 1943 National Pact. Adding up to their dwindling demographics and the emigration appeal among the young, these facts make Lebanese Christians feel—and fear—that time is counted for them. Would the Pact still hold on in case the Christians become a minority in the country created for them and by them in the Middle East? Would Lebanon still be Lebanon without the input and the dynamism of its Christian population? How do Lebanese Muslims perceive the outcome of these eventual changes?

In many ways, the destiny of the Christians of Lebanon condenses the fate of Eastern Christians. This explains why the Holy See, and Pope John Paul II in particular, have braced over the years to save Lebanon and the Christians of Lebanon. Throughout its tumultuous history, Lebanon has been for all persecuted minorities of the Middle East a safe haven where these groups found the freedom that enabled them to blossom and prosper. For many, it has also been their gate to the West, where they finally emigrated. Still, all churches of the Orient have a seat in Lebanon. This country is their anchor to the region, to their faith, to their identity and traditions.

The heads of the Christian churches in the Middle East acknowledge that the success or failure of the Lebanese power-sharing formula in the postwar era will determine the fate of Christian communities throughout the region. They, along with many observers, estimate that if the political endeavor in Lebanon fails to guarantee participation and political representation of minorities in public life, then emigration will accelerate, affecting not only the Christian elite but most probably the modern Muslim elite as well. These developments would inevitably reflect on the cultural landscape of the Arab world, perhaps changing it drastically and condemning it to fall ever farther behind in the competitive universe of the twenty-first century.

Lebanon's failure as a meaningful experience will toll the demise of a once vibrant Arab culture and will impact on the nature of Islam as well, as a once tolerant religion. It will also signal the new era of a "Church of silence," surviving in the land of its Lord but with its voice and bells stifled by the sands of intolerance and totalitarianism, its communities weighed down with the tragedies linked to decades of unmerciful Arab-Israeli struggle. If the foundation of the State of Israel has had terrible implications and incited tremendous sufferings for the peoples of the region, including Christians in Palestine as well as in the rest of the Arab world, very often the Arab-Israeli conflict has also provided a good excuse for the regional rulers to avoid any democratic development in their countries and to exclude minority groups from decision-making.

Most contemporary Arab political systems have indeed failed to handle the delicate problem of ethno-sectarian participation successfully and to provide for a properly inclusive environment. Whereas Lebanon is the sole Middle Eastern country to have engaged in a historical attempt to develop a constitutional modus vivendi for its several religious communities, this political engineering is only the visible part of the "iceberg": it is the translation of a certain equilibrium (numerical, cultural, and economic) between the various sectarian groups and minorities that compose the Lebanese society. Does the Lebanese formula of Christian-Muslim power-sharing still have any realistic prospects for the future? Is it an exception or would it be a model of Christian-Muslim nation-building? What would be the impact of the abolition of "political confessionalism" (a constitutional provision that triggers intense debate) on the future of political participation for all minorities?

To assess the future prospects of political participation, it is thus necessary to embrace all aspects of Christian-Muslim coexistence. In a pluralistic society with an ethno-sectarian representation system, the demographic factor as well as the cultural influence and economic power are the levers that enable each community to assert its political claims. And the debates that stir passion and controversy have more often cultural (and even semantic) features rather than merely political ones. What is frequently at stake in that mosaic country that is Lebanon has more to do with the education system, the demographic patterns of society, the perception one community has of its own cultural role, its own historical claims deriving from its distinct reading of Lebanon's history.

One should add to all these issues the unavoidable dimension of religion that lurks beneath the multiple controversies aroused in postwar Lebanon. Ever since 1991 (right after the end of the war), Christian and Muslim Lebanese have been engaged in an internal introspection, confronting their ideas and ideals; their core values and beliefs; their school system; their social welfare system; their lifestyles; their various and frequently clashing concepts of freedom and democracy, of sovereignty, pluralism, political participation, and cultural heritage; their relations with their Arab environment, with the West, and with each other. But they have been clearly avoiding getting into the theological debate, where the dialogue would necessarily reach a wall and find its own limits, as the head of the Jesuit Order, Father Peter-Hans Kolvenbach, put it abruptly when he addressed the participants at the Synod on Lebanon held in the Vatican in 1995.

Rather, all broad aspects of the national issues have been and are still raised by the contenders, although not always for the sake of "rapprochement" but to "make a point" and underline one's own difference. This dialogue has not been an easy, ongoing one; it is often ruptured by harsh polemics and loaded with suspicion charges. Many observers and analysts wonder whether these altercations are distinctive of a true dialogue or if they are the "defensive" cases in which each communal group seeks to preserve or advance its own interests. Notwithstanding their asperity, these exchanges and arguments mirror the nature of the dialogue pursued after the war, with noticeable efforts of tolerance being deployed to prove that democracy is still alive.

But the success of that democracy requires first and foremost a minimum *vouloir vivre en commun,* according to Ernest Renan's definition, a will of living together. It also requires a set of other conditions: 1) awareness that to preserve the country dialogue is unavoidable, and that dialogue does imply compromise and concession; in a plural society, no one can get it all; 2) the necessity to safeguard the sovereignty of the country and not resort to a foreign power to assert one's claims; 3) the existence of a strong national army; as observed in the Lebanese (and Yugoslavian) conflicts, the fragmentation of a pluricommunal society starts by making the national army invalid and unable to operate. Self-defense of the social body is thus assumed by militias; 4) a common acceptance of a political and cultural lexicon: in plural societies, words and vocabulary rarely bear the same significance and often lead to misunderstanding, tension, and violence; 5) a stable environment, hence the importance of the peace process in the Middle East; 6) a common perception of what foreign relations should be, because there is always a tendency to conflate the sectarian and the foreign policy cleavages; 7) a focus on education in school and university in order to allow the young of diverse communities to open up to other groups' cultures and histories. The temptation of creating isolated cultural islands is too strong in pluralistic societies and it breeds the culture of war, as opposed to the culture of peace, based on the knowledge of the others.

One of the main lessons one can draw from the Lebanese experience is that it highlights the importance of pacts in pluralistic societies: the sufferings of war shared by all groups and the collective memory do not act as an effective deterrent in the absence of an agreement, an accord, a Pact that is the fruit of a consensus. The Dayton accords, the Northern Ireland agreement, like the Ta'if agreement (all have in common being held under U.S. auspices), are perfect examples. They reflect the international dimension of local complex conflicts. The Lebanese case is specific in that it addresses the three dimensions of such conflicts: the internal dimension, which includes the strife for survival and self-assertion of minorities; the international dimension, which turns a local conflict into a "by proxy" war, thus holding a country hostage of a regional and international game; and the institutional dimension, which is the democratic process, the only possible solution to ethno-religious struggles, including Muslim-Christian competition at the political level.

Democracy in Lebanon is being challenged every day and has still to be reinvented. The Lebanese have a natural inclination for freedom of speech and thought and have a common acceptance of democracy as the only possible regime for a plural society like theirs. They have agreed that theirs is a "Covenant democracy" but they're still squabbling over its rules. Although set forth in the postwar Ta'if accords as a prorogation of the post-independence model, these rules fit a transitory phase. The Lebanese have entered somehow into the post-Ta'if phase and the polemics they still engage in show that they just did not come out together with the nature or the type of democracy they want after their long destructive civil strife: would it adopt the rule of majority? Would it preserve the participation of its minorities in the decision-making process? What would be the cultural and historical ground of that democracy? Could the "National Pact" transcend the formal and numerical aspects of the formula?

JOHN PAUL II VERSUS HUNTINGTON

Exactly where concepts clash—unveiling at times, bouts of a "clash of civilization" or "clash of values" within the same society and civilization—lie the cornerstones on which to rebuild a scattered, and yet very much one and alive, nation.

Christians and Muslims have emerged from war clearly aware that living together—for better or worse—was an irrevocable fate. Constrained to coexistence by geography and history, they had *no choice* but to stick together. The question is: how strong is the *will* to live together? In their long and often arduous dialogue, they are discovering that the will of coexistence derives from shared core values, a strong national feeling rather than sub-national allegiances. Is there one image of Lebanon in their mind or are there as many Lebanons as there are Lebanese communities? And could the dictates of one definition of nationalism, of one history book, of one culture (as is advocated by the postwar official discourse) build the new *"homo libanicus"*?

In no other country are ideas more powerful, more vital, more central to the determination of the future. Not in Bosnia, not in Kosovo, not in Northern Ireland, South Africa, Southeast Asia, or East Timor. In all these areas, political agreements, distribution of power, forceful solutions, international intervention, and peacekeeping operations stopped or can stop the conflicts. In Lebanon's case, the internationally brokered Ta'if accords brought an end to the war, but clashing words and concepts still carry Lebanese to the brink of a hazardous tension. This is indeed the only place in the world where ideas do make a difference. For Lebanon itself is born out of an idea; in John Paul II's own words, "Lebanon is more than a country, it is a message."

In Lebanon's postwar era, that message is being challenged by the post–Cold War explosive theory of Huntington, launched from another country, the United States, that is—just like Lebanon—built on one core value, one idea: freedom. Huntington's "clash of civilizations" basically says that Lebanon cannot work. The challenge of the nineties for the Lebanese was to invalidate that theory, to keep it from happening, from being right. One man has given them his active support and used all his might to tip the balance in favor of Lebanon-the-message: Pope John Paul II. His input has been a decisive one.

One of the most significant events in postwar Lebanon indeed has been Pope John Paul II's convening of a Synod on Lebanon in the Vatican under his personal and direct auspices—a crux and a moment of truth in Lebanon's modern history. From the day he called for the Synod, on June 12, 1991, to the holding (by the end of November 1995) of that Special Assembly of all Catholic cardinals and bishops to discuss Lebanon's future and the future of its churches, and then from the post-Synod period till the Pope's visit to Lebanon (May 10–11, 1997), his first to a Middle Eastern country, six years elapsed.

During that "period of grace," as the Holy Father labeled it, both Christian and Muslim Lebanese have been driven to think about their commitment to restart together a joint life in their common (and uncommon) country in mutual respect and understanding. But finding new paths to coexistence is not an easy task. Some say it would take the next generation to build a common ground of lasting values. Others insist that it is up to this contemporary generation, the same that had an unforgettable encounter with Pope John Paul II at the shrine of Our Lady of Harissa and to whom he entrusted the message he addressed to the Lebanese youth, to make straight the paths of hope and bear the responsibility conferred. But what if that generation which is urged to open up to "the other" is the same one that has been and is bred in cultural ghettos?

Contradictory trends exist in Lebanon today; Christian-Muslim dialogue is more than ever a priority and an ongoing endeavor among intellectuals of both sides, but it is also, according to many observers, no more than "ink on paper" and thus it is stalling. For any peace to be sustainable, a new leadership must be committed to peaceful coexistence, reconciliation, and the rule of law. Educational projects that seek to influence future generations to be more accommodative and inclusive are as vital as physical reconstruction and political "mellowing." In order to move ahead and rebuild a reconciled society, some countries, such as South Africa, established a truth commission to deal with the ghosts of its past; other places, like Lebanon, chose national amnesia through an amnesty law passed in Parliament (or "partial amnesia," since only one former militia lord, Samir Geagea, head of the Christian "Lebanese Forces," was tried and sentenced to life in prison).

A "purification of conscience" as called for by the Pope, is yet to come. Is it occurring? And is the idea of coexistence wishful thinking? A continuing struggle? Is it doomed to recurrent violent breakups? In many ways, coexistence today equates living side by side, not living together. For pessimists or fatalists who tend to see the empty half of the glass, all the ingredients of another strife in one or two generations are there; but all the energies and promises for a new, bright future are also looming ahead, for those unfettered optimists who see the full half of the glass and the uncured nationalists who relentlessly work at filling it in. It is hard to guess which prediction would prevail. Only one major factor could make it easy to foresee the future and even bet on it: the unstoppable drive among the Lebanese of goodwill.

This book tells the story of those years that witnessed a series of events which will have their impact through the next coming decade, as surely as the war and its aftermath had theirs. It is an exposé of events, facts, polemics, and trends in postwar Lebanon. These are the groundwork upon which a thesis could be built either to support the optimistic prognosis or foster the darker projection. But Lebanon and the Middle East in general are not the ideal ground for prognosis. Sometimes, people of vision and initiative can outstrip any forecast and shape a better future . . . provided those people exist.

In the first part of this book, I develop the way both Christians and Muslims feel about coexistence, how they perceive it, what they expect from dialogue, and how they disagree on certain concepts that are at the core of Christian-Muslim understanding or misunderstanding, such as Arabity, pluralism, consensual democracy, political participation, political de-confessionalization, cultural difference. One could easily talk about a "war of concepts" that often brings the country to the verge of a new demarcation line; suddenly an invisible yet palpable frontier separates Lebanese anew and the specter of an unbearable tension hovers for days and weeks. What are the limits and hazards of Christian-Muslim dialogue? Is this dialogue based on mutual knowledge of the other's traditions and religion?

In Part II, I present the reality of coexistence through facts and figures. These facts and figures reveal the physical erosion of the Christian presence in the region and in Lebanon as well. Exiled abroad, displaced inside their country, the weakening of the Christians affects the balance of power but also the economic and cultural vitality of their society.

Muslim spiritual leaders in Lebanon (mainly among the strongly emerging Shi'a community) as well as political leaders have been increasingly concerned about the future of the Christian presence and its political participation. They have warned against the danger of increasing emigration and the exclusion of Eastern Christianity from the making of peace in the Middle East. But what were the tangible initiatives they took or oversaw to address that potential dramatic outcome? Lebanese Christians have been watching with anxiety the timid steps taken by Druze leader Walid Joumblatt to allow the return of the displaced in the Shouf mountain villages from where they've been dislodged in the wake of the 1983–84 massacres. The openings of former Prime Minister Rafik Hariri toward the Maronite Church and his recurrent visits to Patriarch Sfeir in his Bkerké residence have similarly captured attention and raised questions on what he can and cannot deliver. And most of all, because of its ironclad dominance of the Lebanese political arena (and its control over the "initiatives" of the Lebanese officials), Syria's frequent attempts to send a signal to the Maronite Patriarch and to reach out to the Christian political parties and opposition have disconcerted the analytical skills of the media. To what extent were these gestures inspired by a genuine will of dialogue and under which terms would that dialogue be initiated? Since the Christian mainstream is the staunchest opponent of the Syrian military presence in Lebanon, which in turn triggers a wave of emigration out of despair regarding a "sovereign" future, Syrian overtures have ushered in perplexed questions about their significance.

In dealing with each other, both Muslim and Christian Lebanese have come to realize that they were not able to move forward together, remove obstacles, and solve certain problems without the support or the "blessing" of their strong Syrian patron. Christian-Muslim dialogue has thus become very often a tripartite dialogue. To many observers, inter-communal dialogue could only be conducted through one central mediator: Syria. If that fact is viewed by many as underlining the positive and stabilizing role played by the Syrian regime in postwar Lebanon, and cushioning the hard feelings that may lead to clashes on the ground, the direct protagonists of that dialogue are also aware that any intermediary or third party in fact prevents true in-depth exchanges from taking place and the emergence of a long-term and unified national vision.

Even states such as France and the Vatican, Iran and Saudi Arabia, who are respectively the traditional allies of Christians and Muslims of Lebanon and the main international interveners in the Lebanese arena, have understood that in order to reach out to the various Lebanese communities and to deal with their Lebanese friends, allies, or political clientele, they, too, have to transit from Damascus.

Yet Muslim and Christian leaders as well agree that Lebanon is not Lebanon anymore without the interaction of its Christians *and* its Muslims. Even the fundamentalist group of Hezbollah has been opening up to various Christian parties, starting with the Maronite Patriarch, and as it (successfully) merged into the Lebanese political landscape, it publicly renounced its stated goal to establish an Islamic Republic, "unless the overwhelming majority of the population votes for it," according to its leaders. With time, will demography prevail?

Having a diaspora larger than their local grassroots is the excruciating dilemma of Eastern Churches. It is also one of the friction points with the Roman Church, which exerts its direct dominion over Eastern Christians abroad. Is Eastern Christianity on its way to getting "Westernized"? "No," says Rome. "Retrieve your oriental heritage, liturgy, and spirituality. Stick to your traditions and to your Arabic environment." That is the essence of the message of Pope John Paul II, in his astounding and historic Apostolic Exhortation to the Catholic Church in Lebanon, released during his groundbreaking visit to the country of the Cedars. Part III of this book tells the story of the visit that took place two years after the Synod held in the Vatican (the history of the Synod is developed in Part II). Part III also explains why peace and prosperity in Lebanon as well as in the Middle East would be unreliable without Eastern Christians. The dramatic decline of the Christian population in the Holy Land from 18 percent in 1948 to less than 2 percent in 1999 raises the issue of the desperate living conditions under Israeli occupation. Peace and justice are the only solution in this beleaguered region. But how could peace reign if coexistence is not there? And without freedom, democracy, and the recognition of others' rights, is coexistence possible? These are central questions that Christians, Muslims and Jews in the Middle East have to face if they want to build a better place for their children. By and large, Lebanon's postwar challenge is also the challenge of a whole region. Could the Lebanese democracy of the National Pact be a model for the peoples of the Middle East and their pluri-ethnic and pluri-religious societies?

PART I

Cognitive Coexistence

Chapter 1

Christian Soul-Searching

The road follows the contour of the wooded hill, makes a right turn, and then crossing the main gate barrier penetrates the park. At the top of the hill stands the vast and modern church with its round dome recognizable from miles and miles away; it is flanked at its left by a pleasant two-floor stone-built building sheltering the administration. On the right, the college with its large classrooms slopes backward to the foot of the hill where the tennis courts, basketball field, and the most sophisticated track-and-field college stadium in Lebanon stretch amid the forest and the scout-camping site encompassed within the walls of the Jesuit domain. For old-timers and alumni students as well as for newcomers, it is difficult to resist the indescribable poignant feeling that floats in the air and the woods and the playing courtyards and the classes of Notre-Dame de Jamhour.

Overhanging Beirut and its suburbs, with an exceptional view over the sea on one side and the Mount-Lebanon on the other side, the Jesuit "Petit et Grand Collège" is credited to have forged generations of highly educated elites who played a major role in Lebanon's culture and history. Most of these elites have then graduated (many as lawyers) from the famous Saint Joseph University, in the Christian heart of Beirut, rue Huvelin. The Huvelin campus was once the location of the college too, before it moved up to the heights of Jamhour in the late fifties, leaving the university downtown. In the year 2000, the St. Joseph University celebrates the 125th anniversary of its foundation by the Jesuits.

I said that the Jesuit college and university is "credited" for having formed the ruling classes of Lebanon during the past decades, but I could also write that it is concurrently being reproached with bringing up a political class that is charged today with the failure of the building up of the nation-state. Whether this criticism is justified or not, one fact is certain:

despite a history of immersion in local traditions, of openness to Islam and of cultural exchanges,[1] the Jesuit school and university have been viewed as being the sanctuary of Westernization, dispensing an education that would cut off the Lebanese from their cultural environment.

Ever since they came to Lebanon in the late sixteenth century, the Jesuits have had a thriving and often hectic relationship with the inhabitants of the country, particularly the Christian Maronites. Their role took on an ambivalent character, both domineering and liberating. At a time when the French consuls and the *Congregatio de propaganda fide* were encouraging the influx of the Latin missionaries in the Ottoman Empire, the Jesuits, who depended directly on the Pope, initiated a bold campaign of French cultural expansion. They also conducted (along with other orders such as the Franciscans) a more or less forced latinization of the Maronite Church, the first Eastern Catholic Church (affiliated with Rome since the twelfth century), which put them at odds with the Maronite clergy, sparked off resistance, and left scathed memories of Father Eliano, Father Jérôme Dandini, and Father Pierre Fromage, the foremen of this enterprise. Old Syriac manuscripts containing the doctrine and spirituality of the Maronite Church were stored in the attic of history and the Synod of Louayzé in Mount-Lebanon (1736) sanctioned the success of the "romanization" of the Maronite Church.[2]

But the overall influence of the Jesuits has been auspicious and marked a turning point in the cultural awakening of the whole region, with the Maronites standing as its vanguard. In many ways, "romanization" also meant modernization. Schools were built, subsidies provided, social and religious foundations established under the Jesuits' auspices. Thanks to the contribution of the Catholic missions in the Levant (the Jesuits in particular but also Franciscans, Capuchins, Carmelites, Dominicans, and Lazarists) and later, in the nineteenth century, of the Protestant missions (whose main contribution was the foundation of the American University of Beirut, the former Syrian Protestant College), the Eastern Christians, especially the Maronites, operated a formidable intellectual leap. The Maronite College of Rome was established in 1584 for the education of the eastern clergy. Those priests who graduated there would disseminate in the Orient the new ideas of modernity, renaissance, and rationalism acquired in the West. They would, in exchange, spread in Europe the Arabic and Islamic literature, philosophy, and science books, thus paving the way for the "Orientalist" trend. The Louayzé Synod would prescribe the creation of as many schools as possible. The first printing presses in the Orient made their appearance in the Mount-Lebanon: at the end of the sixteenth century, in the monastery of St. Antoine of Qozhayya (in Syriac character), and a century later, in the monastery of Khounchara, in Arabic character. Challenged by the competition with Anglo-Saxon and Protestant missionaries who arrived in the Levant encouraged by the American Board for Foreign Missions at the turn of the nineteenth century, the Jesuits set up in Beirut their eminent Catholic press, "Imprimerie Catholique" (1848).

Having already transmitted to the Arab world the philosophical heritage of Ancient Greece and of Antiquity, the Eastern Christians, of whom the Maronites would become the spearhead, were positioned now to convey to the Orient the culture of the modern world and its humanism. This cultural edge would allow them to play a dynamic role in the "aggiornamento" (renewal) of the Arab world in the nineteenth century. From their stronghold in Lebanon, in Aleppo, and in Cairo, they would conduct the awakening and liberation of an Arab nation that had slipped into the lethargy of a four-hundred-year Ottoman domination. George Antonius, whose story of the Arab national movement, "The Arab Awakening" (1938), is a landmark in Arab thinking, writes that "centuries of decadence and misrule had debilitated the collective spirit of its [the Arab world's] population and loosened its former cohesion." He adds: "With the decay of Arab power and civilisation, which received their death-blow with the Ottoman conquest, [the] traditions [of the Arab classical age] were lost . . . and the language itself had degenerated." Antonius notes that efforts had been made by the Maronite Church to provide higher education, "notably at 'Aintura, a village in the Lebanon, where a seminary for the training of ecclesiastics had been founded in 1728 and its management entrusted to the Jesuits," but the college of 'Ain-Waraqa, founded in 1789 by Maronite ecclesiastics, "was easily the most important [establishment]. It made a point of encouraging the study of Arabic literature. Most of the men who in the first half of the nineteenth century rose to distinction in the worlds of letters and scholarship had had their schooling in it."[3]

Analyzing Maronites' role in the Orient and their affinity with the Jesuits, Yoakim Moubarac, Maronite priest and historian, estimates that "the Maronite Church is not a minority (linguistic or ethnic), it is a project. Just like the Jesuit Order, who is rather a movement within the Church, the Maronites are also a movement within the Churches of the Orient. They are and must remain the standard-bearers, the messengers of modernity in the Arab world."[4]

The Arab cultural renaissance (*nahda*) would inevitably lead to the blooming of modern political concepts such as freedom and democracy, human rights, individualism, and nationalism. Christian thinkers, writers, and journalists, almost all of them Lebanese—the Maronites Boutros Boustany, Negib Azoury, Khairallah Khairallah, Choukry Ghanem, Georges Samné, the Greek Catholics Nasif Yazegi, Khalil Moutran, Nadra Moutran, Salim and Bechara Takla (founders, in Egypt, of the Cairo daily newspaper *Al-Ahram,* 1875), the Greek Orthodox Antoun Saadé and Michel Aflak (these last two of Syrian origin), to cite only a few—are at the forefront of the main ideologies that swept across the Arab world: Arab secular nationalism, Pan-Syrianism, Baath Pan-Arabism, state nationalism (such as the one advocated by the Wafd party in Egypt, where two Christian copts, Wassef Boutros Ghali and William Makram Ebeid, militated), socialism, communism, anti-Zionism, and so on.

Needless to say, these political doctrines were highlighting national values and the concept of secular states based on the equality between citizens regardless of their religious affiliation. The French historian and diplomat Jean-Pierre Valognes noted the paradox of the situation of Christian minorities in that context, "since, to be able to survive in their Islamic environment, they had to deny themselves somehow and present religious particularism as completely outdated."[5]

And yet, after the battles for independence fought together by Christians and Muslims, the joint front cracked and Arab nationalism took on an anti-Western connotation, with a strong Islamic component, thus automatically excluding Christians and even reviving some old tendency to identify Christians with the West. The substitution of Islamism for the Arab nationalist theories is more than an ideological defeat to Eastern Christians who tried to build a collective identity encompassing majorities and minorities; it is a threat that gives rise to a secular fear of falling back into the status of *dhimmi,* or second-class citizen under Muslim protection.

Having served in every possible camp and having brandished every possible ideological banner like a battle standard, the Christians of the Orient and of Lebanon in particular, at the end of the twentieth century, have become disillusioned, feeling hapless, with the general conviction that whatever tenet they advocate, they'll be losers. They are tired of feeling compelled every now and then to demonstrate their commitment to an environment ever suspicious of their loyalty, tired of having to climb relentlessly up the mountain pushing the rock before them, like a modern Sisyphus. After all, weren't they the first inhabitants of the land, before the birth of Islam? As Ignatius IV Hazim, the Greek Orthodox Patriarch of Antioch (whose flock includes about 1.2 million faithful in Syria and 400,000 in Lebanon), would often and openly remind people, with a zesty sense of humor: "We were here in the Orient long before Islam. We're the ones who received the Muslims. They've been our guests."

With the general waning of Arab "nation-building," people all around the Middle East have turned to the building of their collective identity. The frustration caused by the failure of political integration of all ethnic and religious components of Arab societies would inevitably reflect on the cultural level too. And in Lebanon, at the end of the fifteen-year-old civil war, there is a strong reemergence of communal identity. Though the modern intellectual and political culture of the Arabs owe much to the input of the Lebanese Christians, of whom the Maronites form the bulk and the core, those have developed an ambiguous and often problematic relationship with Arabity and Arabism that started long before the Lebanese war and continues after the war.

BEING CHRISTIAN AND ARAB

Before being a political concept, Arabity is a cultural fact. It is, for the peoples of that area called the Arab world, a history, a civilization, a language, a distinctive way of perceiving oneself and perceiving the others. The Arabic language is the foundation of their identity and the expression of their specificity. Since its inception, Islam has associated itself with the Arabic language; it is its native tongue and Islam can only be fully learned and embraced in Arabic. As one notorious Maronite priest, scholar, and expert of Islam, Father Michel Hayek, wrote it: "The Arabic language is the genitor of Islam and in turn, Islam has molded Arabism—or Arabity."[6] "For Muslims, the Arabic language is not merely a tool," says Father Hayek, "it is the key that gives access to history, to the understanding of human destiny, to paradise, to real dialogue with God. The Arab and Muslim man dwells in his mother-tongue, his language is his castle and his incline altogether."[7] Even Michel Aflak, the Greek Orthodox founder of secular Arab nationalism, admitted that "Arabism is a body whose soul is Islam."

Arab people acknowledge the importance that Arabic language holds in their life, in their originally oral culture. It condenses the ethos of the nation, of the umma. *Al-hija'* and *'al-madih,* diatribe and appraisal, were long the instruments and attributes of power for the emirs and Caliphs of the Umeyyade, the Abbaside and Fatimide dynasties. Their language is Arabs' privileged way to celebrate their triumphs and achievements, to reflect on the soul of the nation; it is also the instrument of their revenge over the setbacks of history. Thanks to its resonance, it allows them to turn their defeats into victories, the way Egyptian leader Gamal Abdel-Nasser did after the 1967 disastrous campaign against the Israeli army.

The association of the Arabic language with Islam is probably the real drama of Eastern Christians. This drama reaches its peak in Lebanon, where Christians have been at the forefront of the Arabic cultural revival but are also the advocates of cultural diversity and openness and strive to remain the intersection point between Eastern and Western civilizations. "Being Christian and having as a mother-tongue the Arabic language, which is the sacred language of Islam, is one of the fundamental paradoxes that forged my identity," writes the French-Lebanese historian and novelist and holder of the special Goncourt Award Amin Maalouf.[8]

In postwar Lebanon, the cultural controversy on identity has ricocheted between the Christians and their fellow Muslims. The dual challenge of the Christians of Lebanon, voicing the concern of Eastern Christians, is to reach a common understanding with their Muslim compatriots regarding their Arab identity and commitment, and at the same time, explain to the West that one could be Christian *and* Arab. For even the West has a problem dealing with those Christians who have lived in or close to the Holy Land since the origins of Christianity. Ever since their first encounter, when the Crusaders invaded the region, the West and the Christians of the Orient have cultivated a complex relationship. The Maronites, who have been more "Westernized" than the others because of their allegiance as a church to the Roman Pontiff and their special affinity with France, are not excluded from the ambiguous perception and even the uneasiness that the West developed toward the Christians of the Orient. Christian Arab-Americans would attest to that mixture of surprise and discomfort expressed by the average American whenever they identify themselves as such. One logical explanation is that Eastern Christians do not fit the preconceived, clear-cut notion of the dividing line between the Western world and the Islamic world. Where indeed would these Christians stand in the postulate of a "Clash of Civilizations"?[9]

Since the early nineties, books have flourished dealing with the Arab Christians.[10] The main addressees of these books are the Westerners. It is relevant to note that this revived interest takes place at a time when the world is preoccupied with "the West and Islam." The studies echo the anxiety of the eradication of Arab Christianity, under the combined effects of an increasingly unfavorable demographic situation and the emergence of Islamist self-assertion. It is in that context that Lebanese Christians are trying to redefine the notion of being Arab and Christian. "Being Arab and Christian at once is a very specific minority situation, that is not always easy to assume," notes Amin Maalouf.[11]

The Maronites, who are also the only Christians in the Arab world to have gone as far as bearing arms against the Muslims in the defense of their specificity throughout their long history, are torn today between two options: to see themselves mainly as a religious community whose primary aim is to preserve a distinctive identity and a religio-secular unity (without, however, severing their relations with the surrounding communities and Arab states), or to champion a Christian oriental identity immersed in Islam's lands, a "Church of the Arabs."[12]

In this soul-searching and identity quest, what is mainly at stake is the issue of pluralism and diversity. By their history and culture, Lebanese Christians have a tendency to resent any attempt at cultural homogenization. They can only see themselves as the confluence of diverse civilizations, of subtle and sometimes contradictory influences, of various cultural crossings. Maalouf denounces what he calls the "deadly identities," meaning the concept of an exclusive identity, because it is "a concept that reduces identity to one adherence" and denies the multiple influences that shape people's identity. It is a concept that "installs human beings in a partial, sectarian, intolerant, dominating and often suicidal attitude, frequently transforming them into murderers or partisans of murderers. . . . Their vision of the world is biased and distorted."[13]

For the Maronites, should the common adherence to Arab culture and civilization imply the exclusion of any other culture, their spontaneous reaction would be to reject Arabity. In an article that triggered vehement protest by some Arab countries, Michel Hayek wrote: "Arabity has taken its monotheistic view of the world and of its own heritage from Islamic monotheism itself. This is why it aspires to be the exclusive and undisputed value that cements the unity of the language, of the thought, of the affiliation and of the political organization." And Hayek adds: "Arabity denies any ethnic, intellectual or linguistic pluralism," which is why "the most glorious days of Arabity were the polytheistic days, not the monotheistic ones," that is to say, the era of a cultural polytheism that existed in pre-Islamic times.[14]

Some would argue that this is an extreme view of how Islam has transformed Arabic civilization. But underneath Hayek's thesis lies the eagerness of Lebanese Christians to thwart any imposed Arabo-Islamic concept of cultural assimilation and, accordingly, of any political unity that would be justified by it. Lebanon is, after all, the only Arab state ruled by a Christian (Maronite) president.

This is why the theme of Phoenician identity was extensively used and developed by many Maronite writers to assert the distinct and separate identity of Lebanon vis-à-vis Pan-Arabism. A set of brilliant poets and writers (including Charles Corm, Alfred Naccache, Elie Tyan, and Hector Klat) gathered around *The Phoenician Review* they founded and left indelible literary masterpieces written in French. This "Phoenician" historical and cultural claim was the political embodiment of the national aspirations of the Lebanese people and would span from the founding of "Greater Lebanon"(1920) to the post-independence years and even until the onset of the troubles. Some researchers even traced the attempt to link Lebanon to its Phoenician roots to the eighteenth century Maronite writer Tannus al-Shidyaq.[15]

That Maronite cultural trend was to be officially circumvented in the Constitution of Ta'if (1989) that sealed the end of the civil strife. A major concession had been made in Ta'if by the Maronite leadership: for the first time in the history of Lebanon, the Arabic identity of the state was asserted in its Supreme Law. The Constitution clearly stated in its introduction that "Lebanon is Arabic in its identity and its affiliation." For the Christians, this should only be natural, since they claim a historic contribution to the Arabic culture. But their reluctance to admit it was explained by the reluctance of their Muslim counterparts to recognize Lebanon as their final homeland. This latter point was also to be resolved in Ta'if.

And yet the controversy went on in the postwar years on how exclusive or inclusive Arabic identity could be in regard to other cultural influences, especially Western and francophone. The strains started with the stated government policy to impose the so-called "Arabization" of the school programs. Private and Catholic schools were on their guards. They viewed that goal as an attempt to rattle the foundations of a qualitative pluralistic education, which has been the hallmark of Lebanon in the entire region. Archbishop Youssef Bechara, who heads the Catholic Schools Committee, believes that "there is a trend which is fundamentally hostile to private schools, on the ground that they are the hotbed of confessional differences and divisions. This trend assumes that public schools—which it calls "national schools"—are integrationist schools." And yet, "22% of the students registered in Catholic schools are Muslims."[16]

New "civic education" books released by the Ministry of Education stressed the need to reinforce Lebanese identity and Arab identity. For many educators, this posed a delicate problem of reference: what was the Arabic raw-model? Who set the standards of Arabism and what are its criteria? To what extent does Arabism contain a religious Islamic component? Professors in Catholic schools revealed that many students asked them what it really meant to be an Arab.

A bitter and latent dispute flared up within the intellectual circles in March 1997, when the rector of St. Joseph University, Father Selim Abou, gave his annual speech for the celebration of the patron of the Jesuit university. Under the title " The Challenges of the University," he expressed what was lingering for some time in the intellectuals' and academic communities' minds, by advocating communal pluralism and cultural diversity. He also spelled out some major political concerns of the Christians. This is why a brief presentation of his speech undeniably helps understanding much of Lebanon's postwar realities as they have been perceived by both Christians and Muslims.

Strongly criticizing ideological discourses, Abou denounced what he called the "sacralization" of the word "Arabic" and "its derivatives: Arabism, Arabity, Arabization." He said this "sacralization" distorted the historical discourse, the sociological traits, and the political reality of Lebanon. He warned against the confusion between "Arabic" and "Muslim" concepts, because "it dissolves, in the vast Muslim-Arab heritage, the specific contributions of Eastern Christians to the Arabic civilization, especially under the Abbasside caliphate, and the decisive contribution of the Christians of Lebanon to the nineteenth-century Renaissance." He condemned the attempts to "rewrite Lebanon's history starting from the Arab conquest" and "excluding the more ancient historical roots that shaped the specificity of the Lebanese nation." For Christians, explained Abou, "Western civilization, even in its most secular aspects, remains the inevitable depositary of their anthropological and spiritual references." Reproving those who banned the use of the term "pluralism" because they equate it with "sectarianism," he condemned "the fact that the Arabic language is being imposed as the sole education and culture language," adding that "Lebanon will always be bilingual, and even trilingual, or he will not be," just as "Lebanon will always be a multi-communal or multi-confessional nation." According to Abou, "communal pluralism and cultural diversity are not an obstacle to national unity. On the contrary, they're the building block of an idiosyncratic identity."

Finally, Abou said that political reality was hidden behind a "manipulated discourse" of ideological content. He ridiculed the official description of the Syrian troops in Lebanon that refers to them as the Syrian "presence" and Syrian "hosts." He scorned the hackneyed bromides that empty concepts such as "democracy," "independence," "civil society," "human rights" of their content and trivialize repression and dependence. "When the slogan of 'national security' is brandished to justify silencing of the opposition, banning demonstrations, media control, censorship, arbitrary arrests, then democracy is agonizing," he exclaimed, under thunderous applause in the auditorium of the university. Boldly criticizing the assertion that Lebanese and Syrians are "one people in two separate states,"[17] he compared it to the logic that led to the Anschluss. Through the political part of his speech, Abou enunciated as the necessary condition for Christians that the assertiveness of Lebanon's Arabic identity does not mean "subordination" of their state to another state in the name of the "Arab nation's unity."

An unyielding Father Abou (also author of several books) would elaborate anew on these theses in his 1998 speech ("Pluralism in Interaction") and in his 1999 speech, in which he developed the notion of a "differentiated citizenship" based on the equality of the citizens, individual freedom, and an "institutional recognition of the citizens' communal and cultural affiliations" as opposed to a uniform citizenship and a homogeneous culture.

Needless to say, Abou's position unleashed passionate reactions: for months, critics and supporters of the Jesuit rector filled the columns of the newspapers. Diehard "Arabists" chastised "the resurgence of the old political

Maronite confessionalized discourse," although Abou himself is a Greek Orthodox who embraced Catholicism. Even the eminent and liberal Shiite scholar, philosopher and sociologist Waddah Sharara, contended that "the theories of Selim Abou represent a defense by a Lebanese Christianity which is expressing its last breath of life."[18]

Arabism and the cultural identity of the Lebanese people had been a recurring theme of Lebanese rhetoric, and the controversy showed it was not even close to being settled in the near future. At the end of the twentieth century, Lebanon was still engaging in a sterile debate over its Arabity at a time the Arab world itself was gliding away from it. The concept of "national unity" itself was linked to the common acceptance of Lebanon's cultural identity: was it Arabic or pluralistic? As early as 1982, prominent Shiite editorialist Jihad el-Zein had criticized the attempts of those who call for the "unity by fusion," saying this was "impossible." "Why this obsession of a fusion unity, historically and culturally impossible, when Lebanon can mold itself within a coherent unity in the framework of its pluralism?" he boldly wrote.[19]

Maronite Patriarch Nasrallah Sfeir himself did not shun away in defending the sacrosanct right for cultural diversity. "In Lebanon, there are two religions, Christianity and Islam, and each one has its own set of values, its own specific vision of the human being and the world. It is thus fit to say that there are two cultures, one oriented toward the West, and the other toward the Orient, and both cultures merge and coexist in Lebanon, as Christians and Muslims do. And this does not preclude living under one sky, in one country, having a common history and sharing a common heritage."[20]

FRENCH CULTURE AND NATIONAL IDENTITY

One of the centerpieces of the polemics has been the role assigned to French culture and language (the "Francophony") in the Lebanese identity. For some like Selim Abou, it is a fundamental component of the Lebanese identity, whereas others, such as distinguished thinker Phares Zoghbi, viewed the French language as a language of communication and culture. French is "the language which opened up the Maronites to modernity, from the sixteenth century on," wrote priest Yoakim Moubarac, one of the major Maronite scholars and historians. Still today, the Maronite Patriarch presides annually, in the chapel of his Bkerké seat, over a ritual mass in honor of France, attended by the French ambassador, as a reminder of the historical ties between France and the Maronite nation, considered as "part of the French nation" by French king Louis XIV. But French is also the language in which the forebears of

Lebanon's independence and of the Arab world's liberation disseminated the ideas of freedom and self-determination and conducted the nationalistic struggle against the Ottoman Empire at the turn of the twentieth century, right from Paris, where they were established as journalists and writers.

Druze minister, deputy, and former journalist Marwan Hamadé, who masters the French language and is the brother of famous Francophone poet Nadia Tueni, wondered, in a 1992 speech given at a colloquium organized in Beirut by the International Association of French-Speaking Journalists, "whether there is a contradiction between the precept of national unity and the survival of Francophony." "Is the attachment to French language an obstacle for integration in a pluralistic society?" he asked. "And does it reflect an intercommunal chasm and a cultural partition, under the cover of pluralism? The question is at the heart of our national debate." And he summarized his own vision of francophony, as "an opening out to the Universal rather than a substitute to national identity." Whatever the definition of French language and culture in Lebanese identity, the debate was theoretical. There is a new emerging reality in postwar picture of Lebanon, and it challenges the preconceived idea of the "Western" cultural affiliation of the Christians and of Muslims' unimpaired Arabism.

More and more Muslims are French-speaking or eager to teach their children French culture and language while French has been losing ground in the Christian communities. Figures of 1997–98 showed that 20 percent of the students at St. Joseph University were Muslims. The French-speaking Sunni bourgeoisie of Beirut was being outweighed by the Shi'a community, whose wealthy emigrants in French-speaking ("Francophone") African countries were coming back home and sending their kids to French-speaking schools.

According to French ambassador in Lebanon, Daniel Jouanneau, and his predecessor Jean-Pierre Lafon, Shi'a leaders such as Sheikh Fadlallah, but also Hezbollah representatives, have asked the French to open French *lycées* and cultural centers in southern Lebanon. In October 1997, a new *lycée* in the southern suburban town of Nabatyeh hosted 250 students. Another college was to open in Tripoli, in northern Lebanon, and many cultural institutes were sparking across the various regions, such as the Shouf mountain, under the control of Druze leader Walid Joumblatt. The new policy followed by the French after the Lebanese war was to de-emphasize significantly their political as well as their cultural commitment to their erstwhile allies, the Maronites, and to open up to the Muslim communities. By doing so, they followed a "decentralized" geographical approach to education, and thus relocated the "lycées" and Cultural centers throughout Lebanon. More than three thousand Lebanese students were studying in France in 1998.[21] That attitude was clearly dictated by the "Arabic policy" of French president Jacques Chirac, and his close friendship to Lebanese Sunni prime minister Rafik Hariri. In his official speech at the "Summit of French-speaking Nations (Francophony)" in Hanoi (November 1997), Hariri had formally endorsed "the francophone vocation of Lebanon, and its key role in the expansion of the French culture." Furthermore, Hariri reappropriated Christian discourse when he said: "While being proud of its Arabic culture and its Mediterranean heritage, Lebanon perceives 'francophony' as a way of life and thinking."

The picture was changing, yes. And certain prevailing ideas on the francophone community in Lebanon could easily be refuted by the facts. According to a study published in June 1996,[22] 44.4 percent of the overall population of Lebanon speak French, 22.2 percent speak English, and 20.5 percent are trilingual (speaking French, English, and Arabic). When it comes to determining the rate of people speaking good French (the labeled "Francophone" community) to the overall Lebanese population, the survey showed that Maronites represent 49.3 percent of the Francophones in Lebanon, followed (far behind) by the Greek Orthodox community (12.7 percent), the Shi'a community (12.1 percent), the Sunnis (10.5 percent), the Greek Catholics (9.6 percent). The Druzes have a French-speaking percentage of only 2.9.

But when detailing the development of French within each sectarian group, the study showed that the percentage increase of French-speaking people in the different communities is as follows: 25.5 percent of the Sunni, 23.9 percent of the Shi'a, 27.2 percent of the Druze, 27.2 percent of the Maronite, 60.5 percent of the Greek Orthodox, 57.8 percent of the Greek Catholic.

The survey also showed that the larger increase of the average French-speaking people are among the Shi'a and the Maronite communities, and that the number of good-speaking French among the Shi'a community witnessed a five-times increase compared to the older Shi'a generation.

It is certainly relevant to note that, despite their historic role in the propagation of French culture and influence in the Orient, the Maronites have a smaller percentage increase of French-speaking people in their average population as compared to their fellow Greek Orthodox and Greek Catholic counterparts. This is due to the fact that they are the most rural of the Christian communities. Finally, the study confirmed the expansion of English, though not at the expense of French, but rather as an additional and international language for an increasingly trilingual population (85.3 percent of the surveyed said they favored the learning of three languages).

A WESTERNIZED EDUCATION

"De-Maronitize the French! De-Jesuitize it!" the Muslim lawyer Ahmad Kobeyssi said once. That's exactly what was happening in the postwar era. Very much attuned to the realities on the ground, the Jesuits would live up to their reputation of being a progressive Order and to grasp the changes that confronted them: their contribution to the solution of the identity crisis and soul-searching of the Christians would be to revisit their own education standards, to engage into an introspection of their own role and mission in Lebanon. After all, hadn't they also paid a blood tribute to the war during which they lost six priests?[23] In the wake of Pope John Paul II's call to the Lebanese Catholic Church for a "conscience-screening" and self-questioning (June 1991), the Jesuits developed a renewed sense of their responsibilities. And their leading role will be enhanced at the Synod on Lebanon (November-December 1995), at the end of which the Pontiff would ask the Christians of Lebanon to rethink and reassert the terms of their Arabic commitment (see Part III, Chapter 12).

The "General" of the Jesuit Order, Peter-Hans Kolvenbach, S.I., was one of the preponderant speakers at the Synod. He confirms that "after the recent holding of the general Congregation, the Jesuits have made their choice.... In the new emerging Lebanon, the Jesuit priest will try his best ... to be a man of dialogue, and to contribute to conviviality, in the name of the gospel. As he is aware of a certain breach between faith and ambient culture, he will strive to translate the message of Christ through the oriental tradition and in Arabic within the Lebanese culture. On that particular point, the Synod reasserts the orientations of the Society of Jesus."[24]

Kolvenbach rebuts nonetheless the criticism targeted at the Jesuit education by their detractors.

Is it fair to make an educational system accountable for some political failures, especially a system like the Jesuits', that dispenses a critical sense of the responsibilities? Isn't it significant that the Jesuits "alumni" are found in different political sides, and that they still share a common platform which allows them, despite everything, to remain in touch, to listen to each other and to agree on specific issues? Maybe, somehow, this open education [of ours] has enabled the students to feel at ease on the riverbanks of the Seine as well as on the Beirut river's, and that might have facilitated the exodus. But is it reason enough to provide a close and confined education? It wouldn't be a service rendered to Lebanon. In any case, the problem does not lie in the educational system; Lebanon has unjustly bore the bloody brunt of a war whose roots originated in the Palestinian problem rather than in Lebanese soil. We know today that the solution passed by the White

House, not by the European West, who's always been a friend, albeit a helpless one.[25]

At Notre-Dame de Jamhour, once the bastion of the French Jesuits' cultural and physical presence, a change in the orientation of the Jesuit policy soon became perceptible: the few remaining French priests were being incrementally replaced by Jesuits coming from the Netherlands. Those were in excess, since the decision was taken not to send Dutch Jesuits anymore to Indonesia (a former Netherlands colony). Meanwhile, Lebanese "missionary" vocations were being encouraged and trained so that a new guard of local Jesuit priests would progressively replace the old Western "crew." Also, lay people were assuming increased responsibilities, "in accordance with the directives of the general Congregation and with the Holy Father's will for the Third Millenium."[26]

On the other hand, programs were being adapted to the Arabic and Muslim environment, "so that the Christians would re-discover their mission in the Orient," as one of the Dutch Jesuits put it. A self-critical exploration of their education had led Jesuit educators to believe they had formed an elite knowing French literature and history better than the French themselves, but cut off its cultural roots. Many Christians did not even speak, read, or write proper Arabic. "This has developed a certain schizophrenia of the Lebanese Christian personality," one Jesuit priest would comment. "Many of our former students would tell us: we've acquired a thorough grounding in Western culture and a great education but somehow we became strangers to our direct environment."[27] The real challenge of the College of Jamhour today—as an example for all other Catholic and French-speaking schools—will be to maintain the same level of quality in education while shifting to a more "Arabist" system. In other words, combining Western and Arabic cultures.

The "Westernization" of the Maronite elites is reflected also in the training of its clergy. The late Yoakim Moubarac, one of the strongest advocates for an internal synod of the Maronite Church, deplored the fact that Maronite priests who studied in Rome ignored the theology of the fathers of the Eastern churches: "They know better Ignatius of Loyola, Alphonse Ligure, St. Thomas Aquina, than Jacob of Sarrouje, Isaac the Syriac (As-Siriani), St. Ephrem or Youhanna Delyati."[28] Preaching for a renewal of their mission in the Orient, Moubarac would call on the Maronites "to take the bold initiative of the Arabization of the programs in their own hands," and by so doing, "they would reassert the leading role they played in the Golden Age of the Arabic culture and in the *Nahda*." They would also and especially "rebut the assertions of those who underline the Islamic feature of the Arabic language and claim that it would not be "christianized."[29]

Ironically, the incentive to "rediscover the deep roots of their faith" will be provided by Rome itself, when the Holy Pontiff will ask the Patriarchs and Bishops of the Eastern Catholic Churches "to fructify the spiritual richness of the ancient Eastern churches, these cradles of our faith"[30] (see Part II, Chapter 6). Yet it is relevant to note that French language will be the official language of the Synod on Lebanon. The Pope was quoted, saying to Maronite Patriarch Cardinal Nasrallah Sfeir, this was the first time that a Synod was entirely French-speaking.

THE MARONITE IDENTITY OF LEBANON: IS IT OVER?

In order to assess the Maronite's state of mind in postwar years, one should appraise the nature and depth of their kinship and association with their fatherland, Lebanon—also assimilated in their historical memory with Mount-Lebanon. For the Maronites, there is a specific Lebanese identity, which is a blend of all civilizations, cultures, and beliefs that crossed the region. Lebanon could only be different from Arab countries, even if it belonged to its geographical and cultural references. What makes that difference is mainly the massive presence of the Christians (relatively to its population), and the fact that Lebanon is the only country in the Arab world in which the civil liberties of Christians were guaranteed. For that reason, Lebanon is an absolute necessity, not only for Christians, but for all minorities in the Arab East. Christian presence leads to a civilizational and cultural interaction with the West, and also between Christians and Muslims themselves. The Lebanese society has thus a distinct feature of "pluralism within unity." "The real identity of Lebanon is the genuine coexistence between its various groups," says the former president of the Law Bar Association Chakib Cortbaoui.[31] Mount-Lebanon bears a particular significance for the Maronites; it is their historical refuge, the birthplace of the Lebanese entity and the symbol of independence and of Lebanese nationalism. They also consider it a holy place for the great religions, Christianity and Islam.[32] Mount-Lebanon indeed not only sheltered Christian hermits and monasteries, but it harbored some Muslim Sufis as well, and the Syriac language (the primary language of the Maronites and still their liturgical one) has historically been the contact language with Islamic Sufism or mysticism. It is the transition language that enabled Greek philosophy to be translated into Arabic.

"The Maronite identity is intrinsically bound to one land, and that is Mount-Lebanon," writes Archbishop Antoine Hamid Mourani.[33] This is why the Maronite presidents of the Lebanese Republic have traditionally been from Mount-Lebanon. By their geographical affinity, they embodied the core spirit of Lebanese nationalism.[34]

The exclusive and unique relationship between the Maronite community and Lebanon—the national entity and then the specific state—granted the Maronites a special position in the formation of the Lebanese nation. Maronite monks, priests, and patriarchs, such as Bishop Youssef Debs, Bishop Germanos Farhat, and Patriarch Etienne Douaihy, played an instrumental role in setting the political and cultural framework of the Lebanese entity of Mount-Lebanon. Maronites have culturally, ideologically, geographically and politically established the ground basis of Greater Lebanon born on September 1, 1920. The full potential of the Maronite community resides in one single country, Lebanon, and the Maronite and Lebanese destinies are identical. Maronite Patriarchs played a central role at crucial turns of Lebanon's history. Patriarch Elias Hoyek is considered as the inspirational figure of "Greater Lebanon": in 1919, he headed the Lebanese delegation at the Versailles Treaty in Paris and obtained a letter of assurance from French premier Clemenceau pledging the creation of Greater Lebanon. Patriarchs Antoun Arida in the forties, Boulos Meouchy in the seventies, and Nasrallah Sfeir in the nineties, took a genuine interest in social issues and on the political level, they reasserted the national identity of independent Lebanon, as a promoter of Arabic civilization but unshakably opposed to any Pan-Arab or Pan-Syrian unionism. Yusif Sawda, one of the main Maronite political ideologues whose life spanned Ottoman occupation, French Mandate, and independent Lebanon, stated in 1956 that the future existence of the Lebanese entity based on coexistence depended upon preserving Maronite dominance within the state. This was all the more important, he argued, because the Muslim community had not yet definitely committed itself to the existence of Lebanon. Thus, any challenge to Maronite dominance would be a challenge to the Lebanese entity itself. Lebanese nationalism became organically dependent on the existence of the Maronite community.[35]

But the once-dominant and self-confident Maronites were emerging from war as an embattled community, illusions shattered by the internal fighting that culminated during the final throes of the war, in 1990,[36] wrapping up a long, bloody strife against Palestinian and Muslim militias as well as Syrian troops. After having been the leaders and builders of Lebanon, "the angels and the demons" of a country made by them and for them, they now saw themselves as a minority fearful of the future, yielding to the atavistic reflex of insulation, of refuge in their sacred Qannubin Valley, their fortress and spiritual retreat, where they historically hid for four centuries to flee persecution, when the Mamluks invaded the littoral, destroyed their villages, and burned alive one of their Patriarchs.

The best analysis of the Maronite postwar crisis of identity and crisis of existence has been provided by Archbishop Mourani.[37] "The crisis reflects an internal divide or dilemma and it requires a renunciation of parts of the past that do not fit the identity or the core personality anymore. It calls for a renewal in the personality." In other words, Maronites have a noncontemporary perception of themselves that they need to adjust to the present. They did not find themselves in the new Lebanon that surfaced from war. They needed to know, for instance, what is their mission at the dawn of a new era in Lebanon, an era not really appealing to them. Will the dusk of the twentieth century also bring about their decline? How could they carve their way through the next stage of history?

Mourani explains that the historical isolation of the Maronite community in Mount-Lebanon is being replaced today by a compelling drift toward Arabic adherence. "This raises the question of the relation between the Maronite identity and the history to which we belong." Quoting the late president of the Republic Elias Sarkis, who said, "Arabity is our fate," he compared "the Muslim who is Arabic by tradition since his birth" and the Christian who becomes Arabic out of historical, sociological, and political necessity. Thus "Lebanon's past is Maronite," he wrote, "its present is a tension between various opinions and horizons, and its future is Arabic." But Lebanon's Arabity is different from that of other Arab countries, in that it is "critical and democratic." "Lebanon has a mission towards the Arab world, it is to be his critical mind, telling the truth to the Arabs from a position of strength conferred to him by his deeply rooted diversity and the freedom of his citizens." And that mission is to be the Maronites' contribution to a new Arabic twenty-first century renaissance. Their new Arabic commitment should be "freely embraced" rather than viewed as an inescapable fate.[38] This "mission statement" was inspired from Pope John Paul II's exhortation to the Christians of Lebanon (see Part III, Chapter 12).

Yoakim Moubarac, who was advocating an *aggiornamento* of the Maronite Church and a reassessment of its mission and role in the Levant, believed that Lebanon is not only an asylum of minorities but that it is an experiment of a role model society. He insisted that the Christian features of Lebanon should not reflect a confessional look, but the image of modernity. But did the Christians in general, and the Maronites in particular, still have the means and the drive to carry on such a responsibility in an Arabic environment that was equally experiencing a cultural and existential crisis? And were they to bear all alone the brunt of that daunting task?

Chapter 2

Muslim Self-Assertion

Sitting on the shoulders of the Galilee, and overlooking Palestine, Jabal 'Amel spreads its cliffs and rugged terrain in South Lebanon, casting its spiritual bearing as well as its rebellion-drenched history on Shi'a conscience. Jabal 'Amel is for the Shi'a community what Mount-Lebanon is for the Maronites: their geographical and historical cradle and a sacred place that condenses the spirit of the "nation-community."¹

A symbol of opposition to the French mandate, it has also been a breeding ground of reformist ulema and prominent scholars who contributed to the development of Shi'a theology *(al-fiqh)* in Najaf (Iraq)—once the center of Shi'a scholarship—and in Qom (Iran), ever since the establishment of the first Shi'a regime in Iran in the sixteenth century with the Safavid dynasty. Names such as Sayyed Mohsen Amin, Abdel-Hussein Charafeddine, Sheikh Ahmed Rida, and Sheikh Ahmed 'Aref el-Zein, are evoked as having been the pioneers of the Shi'a religious *Nahda*. The historic ties of Lebanon's Shi'a with Iran will reach a grass-roots expansion after Khomeini's revolution, viewed by many Shi'a scholars as the political *Nahda*, the one that quenches the Shi'a's thirst for justice *('Adl)*. Throughout their history, the Shi'ites have developed an extensive sense of injustice that is most vividly expressed in their celebration of *'Achoura*.²

In the organization of the state, justice could only be attained under a ruler inspired or guided by the *faqih*. This happened under the Safavid dynasty. But the ideal is to have the *faqih* become the *wali*. The concept is known as *wilayat al-faqih*. It was achieved under Khomeini. The Iranian revolution draws from the historical claim of the clergy to be part of the state, and the "reconciliation" between the political body and the religious one was achieved by the Iranian revolution. A far cry from the Western concept of separation of state and church!

Those among the Shi'ites of Lebanon who were militarily backed by Khomeini's Pasdarans became well-known to the wide world as hostage-takers and terrorists. All other aspects of the Shi'ites claim and of their historical background was ignored. At first, they took pride and satisfaction in their recently (mid-eighties) acquired notoriety. But these feelings progressively commuted to anger and frustration for being so clearly misunderstood in their fight against Israeli occupation and against injustice represented by the West's behavior regarding the Palestinian issue.

Representing roughly 9 percent of the total of the Muslim world,[3] the Shi'a have emerged from the Lebanese war as the largest minority (some evaluate it at 35 or even 40 percent of the Muslim population and over 25 percent of the total Lebanese population). Since figures are still a taboo in Lebanon, and the last official census goes back to 1932, their number is roughly estimated around 900, 000,[4] out of a total (and disputed) semi-official estimate of more than 3.1 million inhabitants.[5]

Through their demographic rise, the Shi'a have jostled the Sunnis, and the postwar years have witnessed a political, economical, and cultural Shi'a-Sunni competition.[6] The main parties of the Shi'a, especially the Hezbollah, overshadowed the moderate Muslim bourgeoisie of Beirut, Tripoli, and Saida, and their main challenger in the postwar years has been Prime Minister Rafik Hariri—until his stepping down from office late 1998 (see Part II, Chapter 9). The Shiite youth was particularly eager to assert itself, to learn and to catch up with other communities in Lebanon. Hezbollah's educational platform and social activities would provide it with the means and capacities to do so.

The 1943 National Pact had been viewed by many as a Sunni-Maronite alliance, forged at the detriment of the Druze, the historical partner of the Maronites in Mount-Lebanon, and of the Shi'a, feeling misfit and left embittered, downtrodden by their own feudal leaders.

The Shi'a community has always been torn between its inner aspiration for integration into the social and civil body of the state, and its visceral rejection (*rafd*) of any established order, of any legal authority, explains Sayyed Hani Fahs, a Lebanese Shiite ulema and expert of the Iranian revolution.[7] Hence, the stature of a man like imam Musa Sadr, who will give this community a role and a mission by establishing the movement of the "deprived." The concept of the "disinherited" as set forth by Musa Sadr would become part of Shi'a political discourse to the present and would even appeal to prominent Christian intellectuals and priests.

In his first years as a diplomat, former Assistant Secretary for NEA Edward Djerejian was based in Beirut. He says he'll never forget the day he met with Imam Sadr. The meeting took place in Tyre, near the seashore. "For two hours and a half, sadr spoke about the aspirations he had for the

Shi'a community and I listened. It is at that moment that I realized the social and Shi'a dimension of the Lebanese problem."[8]

Before the war, the political activities of the Shi'a youth revolved around the main Lebanese parties headed by Christians (Bechara el-Khoury, Camille Chamoun, Raymond Eddé), and they would often find themselves in antagonist camps of leftist ideologies (Baath, Marxism, Pan-Syrianism, Pan-Arabism). Despite his Iranian roots, Sadr was instrumental in mobilizing politically the Shiite in the South, the Biqaa and the southern suburbs of Beirut into a movement of their own.[9] He shed their hidebound political and feudal structures.

The Shi'a awakening will start from the southern suburbs of Beirut, greatly influenced by their demographic explosion, the frustrations about moral decay and poverty, the successive Arab defeats in Muslim conscience, the fighting between Israel and the Palestinians, and periodic Israeli incursions into the country. During the Lebanese war, the Shi'a youth enrolled in "Amal" (the Arabic acronym for "*Afwaj al-Mouqawama al-Lubnaniyya*"— the brigades of the Lebanese resistance) founded by Sadr in 1975. Although Sadr strongly supported the Palestinians' fight against Israel, he became aware of their growing military and political clout in Lebanon. It is said that "Amal" was meant not only to resist Israel (whose first occupation of southern Lebanon occurred in 1978) but also to counterbalance Palestinian influence in the South. For rancor against the Palestinians' exactions had extended among the Shi'a, who often shared the squalid refugee camps of the Palestinians or lived in their immediate neighborhood, whereas the Sunni community identified with the Palestinian Resistance and viewed it, one way or another, as its proxy militia, using it against the Christians during the war. Musa Sadr's famous hunger strike against the internal Lebanese strife at the onset of the troubles remains in Lebanese minds.

Two events have impacted durably on the life of Shiites and their political evolution: the creation of Israel in 1948 and their subsequent exodus from the South and the Biqaa Valley. "After the establishment of the state of Israel, the small artisans and merchants of Bint-Jbeil, Nabatyeh, and Areyssi, could no longer sell off their goods in towns like Safad and Akka (in Palestine)," tells historian and writer Ahmed Beydoun.

> Job opportunities dried up for the Shi'a of Jabal 'Amel and rural depopulation accelerated. So they came to Beirut's suburbs (Nab'a, Bourj Hammoud, Haret-Hreik, Ghobeyri, Chyah, Bourj-Barajneh). The urbanization accelerated the dismemberment of the Shi'a families. But a movement like the "Amiliyyeh," established by Rashid and Mohsen Beydoun, played an important role in Shi'a self-assertion. The printings also took in charge the political

education of the masses. The Shi'a magazine "Al-'Irfan" had a prominent role in that respect.

It is meaningful to note the role of the towns (the "medina"), such as Beirut and Tyre, in the political mobilization of the Shi'a community and the emergence of a new leadership and a new solidarity that replaced the clan system of Jabal 'Amel and Baalbeck. It is thus adequate to say that Shi'a political confessionalism grew up in the suburbs of the Lebanese towns.[10]

From the docile Shi'a youth of the Lebanese *rif* (countryside) held tight into the grip of tradition to the suicidal militants of Hezbollah, one big leap had been taken in a few decades. Hezbollah's influence on the Lebanese arena started in 1983. The political dynamics of Islamic activism in Lebanon received a further reinforcement from the victory of the Iranian revolution. Early "revolutionary" cells in Lebanon had paved the way for the Iranian influence.

But competition surfaced quickly between Hezbollah and the traditional representative Shi'a institution (the Islamic Shi'a Supreme Council) that brings together the clerics and the lay leaders of the Shi'a community, including the speaker of Parliament and "Amal" leader Nabih Berri. The council, established by government decree in 1967, was originally led by the charismatic Imam Musa Sadr, elected in 1969 as its first president. Since his disappearance in 1978, Musa Sadr has been popularly regarded as the "hidden Imam." In May 1994, Sheikh Mohammed Mehdi Shamseddine, who had functioned as deputy president of the council, was elected president. In that capacity, Shamseddine is the official head of the Shi'a community.

With the rise of Hezbollah, the council's authority has been frequently challenged. In areas controlled by Hezbollah such as the Biqaa Valley and Beirut's southern suburbs, many of the council's spiritual, philanthropic, and legal functions are challenged by rival sheikhs who embrace radical doctrines and interpretations. All too often Hezbollah leaders issue *fatwas* without reference to the council's authority, in view of its ties to Amal. Divergence in the line of conduct (regarding "flagellation," for example) shows on occasions such as the *Achoura*. But the rivalry would become all too blatant and would lead to clashes on the ground in the southern suburbs of Beirut and in some villages in Southern Lebanon on political occasions, like during the municipal elections in the spring of 1998.

A veiled competition gradually extended to the persons of both Sayyed Mohammad Hussein Fadlallah, who has been labeled "the spiritual Guide of Hezbollah" (although lately he distanced himself from the party), and Sheikh Shamseddine. Also Sayyed Hassan Nasrallah, the general secretary of Hezbollah and leader of its militant group, will emerge first as a military, then as a political leader. His *aura* increased after the loss of his son on the battlefield in 1997 during an anti-Israeli operation.

On the doctrinal level, both Shamseddine and Fadlallah are the products of the Najaf *hawzat* (teaching circles), but while the former and his vice president, Sheikh Abdel-Amir Qabalan (who is also the Supreme Mufti of the Ja'fari tribunal), remained linked to the traditional *marjai'ya* (reference) of Najaf, in Iraq, the latter opened up to Qom and Khomeyni's Iran.

And while Shamseddine is rather steeped in the Lebanese political establishment, strapped into an institutional role and gets involved in local politics, Fadlallah considers himself as a *marja'*, exercising a religious and legal authority on a regional scale, and even embracing the whole Islamic world. People flock to his door, he rarely knocks on other doors.

And yet, both Shamseddine and Fadlallah have ultimately referred to Syria, particularly on things related to political and military issues, since their organizational constituency ("Amal" and "Hezbollah") are involved in military resistance against the Israeli occupation in the South.

Tainted by the hostage-taking terrorist activities it has been identified with by Western media during the war, the Hezbollah (which has constantly denied having led such activities) would change its image after the war. It would progressively acquire a feeling of pride and a national legitimacy in its increasingly sophisticated military resistance against the Israeli occupation starting in 1992. It would become a major player in Parliament, would fill the TV screens, affect the government's political agenda, have its own media and its own Internet Web site, and strongly appeal to the youth. Other Islamist factions who also emerged as sizable pressure groups, such as the two Sunni fundamentalist adversaries "Al-Jama'a al-Islamiya" (close to the Muslim Brotherhood) and the "Ahbash" (from Ethiopian origins), did not enjoy the prestige of Resistance against the Israeli enemy the Hezbollah had, and also were less inclined to reach out to the Christians than were the Hezbollah leaders. Christian and Muslim intellectuals estimate that although Shi'ism is a more mystical and more revolutionary Islam, Sunni fundamentalism is theologically more strict, less tolerant, and even adamant on certain issues, especially regarding the Islamic State, the Ijtihad (interpretation of the shari'a), the status of women, and minorities' rights.

In its ideology, as formulated by Sayyed Mohammad Hussein Fadlallah and other sheikhs, Hezbollah advocates "Islamic revival" rather than Islamic fundamentalism. Integrism (the European name of fundamentalism) is described by Fadlallah as preserving the "integrity" of faith. For many analysts, Lebanese Shi'a fundamentalism has more political attributes than the Sunni's: resistance against Israel and opposition to the West (mainly America) remains atop its priorities, while Sunni fundamentalism is less directed against the West in its doctrine (probably because of the policy and constraints of its Saudi sponsors) and is often associated with internal violence such as the one that has occurred in countries like Egypt, Algeria, Sudan, Afghanistan. "To my opinion, groups who are financially or politically related to Saudi Arabia do not have the revolutionary impetus open to concepts such as freedom and justice, in their confrontation with Western and American arrogance," commented Fadlallah a few years ago.[11] Arrogance (*al-Istikbar*) is the specific word used by him to describe Western behavior, and particularly the U.S. attitude regarding the Third World. This political fundamentalism explains Hezbollah's links with Hamas and Islamic Jihad, for example, both groups that have also been associated with resistance against Israel in the West Bank and supported by Iran.

A lot has been said and written about the repercussions of Zionism and of the foundation of the State of Israel on Arab consciousness and on Islamic resurgence. Some developed the theory that it is precisely Israeli fundamentalism that triggered Islamic fundamentalism. The establishment of the State of Israel in Palestine generated a powerful and virtually unending anti-Western sentiment. Since 1967, Israel has been increasingly identified with the West. And thus, the strains that characterize relations between the West and the Arab world owe a lot to the Palestinian tragedy. The unsolved Palestinian problem illustrates "the persecution, exploitation, oppression, arrogance of the West towards the Arab and Islamic societies," to use the common Islamic lexicon.

In that context, says Shi'ite cleric and scholar Sayyed Hani Fahs, the strategic geographical location of the Lebanese Shi'ites—bordering Palestine/Israel—was of great importance to the Iranian leaders and accounted as one big asset the Shi'a community of Lebanon had as compared to the Shi'ites of the Gulf countries or even to Iraqi Shi'ites.[12]

For here was exactly the point of confrontation with, not only Israel, but also America. From that very strategic vicinity to Israel, the Iranians would directly face the West and its aims and politics in the region. The Lebanese Shi'a community would thus become one major catalyst of the "internationalization" of the Islamic condition.

HUNTINGTON CHALLENGES LEBANON

With the West, Muslims of the Middle East have a kind of attraction-repulsion relation, full of paradoxes. On the one hand, this relation has been hectic and confrontational throughout history, riddled with disillusions generated by false British promises to Sherif Hussein of the Hijaz, by Lord Balfour's pledge for a Jewish homeland, by the French mandate on Lebanon and Syria, by the U.S support to Israel, and finally by the "globalization" perceived as the "Americanization" of the world. On the other hand, Muslim leaders and clerics cannot ignore the West's lustrous appeal to the youth and to their intellectuals seeking freedom of conscience and belief.

This conflicting relation had inevitable repercussions on the Christians in Lebanon. They are regularly confronted with the ever conspicuous theory of conspiracy with the West against Islam.[13] "Some Islamist groups have a tendency to eyeball Arab Christians with suspicions, and to view them as the bulwark of the West (or the cat's paw for Western influence). They are not. Nor are they the fifth column of colonialism. . . . Christianity is not an ideology imported from the West," writes Mohammad Sammak, a Lebanese Sunni advocate of Christian-Muslim dialogue and one major adviser of the Mufti of the Republic at Dar el-Fatwa (an institution that tops Lebanon's Sunni establishment) and of former Prime Minister Rafik Hariri.[14]

Muslims' recurrent mistrust toward the Christians could only be explained by the trauma left in Islam's psyche by the Crusades: "900 years of confrontation did not even end in the twentieth century," advances Sammak. He quotes British general Allenby, who allegedly said when he entered Jerusalem in 1917, "Now the Crusades are over," and French general Gouraud, who displayed a sense of revenge when he entered Damascus in 1920 after having crushed Faysal's rebellion in Maysaloun: "We're back, Saladin."[15]

But then the Crusades are also a bad memory to many Arab Christians, and specifically to the Greek Orthodox, who still evoke the seizure of Constantinople by the knights of the Fourth crusade in 1204 and some atrocities committed by those who claimed to liberate the Holy Land. The Crusades' anthology is so vivid that some Christian writers such as Elias Khoury urged that "we must remove the Christian-Muslim dialogue from the context of the Clash between the Islamic Orient and the Christian West that has imposed itself since the Crusaders. Unfortunately, this language is being renewed by the American Empire, who is inventing an enemy, Islam, in order to justify its dominance over the world. Dialogue is not between East and West, it is between two Easts: the Arab Christians are not a foreign colony, and their presence need not be supported by the West. Arab Christianity is an organic part of Arab culture."[16]

One positive aspect in the relations of Islam with the West is the importance given by Muslims to the Vatican II Council. Through the Council documents (mainly the two groundbreaking Constitutions on the Church, *Gaudium et Spes* and *Lumen Gentium,* and declarations such as *Ad Gentes* and *Nostra Aetate*), the Catholic Church opened up to other religions and called for dialogue with non-Christians after fourteen centuries of clashes between Islam and Christianity, of "Holy Wars" and "Jihad." "These Christian texts opened new venues for a warmer dialogue with Islam," writes Mohammad Sammak.[17] But he also deplores the "lack of courage (of the Catholic Church) to denounce the crimes committed by the Crusaders until present times, with the Balfour declaration, then the Sykes-Picot accord—just as it apologized for crimes committed by the Nazis against the Jewish people."[18]

After the collapse of the Soviet Union and the end of the Cold War, Muslims in Lebanon have been keenly interested in the many theories formulated by Western intellectuals and NATO strategists who presented Islam as the next number one enemy. Samuel Huntington's paradigm of a Clash of Civilizations challenged them particularly. "The West needs an enemy to justify its policy in the Third World," argued Sheikh Fadlallah. "It is over-inflating the importance of the Islamist trend, as if that stream were able now to defeat Western civilization. What I see is a clash of interests in which the Third World, including the Islamic world, tries to develop its resources and get its economic independence, and hence, take its own security in charge while the West opposes this endeavor. The West would even go as far as to create or support some Islamist groups, like in Algeria, where the real clash is between French and U.S. interests."[19]

Fadlallah clearly says he prefers a strengthened Euro-Islamic relation rather than a U.S.-Islam relation, "because of common civilizational, religious and historical ties with Europe." Even Sayyed Hassan Nasrallah, the general secretary of Hezbollah and head of its militant (and military) faction, stated that "Europe has a primary role" in the Middle East, as opposed to the United States, who remain "our number one enemy."[20] This attitude reflects a general standpoint in the Iranian regime. (It is relevant to note in that respect that Iranian president Khatami's first visit to a Western country was to Italy in March 1999, followed by another one to France in October of the same year).

In his book entitled *Horizons of Islamo-Christian Dialogue,* Fadlallah argues that America is a greater danger for Christians than Islam. For him, "the aim of dialogue with the Christians is to search their solidarity against the West in order to confront its arrogance (the Shi'ite's term for Imperialism)," writes John J. Donohue, S.J., who analyzes Fadlallah's thinking.[21]

Actually, many Muslim thinkers seem to be lukewarm when it comes to dialogue with the Arab Christians. They would rather engage in conversation with the West, first because "they still crave recognition," and second because the West is the center of decision-making.[22] Eastern Christians are either connected with Western influences (so, in that case, it would be more meaningful to "speak to God rather than to His Saints") or too weak, with problems of their own. The only Christians in the Arab world who still hold political and cultural leverage are the Maronites of Lebanon. This explains why Hezbollah leaders have been attentive to keeping in touch with the Maronite Patriarch (see Part II, Chapter 9).

Criticizing that "utilitarian" approach (i.e., Islam addressing the West and neglecting Eastern Christians), Mohammad Sammak holds the West responsible too for "diminishing, or even setting aside the role of Eastern Churches." "The Arab Church," he argues, "is needed by the West whenever relations with the Arab world go through some strains, and so the West poses itself as the protector of Eastern Christianity in order to put pressure on Arab states. But when the West's strategic interests are safe, the need for the Arab Churches fades away."[23]

Sammak also states that "it is a common error to think that the West represents Christianity." "This misconception is rooted in Arab minds," he writes.[24] Sammak's opinion is shared by a great number of Muslim as well as Christian intellectuals and religious leaders. The West has been increasingly viewed as a secular and materialistic world, not as a Christian world. However, despite the frequent denunciation by some Eastern Patriarchs of the consumerist and radical capitalistic aspects of Western societies, the Western world in general is still considered as a model of pluralistic conviviality. A model only Lebanon could herald in the Arab and Muslim world.

ISLAM, PLURALISM, AND LEBANON

And here are precisely the fundamental questions that lingered on Christians' minds: did the perception of Lebanon evolve in Muslims' thinking? Were Muslims feeling more "Lebanese" after the war? And what did Lebanon mean to the Islamists, more specifically? Was there some room for nationalism in the tenets of a religion-based movement? In other words, could an Islamist party be "Lebanonized" or have a national Lebanese agenda?

Ever since the establishment of Greater Lebanon, Muslims have grudgingly accepted, after having bitterly opposed, the new national entity because they aspired for Arab unity. The "Hojair conference" and the "Sahel conference"[25] stamped that historical attitude. The French mandate period had been marked by the alienation of the Muslim community as a whole from what they saw as a French-Maronite hegemonic project. But the 1943 National Pact brought the Muslims into the system as Lebanon embarked on Independence.

However, it is only in the seventies and the eighties that Muslims recognized Lebanon as their definitive homeland (in a November 5, 1977, meeting of the Islamic Shi'a Supreme Council, and then in a meeting held on September 23, 1983, at the Sunni Juridical Office of Dar el-Fatwa, where the main Muslim leaders representing Sunnis, Shi'ites and Druzes—Selim Hoss, Hussein el-Husseini, Adel Osseirane, Sheikh Shamseddine, and Sheikh Halim Takieddine—gathered under the auspices of the late Mufti of the Republic Hassan Khaled and laid down the "Islamic principles"[26]). And yet, the long-awaited official recognition of Lebanon as "the final homeland for all" only came in 1989, to be framed in the revised Constitution of Ta'if.

From the sufferings and the atrocities of a merciless war, the various sectarian groups have emerged more Lebanese indeed. This is probably the only positive consequence of the Lebanese internal and internationalized strife. The Shi'ites in particular have developed a sense that they have no other alternative, no other homeland than Lebanon. Some historians would date back the Shi'a "institutional enrollment in the State" to the creation of the Islamic Shi'a Supreme Council.[27] Others argue that their "Lebanonization" started when they clashed with the Palestinians, who, at one period, had become the real masters of the country. Espousing the cause of Palestine would not be at Lebanon's expense as the leader of "Amal" movement Nabih Berri had reminded it earlier on: "Palestinian blood is not more sacred than Lebanese blood."[28]

Shi'a's nationalistic conscience has increased significantly since the end of the war and it has inspired the political discourse. During a "Conference on Islamic Conveying" (*Tabligh*) held in 1997, muftis and sheikhs from different Lebanese regions publicly acknowledged that "despite its flaws, the situation of Muslim Shi'ites in Lebanon is incomparable to any other place in the world, and the freedom we are enjoying in Lebanon, we have not enjoyed it under any sky, and the deprivation we've been decrying and suffering from, is mostly to be blamed on our misbehavior or inexperience."[29] Analyzing the Shi'ites' mindset, Augustus Richard Norton makes a parallel with the Maronites' when he writes: "Like the Maronites, the Shi'a are a minority in a predominantly Sunni Arab world; for both sects, Lebanon is a refuge in which sectarian identity can be preserved and security ensured. It is not surprising that many Maronites saw a natural ally in Imam Musa, especially before he organized his own militia in 1974. (Musa Sadr) often noted, "For us Lebanon is one definitive homeland."[30] Norton also quotes a Lebanese Christian politician and analyst, Karim Pakradouni, explaining that Musa Sadr

> recognized the insecurity of the Maronites, and he acknowledged their need to maintain their monopoly hold on the presidency. Despite his appreciation of the dramatic demographic shifts that had made the Shi'a community the largest plurality in Lebanon, he declined to call for a new census. Yet he

was critical of the Maronites for their arrogant stance toward the Muslims, and particularly toward the Shi'a. He argued that Lebanon's Maronite-dominated governments had neglected the South since independence and had rendered the Shi'a a disinherited subproletariat in Lebanon.[31]

Within the Shi'a community, there is today a strong sense of having earned their Lebanese citizenship by their ongoing struggle against the Israeli occupation with all dire consequences attached to it, such as loss of lives and properties. Suddenly, the Shi'ites no longer sensed they were "on the margin" or "on the edge" of the country (*al-atraf*) as they used to, when they also resented the fact that Mount-Lebanon was the throbbing heart of Lebanon. Eager for recognition, they had imposed themselves. *They were the rising force* and their rich emigrants were coming back from overseas and investing in their hometowns and villages in the South as well as downtown Beirut. This firm "national" commitment has been confirmed by Shamseddine, who repeatedly pledged that the Shi'a community "has no other project than Lebanon." That statement also implied that Shi'ites' political ambitions would only be fulfilled through the Lebanese system and that they would be attentive that the new mold of Lebanon bear their features too. Now in postwar Lebanon, they displayed such self-confidence in their future, formulating what they believed were their rightful demands and seeking satisfaction, that soon the political discourse started mentioning "Political Shi'ism," as replacing "Political Maronitism," which prevailed in the prewar period.

Even the Hezbollah went through the "Lebanonization" process. Sheikh Fadlallah was reported to be behind that process.[32] Since its inception, Hezbollah had rejected the idea of a Lebanese state, calling instead for the establishment of an Islamic Republic. But as soon as Iranian president Rafsanjani pressed for openness and relaxation of Iran's foreign relations (soon to be joined by the Iranian Guide of the Revolution Ayatollah Khamenei, who would dismiss the idea of "exporting the Islamic revolution"), the Hezbollah sought a foothold in the Lebanese political system and reached out to political and religious leaders outside the fundamentalist camp.

Its rhetoric regarding the advent of an Islamic state toned down as the party adopted a non-committal position on the issue (see Part II, Chapter 9). As Fadlallah would put it, "the main characteristic of the Islamic movement in Lebanon is its rationalism and its pragmatism. It is able to think politically."[33] He even believes Lebanese Islamists should be a model for other Islamist groups in the Arab world who resort to violence, which he condemns.

Sociologist and writer Waddah Sharara, who has focused in his work on Islamic political thought, estimates that "the idea that Lebanon is a 'federation of minorities' has taken hold, even among Lebanese Islamists."[34] This development has only occurred after a consistent period of political merging in the Lebanese confessionalist and political system. Now that Muslims in Lebanon were reaching a point of "political maturity," to use one of Fadlallah's expressions, was there a "Lebanese path" for Islam, somewhere between copying Western secularism and falling back on fundamentalism?

Undoubtedly, Lebanese Muslims have developed throughout their longtime coexistence with the Christians patterns of behavior different from Muslims in other Arab countries, and they are the first to acknowledge that, even priding themselves on it. They are more liberal, more "modernized" or "Westernized" (although these aphorisms ought to be used very cautiously), meaning that they are more directly in touch with Western concepts and way of life, more accustomed to be in a pluralistic environment than their fellow Arab Muslims. Sammak clearly observes that "Arab societies do not have the same sense of what the coexisting experience could be, . . . because they are not used to the phenomenon of religious diversity."[35] In a country where Muslim and Christian celebrations are official holidays, religious diversity has led Muslims in Lebanon to celebrate Christmas with their fellow Christians, flooding the capital's streets with decorations and lighting; politicians like former Prime Minister Rafik Hariri would even flaunt a Christmas tree in their private homes. Examples are also given about the influence of Christian rituals on Muslim's social events.[36] And the reverse is true. What makes it easy for Lebanese Christians to deal successfully with the Arab world as businessmen and intermediaries is their exposure to Muslim traditions and lifestyles. As the Maronite Patriarch worded it, in a much celebrated saying: "In each Lebanese Christian there is a Muslim facet, just as there is a Christian facet in each Lebanese Muslim." Many are all the more convinced that Christian Lebanese are closer to their Muslim Lebanese partners than they are to Christian Americans, and vice versa: Lebanese Muslims feel closer and more related to Lebanese Christians than to the Saudis or the Iraqis. But then, how to explain the kidnappings and terror of more than fifteen years of war? Were the Lebanese completely overwhelmed by the external interventions to the point that they totally lost control of the antagonisms that ravaged their country? Is coexistence mere wishful thinking more than it is reality? Or have things really changed after the long bloody strife?

One can easily notice that an evolution in political thinking is currently under way. Muslims of Lebanon agree today that there is a Lebanese specificity, although "certainly unachieved," as Waddah Sharara put it. He states that "contrary to a widespread belief, the idea of Lebanon has been in the air for three centuries. Ach-Chana'a al-Mariahhi, an 18th century poem depicting the resistance of Jabal 'Amel Shiites against Ottoman rule, was written in Lebanese vernacular." According to him, the roots of that Lebanese specificity lay in "the relative weakness of clan cohesion (caused by the special regime of land ownership enjoyed by Lebanon for centuries), the modernizing role of the Christian monastic orders (which dealt a big blow to the rule of feudal lords), and the early emergence of municipal centers (Zahleh and Deir el-Kamar were the first municipalities in the Levant)." Sharara is convinced that "the Lebanese people can create a common political culture which is not based on ethnic or religious 'assabiyya'. They have to build what Habermas calls a 'constitutional patriotism' which will allow them to manage their diversity."[37]

By and large, a set of intellectuals and academics are stressing on the fact that Lebanese Muslims bear a responsibility towards the Arab world, in setting an example of coexistence and respect with the Christians. Lebanon, as Sammak put it, should be the yardstick by which to measure Arabic experiments. So Lebanese Islam, too, has a modernizing mission within the Arab world. In his speech addressed to the representatives of the Arab and Muslim countries attending the "National and Islamic Conference" held in Beirut in 1998, the Lebanese prime minister Selim Hoss pointed out that "Lebanon differs from other Arab regimes in that it is a democratic country."

A strong sense of urgency to challenge Huntington's theory—that Islam cannot live with others and that it is a monolithic world—is developing among Lebanese Muslim intellectuals. "This is all the more a reason to succeed in our Muslim-Christian coexistence," urges Sammak. And he points out that the first dialogue with the "People of the Book," that is, the Christians, was initiated by the Prophet in the city of Najran. Another renowned attempt at dialogue is the theological confrontation that took place between the Abbasid caliph Al-Mahdi and the Nestorian Patriarch Timotheus I.[38]

The initial tolerance of Islam is evoked with nostalgia by many writers. For centuries, Arab and Persian civilizations have constituted, in the Middle East, Africa, and Asia, a powerful factor of unity, because they carried an authentic universalism and a humanist creed. Under the Abbassids, religious discussions were frequent and they often took place in the mosques of Basra and Bagdad. Muslim cities such as Bagdad, Damascus, Cairo, Cordoba, Tunis, and Istanbul, were crossroads for artists, scientists, and liberal thinkers. "When Arabs were triumphant and had the thriving feeling they dominated the world, they interpreted their faith in a spirit of tolerance and openness," observes Amin Maalouf.[39] Arab Muslims like to remind their fellow Christians of that "golden age," when Christian minorities were not only tolerated and protected but were active founders of the Arabic civilization and had even been the administrative architects of the Umeyyade Empire.

Some Muslims, like Fadlallah, wish that Islam would play, with the same success, the same role once upheld by the Arabic civilization. So he would subtly reduce the Arabic *Nahda* to a mere political endeavor and would deprive Arabity from any specific project or definition of its own in order to intertwine it with Islam. "When it started during the *Nahda* as a political and a cultural trend aimed against the Ottoman State, Arabism did not uphold any doctrinal or intellectual content, except the issues of liberation and independence. Later on, it adopted Marxist and socialist ideals," he said.[40] And he added: "God sent the Kuran in Arabic. Arabity can only be achieved and would only find itself in Islam."

This tendency to blend Arabity and Islam is indeed the most sensitive issue the Arab civilization has to deal with at the turn of the twenty-first century. Ultimately, many "Arabists" see that the big victim of Islamic fundamentalism could well be Arabity itself, not the Christians. Arab Muslims specifically are the ones who should be concerned by the replacement of their old ideological reference, because fundamentalism is stripping them of their Arab identity. Arab Muslims are actually a minority in the vast Islamic ensemble *Umma* (they represent 20 percent of the Islamic world)[41] although they occupy a central position in it, culturally, emotionally, and geographically.

Despite the influence of the fundamentalists, the vast majority of Lebanese Muslims are secular. They want to hold on to the paradigm of Arab diversity and pluralism and they do not hide their anxiety. Some of their intellectuals directly confront "the one and unilateral thinking."[42] Others question the ability of "late century's Islam and its twin brother Arabism" to open up and "admit the historical diversity of the Arab world."[43] "What innovating bid has the Islamic world (stretching from Indonesia to Morocco) undertaken (to counter the West or meet it halfway) except waiting or reacting?" wonders Sammak.

Speaking at the meeting of the Islamic Conference Organization in Tehran, December 1997, former Lebanese President Elias Hrawi (the only Christian head of State to attend that conference), urged the Islamic world "to open up" and "to show the real face of Islam," to "rehabilitate women's role" in society, and to "engage into a cultural contest that goes beyond mere Arabo-European dialogue."[44]

In their effort to tackle the fundamentalist wave, Muslims are clinging today to the unique and meaningful experience of Lebanon. The Iranian President himself, Mohammad Khatami, has, on various occasions, lauded Lebanon as "a cultural beacon for the whole region." Hence, the Christian presence becomes a major concern for Muslims too. Christians, especially the Maronites, are geographically spread all over the country, living in mixed villages with Sunnis, Shiites, and Druzes, whereas it is exceptional to find mixed Muslim villages. Sharp contrasts and wide historical gaps separate the various Muslim groups even if the Lebanese entity has brought all communities together. "The Maronites are the only community that is scattered across Lebanon, from Hadath el-Jibbi to Ain-Ebel, forming a kind of spinal cord for Lebanon. This explains their prominent role," observes Sharara.[45] This is why it has been said that Lebanon is a mosaic in which the Christians are the cement. If they leave, wouldn't that erode Lebanon's uniquely pluralistic society? Kamal Salibi, one of Lebanon's premiere historians and authors, considers that "Lebanese Muslims are terrified by the emergence of Islamic clericalism, so they have an umbilical attachment to the Christians as the preservers of secular government and more importantly a secular way of life."[46] And a secular life simply means enjoying the freedom of having a drink at a bar, watching movies, reading books, and choosing the culture you want. These are basic elements of a modern identity.

It is in that perspective that Lebanese Muslims feel increasingly responsible for the preservation of the Christian presence in Lebanon and in the rest of the Arab world. In his book, Mohammad Sammak criticizes some Islamist groups who are in fact "political movements but are essentially exploiting religious sentiments to achieve their political objectives."[47] This is why, according to him, the response of Arab Christians should be expressed within a broader and common Arabic Muslim-Christian context, aimed primarily at educating Arab society. There is a wide consensus among both Arab and Western intelligentsia that fundamentalism is the expression of a crisis of identity of a Third World trying to face the expansion of Western civilization, of its living standards and set of values. In that perspective, secular Muslims (and even "modernists" or reformists within the fundamentalist trend) find themselves standing first in line facing extremism, next to the Christians.

In a critical article, Radwan el-Sayyed, one of the liberal thinkers among the Muslim intelligentsia in Lebanon, asks point-blank: "Is Arabity (or Arabism) of this end of century able to accept the historical diversity that characterizes the Arab homeland?" "Although Arab and Muslim views calmed down and opened up a little in the nineties, the acuteness of the debate concerning the peoples of the Book and of Dhimmitude shows that the question of the identity is still unresolved and that painful times await us," he grimly concludes.[48] Is he right? And can the Christian-Muslim dialogue head off the landslide?

Chapter 3

Dialogue: A Necessity or a Burden?

Despite Lebanon's embedded tradition of inter-communal coexistence, "Christian-Muslim dialogue" is an expression that triggers a mix of derision and skepticism when it is evoked. Most of the Lebanese are scathing on that subject. They have attached to dialogue whimsical labels such as "mutual deceit" and "reciprocal trickery," signaling through contempt that dialogue hasn't so far led to an open and frank national debate. The general conviction among Lebanese at various levels is that dialogue has been a coddling exercise that avoided raising the thorny but fundamental issues.[1] Many sense that, despite the involvement of the country's most prestigious names and prominent religious leaders and scholars in intellectual exchanges, dialogue has not prevented fanaticism and war in the near past, and is not precluding the resurgence of sectarian behavior in the postwar era, even after the convening of the Synod on Lebanon in the Vatican at the end of 1995, under the auspices of Pope John Paul II.

On the very day the Holy Father was scheduled to arrive in Lebanon, where he would release his Apostolic Exhortation (May 10, 1997), the first Lebanese daily, *An-Nahar,* published a special issue, significantly titled, "The Pitfalls of Christian-Muslim Dialogue in Lebanon." It is only relevant to pick up the headlines of the articles signed by major experts and men of religion who contributed to that issue. They speak by themselves: "Yes, dialogue is in trouble," "National dialogue is jammed at all levels," "Dialogue does not reinforce national unity," "In order to stop reciprocal guile," "Dialogue is unable to resolve Lebanon's existential crisis," "What can we do?" and "The faked dialogue."[2] Like an undesired child, dialogue has been rebuked by those who practice it. Baffled by its manifold demands, they would surrender at times to the temptation of giving up, of laying down the burden.

Yet, one shared conclusion had surfaced from the infernal circle of war: there is no other alternative to dialogue. This conclusion was politically translated in the Ta'if agreement, which redesigned the 1943 Covenant. All radical ventures had been tried, from ethno-religious cleansing to sectarian "gerrymandering." Once they'd set their fiefs, Christian warlords turned against each other and so did the Shiite militias, in a compelling drive to shore up their exclusive hegemony over their own community. And so, Lebanese are bound together by the unpleasant memory of their inter- and intra-sectarian antagonisms and the desire to keep them at bay. But is it enough to engage in nation-building?

One of the politically correct trends is to deny the Lebanese "identity" of the war, in order to produce an image of integration. One myth simply held that there had been no civil war in Lebanon, but to quote former President Elias Hrawi, "only a war of others on our territory."[3] This slogan had been launched in the eighties by famous journalist and former Lebanese ambassador to the UN, Ghassan Tuéni.[4]

The international and regional interference in Lebanon and the active involvement of numerous players in this war is undeniable. The best proof lies in the Ta'if accord itself.[5]

It is also true that, unlike in Bosnia, back-channels always existed between the in-fighting parties, and hatred was not widespread and was not propagated by the intellectuals to set the ideological platform of the militias. But, as Ahmed Beydoun put it: "How could the seed [of war] grow if it were not sown in fertile soil?"[6] Could the Lebanese candidly shirk responsibility and dissociate themselves from the causes of the war they fought? In short, could they heal the wounds without the "purification of conscience" required of them by Pope John Paul II? How could they be immune to future interventions that would bring them into collision with each other again? And would the inter-religious dialogue in which they engage be truly open and candid? How straightforward can a dialogue be, without wounding others' feelings and tweaking their convictions? What are the limits and hazards of Christian-Muslim dialogue?

THE LIMITS AND HAZARDS OF DIALOGUE

The first Christian-Muslim dialogue in Lebanon officially took place in July 1965 at the prestigious forum "Le Cénacle Libanais," where foreign leaders and intellectuals have often been speakers. Eight participants representing various Lebanese communities expressed their belief that "Lebanon is the chosen land for this Christian-Muslim dialogue." They also asserted that Islam and Christianity "meet together in their belief in one God and aim at consolidating the joint spiritual and moral values that safeguard human dignity."

Although dialogue took the form of eight lectures, the conference set in motion a daring rapprochement. "It was the first Lebanese attempt, if not the first Arab attempt, to establish a comparative theology," wrote the Greek Orthodox Bishop of Mount-Lebanon, George Khodr, who was one of the lecturers.[7] This historical attempt had also lined up eminent figures such as Imam Musa Sadr and Maronite historian and priest Yoakim Moubarac (whose mentor had been French Orientalist Louis Massignon). Sadr defended an Islam that was able to open up to the cultures of the lands it conquered because it was strong. He warned that if Islam shuts the door to modern civilization, it would be a sign of weakness and a loss of self-confidence.[8] Moubarac developed the idea that "an exclusively Christian or exclusively Muslim Lebanon would loose its raison d'être and would condemn itself, like Israel did."

After that milestone was set, the first international Christian-Muslim conference was held in the summer resort of Broummana (Mount-Lebanon) in 1972.[9] From the very beginning, the question of the representability of the participants was raised. In 1972, the 46 participants who came to Broummana from over 20 countries insisted that they only represented themselves. The same thing had happened in 1965, when the eight participants underscored the fact that their dialogue had no official quality and they had no representative capacity. "We were only expressing our own personal opinions," stressed bishop Georges Khodr.[10]

Capital issues regularly upheld by the Catholic Church,[11] such as the necessity of reciprocity and the respect of religious freedom, would become the keystones of any inter-religious gathering ever since. The religious freedom was a fundamental principle proclaimed at the 1972 conference of Broummana.

The responsibility Lebanese religious leaders bear in boosting national and inter-religious dialogue is critical. And Bkerké, the siege of the Maronite Patriarchate, has an undisputed lead in that regard. Considered as "primus inter pares" among the spiritual authorities of the country for its role in the foundation of Greater Lebanon, the Maronite Patriarch is regarded as "the Patriarch of Lebanon" even by the Muslims. In 1958, hosted by Patriarch Meouchi, Muslim leaders gathered in Bkerké and prayed there to assert the unity of the Lebanese people. It is also in Bkerké that the first postwar spiritual summit was convened (August 1993), in the wake of the Israeli attack on Southern Lebanon. It assembled all Christian and Muslim religious authorities and issued a joint statement condemning the Israeli aggression. But also and essentially, the summit established "the national committee for Christian-Muslim dialogue," in which the main Lebanese communities would be represented at a formal level, directly linked to the religious hierarchies.[12] Then, for the first time in the history of the Vatican, the three Muslim representatives in the committee attended the Synod on Lebanon held within the walls of St. Peter Square (November 26 through December 14, 1995) and participated in the colloquiums and debates in their official capacity as "observers." They also were the first Muslim guests to the dinner table of the Holy Father in his private apartments. They—with their Christian counterparts in the committee—would also play an important role in appeasing the inflammatory reactions that erupted when the Final Message of the Synod was issued (see Part II, Chapter 7).

The unimpeded power of religious leaders in Lebanon is all the more astonishing for a Western observer. Bishops and priests, sheikhs and imams have become the spokespersons of their communities in postwar Lebanon, when political parties through ideological bankruptcy fell into discredit. No initiative would be politically endorsed if not hallowed by them, no dialogue can really occur and have some impact without their consent and even blessing. They are also the ones who give legitimacy to political leaders.

All throughout the war, the official religious authorities on both the Christian and Muslim sides refused to warrant any militia, held on to the symbolic pledge of "the Lebanese unity and sovereignty," and tried to keep the channels open between them (a spiritual gathering in Bkerké was even held in October 1975, the first year the fights started). Some paid a heavy price for their unyielding "national" and anti-partition position.[13]

In postwar years, the Maronite Patriarch, the Maronite Orders, the Jesuits, the Apostolic Nuncio, and above all Pope John Paul II himself, are the main players on the Christian side, whereas Sheikh Shamseddine, Ulema Fadlallah, and the lay advisers of Dar el-Fatwa and the Shi'a Supreme Council, Mohammad Sammak and Seoud el-Mawla, as well as the invisible hands of Syria and Iran, on the Muslim side, will set the tone of Muslim-Christian dealings.

It is rather paradoxical to imagine a democracy like Lebanon, yielding at times, to theocratic temptations, surrounded by autocratic and Islam-driven regimes, claiming secular orientations! (Not to mention the Jewish state of Israel.)

Separating religion from politics in Lebanon? It might look like a fancy intellectual exercise. How indeed is it possible to ignore that all minorities of the region sought asylum in Lebanon to preserve first and foremost their freedom of belief, of expression, their right for political participation, and their specificity? No wonder that the Apostolic Exhortation, in its very first section, clearly refers to "the religious roots of the Lebanese national and political identity." It is actually John Paul II's appeal for a work of preparation for the Synod that will determine the content and the mechanisms of postwar Christian-Muslim dialogue.

DIALOGUE WITHOUT KNOWLEDGE

No one knew what the word "synod" meant except the initiated, i.e., the Christian clergy. So when the Synod was convoked by the Holy Father on June 12, 1991, an information campaign was launched through the media to familiarize the masses with that idea. Moreover, considerable efforts were deployed to defuse Muslim apprehensions that no Western plot was under way and that the Assembly's aim was to discuss the situation of the Catholic churches in Lebanon and the region. Muslim authorities would soon be asked to join their efforts and formulate their remarks to the document for reflection referred to as the *Lineamenta,* a first step in the synodal process (*see Part II, Chapter 6*).

This episode highlights one of the main difficulties facing an enlightened dialogue. It is summed up in one basic question: is there substantial mutual knowledge of the other's religion and traditions? "Most frequently, the Western Christian interlocutor (be he Catholic or Protestant) is an expert on Islam, deeply abreast of its doctrine, its *fiqh* and the *chari'a*. Whereas his Muslim counterpart has a knowledge restricted to the Kuranic text. Studying Christian theology and philosophy has often been alien to Muslim culture," deplores Mohammad Sammak.[14] This self-critical view is shared by Radwan as-Sayyed.[15] Christian religious figures engaged in dialogue confirm that theory: Muslim dialecticians, they say, rely on the Kuran, the *sunna* and the *hadith,* when they address Christianity. Besides, they act as individuals. Whereas Christians do not argue on the doctrinal level, they base their dialogue on principles of human respect, tolerance, and recognition. In doing so, they also reflect positions endorsed by international religious institutions.[16]

On the general level as well, "cultural and religious dialogue still does not exist, except in some second-grade schools. Few of the Christian students know anything about Islam. And few of the Muslim students know what Christianity is all about. Schools need to have books that deal with religion in a scientific and objective way, and do not scoff at others' religion," notes Greek Catholic bishop Gregoire Haddad, the most progressive figure in the Greek Catholic Church.[17]

The pioneers of the Christian-Muslim overture at the 1965 conference had dispensed then an unheeded recommendation: the creation of an Institute for inter-religious studies and comparative theology, where Christianity and Islam would be taught. They knew that "ignorance leads to distrust, which in turn gradually shifts to prejudice, polemics, then nurtures a self-defense instinct, hastily replaced by a desire for power and stamped with fanaticism, which in turn confiscates religion."[18] Bishop Khodr reveals that the participants had also suggested the drafting of a common book on religious education to be circulated in all public and private schools. "Unfortunately, despite the enthusiasm of the President of the Republic at that time, our suggestion never came to light."[19]

Another impediment is that dialogue is confined to restricted intellectual and academic circles. The question of how exactly representative are the participants in the dialogue and what leverage do they have is a core one. Are they able to commit their communities and the decision makers? Without a "culture of dialogue" spreading at the grass-roots level, it is like "building the roof before laying down the foundations of the house," to paraphrase Jean Corbon.[20]

The objectives of Christian-Muslim dialogue as well as its initiative are also major points of contention. More and more frequently, this dialogue is seen as an attempt of the West to impose its values and conditions on the Muslim world. Summarizing what he presents as the Muslim position in the Christian-Muslim dialogue, Sammak considers that Islam frequently stands on the defensive in an "unequal exchange." According to him, "the Christian negotiator essentially sticks to a Western agenda" and thus "Islam is charged in advance of violating human rights and women's rights."[21] And he adds: "For the West, dialogue aims at knowing better how Muslims think and how their analyses evolve, so as to be able to contain and subjugate them. Whereas the Muslim's intent is to show his good faith in dealing with Christianity, and subsequently, with Western civilization, or to alleviate the European guilty conscience toward the Jews, in order to break the linkage between Western Christianity—particularly some American evangelical churches—and the Zionist movement."

This is why some Arab Muslim intellectuals make a point by separating the dialogue they are engaged in with Western Christianity from the one they have with Arab Christianity, since the latter shares the same ethnic, historical, and cultural background as Islam. "It is no good opening an Islamic dialogue with the Western Church if it should bypass the Arab Church, because the Arab Church is the bridge that leads to any understanding," insists Sammak.[22]

But on the Christian side, there is a broader feeling that dialogue is a "one way ticket" when assessing the end result. Reciprocity of treatment remains in fact a pivotal demand heralded by Pope John Paul II himself. Many consider that dialogue has brought about a deeper understanding of the Muslim world and greater solidarity with it, as well as a better acceptance of Muslim emigrants in Western societies and a recognition of their religious rights and cultural traditions.[23] Meanwhile, Islam witnessed a divergent evolution, characterized by radicalism and fundamentalism, and Christian minorities in the Islamic world still face discrimination and inequality of chances and treatment.

Some would explain the absence of reciprocity by the fact that dialogue is essentially a Christian initiative—if not even a Christian concept. They add that, because of the Christian presence, "dialogue is what distinguishes Lebanon from the rest of the Arab countries."[24] Sammak seems to confirm that view when he deplores the lack of initiative on the Muslim side.[25]

Notwithstanding the involvement of spiritual leaders in it, and despite an inclination to dwell on the Abrahamic roots of the three monotheistic faiths, dialogue is carefully designed to avoid the theological aspect. It is one of its first and most sensitive limits. In his presentation at the Synod, the Jesuit "General" Kolvenbach made it clear that "radical divergences—deriving precisely from their interpretation of their Abrahamic ascendancy—separate Islam from Christianity," which makes a theological debate "unrealistic."

"True dialogue can only take place between persons and communities, not between systems or religions," writes father Maurice Borrmans, the director of the Pontifical Institute for Arab and Muslim Studies in Rome, who also publishes the magazine *IslamoChristiana*.[26] According to him, it should insist on shared values, without resorting to a religious syncretism. His opinion is shared by many Christian and Muslim figures.[27] "Religions are not meant to dialogue, because dialogue means compromise, and how do you compromise on the absolute truth on which religion is built?" wonders Hassan Kobeyssi.[28] "The problem is known: it stems from Islam's negation of the divinity of Christ, and Christians' denial of the prophecy of Muhammad," adds Ahmed Beydoun.[29]

Sammak's own attempt to venture into the muddy sands of the core religious beliefs was bashed by the Christian episcopate on summer 1998. (He had raised the issue of the Trinity and the Virgin Mary's place in it. A similar attempt from the Christians to read Muhammad's prophetic character would undoubtedly have the same fate.) This is why it's been said that this is not a dialogue between Islam and Christianity, but between Muslims and Christians. It has even become at times a dialogue between confessions, since people define themselves by their sectarian affiliation. "This is why dialogue has turned into a means to score points and to assert oneself as opposed to the other," contends Sayyed Fadlallah.[30] One of his favorite themes is that "in Lebanon, there is a lot of sectarianism, and not much religion."

He's not the only one to lash the current Christian-Muslim debate. Many resent that it has turned into feuding over power, public posts, and private profits. As such, Christian-Muslim dialogue in Lebanon is directly linked to political confessionalism. Could it be otherwise? In Kolvenbach's eyes, "inter-religious dialogue in Lebanon is rather an expectation than a reality."[31]

PLURALISM IS THE REAL ISSUE

Navigating the thicket of Lebanon's religious quagmire is not a comfortable task. At the end of the day, it all boils down to one matter: pluralism is the real issue, or rather its acceptance. The Greek Orthodox Bishop of Beirut, Elias Audeh, believes that the very fact Lebanese keep talking about coexistence, analyzing its scope and meaning, means that there is still a problem somewhere. Are Lebanese able to move beyond simple coexistence and generous tolerance to a deeper recognition and mutual support?

One of the many paradoxes of Lebanese society is that political pluralism is working and has an integrative power, even on Islamist groups such Hezbollah and the "Al Jamaa al-Islamiya" (close to the Muslim Brothers). But admitting "cultural pluralism" still irks some Muslim sensitivities (see Chapter 1) so much that this concept, referred to in the Final Message of the Synod, had to be replaced in the Apostolic Exhortation by "cultural diversity," a phrase that is better accepted (see Chapter 7). And yet, sectarian pluralism is a fact that has been sanctioned by the Constitution. One would wonder: what kind of dialogue is that in which words do not carry the same significance on both sides? Christians and Muslims do not have the same approach nor the same vocabulary in describing the Lebanese consensus, so Lebanese definitely need to produce a common lexicon.

The Christian speech (shared by Muslim intellectuals and modernists such as Nawaf Salam, Waddah Sharara, Wajih Kawtharani, and Radwan Sayyed) highlights and praises the "pluralistic" aspect of the Lebanese society, while the word "pluralism" is a loaded term for Muslim leaders. It contests the integrative philosophy of "one people" and jeopardizes "national unity." In their minds, it still carries the "federalist" speech pattern—equivalent to a "partition" of the country—defended by the Christian militia of the "Lebanese Forces." Sheikh Shamseddine is adamant about it: "This is why," he explains, "I do not accept the use of the pluralistic concept, neither in Lebanon, nor in Egypt or any other Islamic or mixed society."[32]

"The old notion of national unity that refuses to acknowledge the differences and tries to obliterate them would only lead to clashes and outburst of violence," warns Samir Frangié, a Maronite politician and intellectual.[33]

Maronite Patriarch Sfeir, a firm advocate of cultural pluralism but a staunch opponent of any partitionist project (after all, is not the Maronite

Patriarchate the godfather of Greater Lebanon?), addresses Muslim concerns by reasserting that "no one thinks of partitioning the country, because Lebanon would not survive in case it is divided. That idea is a relic of the past."[34]

Islam's inability to deal with pluralism today may well derive from its loss of self-confidence predicted by Musa Sadr. Will a newly emerging "Western" Islam revamp the entrenched oriental Islam? "Classical Islam developed a theology for a majority religion sovereign in its own land," the Mufti of Marseilles, Soheib Bencheikh, is quoted as saying in *Time* magazine.[35] "We have no theology for being one minority among others in a secular space. We need a new theology to bring the Muslim faith into line with these new realities."

BRIDGING THE POLITICAL GAPS

The real dialogue able to bear fruit would rather be dealing with common social and economic matters, advancing the cause of individual rights and freedom, building on shared values, exploring the notion of human rights, democracy, political participation. In a word, establishing "the culture of democracy." To use one of the renowned maxims of Prime Minister Selim Hoss, "in Lebanon, we have a lot of freedom, but little democracy." And Sayyed Fadlallah would add: "We have the freedom of speech, not the freedom of change." At that level, sectarian boundaries would disappear and give way to other dividing lines within a community group: on the Muslim side, there are those who advocate secularism, civil rights, separation of powers, and democracy, and those who want to base social and political development on the precepts of Islam and of the chari'a.

For academics such as Ahmed Beydoun and Nawaf Salam, the dialogue could only be true if it overruns confessions and sectarianism and tends toward building a secular democratic society, where the person is genuinely free from sectarian bonds and the unshakable authority of the religious.

The "Observatory of Democracy in Lebanon," a project launched in 1997 by a Lebanese nonprofit organization[36] with the cooperation and support of the European community, aims at "discerning the Lebanese democratic legacy," as explained by Antoine Messarra, eminent professor at the Lebanese University and director of the project. He says that "the research on Lebanese democracy is hindered by a complex of shame toward sectarian pluralism and by cultural alienation and dogmatism." Deeply convinced that "any setback of democracy in Lebanon threatens the future of inter-religious relations in the region and favors the return of war," he has compounded seminars, TV talk shows, editorials, and surveys to prod a political debate on the system of government "rather than sinking into a sterile intellectual rumination."[37] At one of his seminars, a Hezbollah representative asked, "Why is this project being sponsored by the European Community and handled by Christians?"

The answer: "Well, if you know of any Arab country willing to sponsor an Observatory of Democracy that would scrutinize public life and publish regular reports on the compliance of the state with democratic standards, let us know." Messarra ended up being invited to talk about civil society on the Manar TV network of Hezbollah, and confronted direct questions about "this Westernized notion of civil society" and what it did imply and how it matched the Islamic goals of justice and social integration.

"Why the Christians?" At each and every stage of the nation's evolution, that question of the Christians being at the forefront of the struggle for civil liberties arose. But Christians have always highlighted that theirs was a joint struggle led with their Muslim counterparts and that they all shared common goals. Very often though, disputes would erupt on issues such as "independence," "sovereignty," and "freedom," particularly if these words related to the Lebanese-Syrian relation and the presence of Syrian forces on the Lebanese territory; a "presence" the Christian mainstream would designate as "occupation."

The Final Message of the Synod provoked alienation of the Mufti of the Republic, of Sheikh Shamseddine, and of political leaders such as Prime Minister Rafik Hariri, Speaker of Parliament Nabih Berri, and Druze leader Walid Joumblatt, because it mentioned (among other things) the "withdrawal of the Syrian forces from Lebanon." The controversy reached all levels. Editor in chief of *As-Safir* Talal Selman, a key media figure in Lebanon and a prominent debater in the Shi'ite community, often protested the fact that Christians would have "a preemption right on freedom and independence. . . . Do Christians think the Muslims are more inclined to live under oppression?" he argued, putting forth the fact that the stationing of Syrian troops in Lebanon is viewed by a larger portion of Lebanese as a fraternal presence, not an occupation force. This divergence of opinions on a key aspect of sovereignty is critical indeed as is the question raised by Selman: is independence a Christian claim? Is there a different "Muslim concept" of independence, especially when it comes to Syria (given that all Lebanese are united in considering the Israeli occupation in the South a major infringement upon Lebanon's sovereignty and territorial integrity and that getting rid of it is the number one priority)? What does the word "independence" really imply? Do Lebanese agree on the same definition of it?

Ever since its independence, Lebanon has had difficult times conducting its foreign policy because of this tendency to conflate the sectarian (Christian-Muslim) and the foreign policy (Arabism-Western) cleavages, although the National Pact of 1943 stipulated that Christians would abjure striking alliances with the West and Muslims with the East (meaning Syria and the Arab-Muslim world). But, as famous journalist Georges Naccache put it then : "Two negations do not build a nation."

"The genius of the al Khuri-al Solh National Pact was that it enunciated the one, unvarnished truth about Lebanon—it is separate and Arab," writes Charles Winslow in "Lebanon: War and Politics in a Fragmented Society." According to Winslow, "in order to regain their independence, Lebanese should set the following priorities: to demand the reconstitution of the fully independent Republic; to organize it according to the conception of the National Pact; to engage into non-sectarian politics and to manage, if possible, to have the top leadership position in the movement held by a Muslim." And he adds: "Comment is perhaps needed only for the last of these priorities: such a movement, if necessary, would only meet with success if most of the members of the Muslim communities in the Republic felt Lebanese. Christians should assume, therefore, that a time would come when Muslims also wanted to reconstitute a fully independent Lebanon, one that was their country too."[38]

In postwar Lebanon, the Christians have been passing tests in order to move freely on the political stage: they have been constantly solicited to reassert their Arabic commitment, culturally and politically. This requirement, along with the reiterated common position against Israeli occupation[39] and the support to the activities of the Resistance in southern Lebanon, as well as the consensus on Syria's role in Lebanon have become the main yardsticks of Christians' integration in the new political landscape produced by the Ta'if accords. However, they still had the feeling that they were downsized and even excluded from decisions affecting Lebanon's future and their own.

It is thus all too blatant that dialogue has an inevitable political dimension and that the state is a major interlocutor since it has a responsibility in bridging the gap between its citizens. But the postwar regime did not try to foster dialogue, and favored instead "authoritarian integration" and so, writes Seoud el-Mawla, "the national committee for dialogue laid down a draft paper containing a set of bold ideas that became the guidelines of the spiritual authorities from 1993 to 1996. The main point was the acknowledgment of a political imbalance and the call for the inclusion of all in the State institutions to avert further threat to the unity of the country and to the principles of coexistence."[40]

As he worried for the "non-dialogue situation" that had spread throughout the country at the eve of Pope John Paul II's arrival, Seoud el-Mawla, the Shiite representative in the committee, was alarmed that protest had extended to the Greek Orthodox church.[41]

GREEK ORTHODOX AND MARONITES: COMMON WORRIES

Indeed, the once reserved Greek Orthodox Church of Antioch, through its Patriarch and bishops, was suddenly voicing its discontent and concern for the future of Christianity in Arab lands, including Lebanon. Most unexpectedly, the Maronite apprehensions were being relayed by the Greek Orthodox.

Traditionally, the Greek Orthodox Church of Antioch has always considered itself as the heir of Byzantium but also (and like the Maronites themselves) of the Antiochian spirituality, very much inspired by the Syriac fathers of the Orient. It has always stressed its Arabic identity and was prone to highlight its Arabic commitment and its ability to live in harmony with Islam.[42] The Patriarch of Antioch, Ignatius IV Hazim, who resides in Damascus, was thus eager to distance himself from the Greek Orthodox Serbs, who were jeopardizing, by their behavior in Bosnia and Kosovo, the centuries-long coexistence of the Antioch seat with Islam.

Parallel to that, the Greek Orthodox Patriarchate of Antioch has displayed deep contempt toward the West. "What was once called the Christian world does not exist, in my view," Patriarch Hazim bitterly comments. "There are no more Christians in Europe and those few who still are Christians have great merit because they live in an environment fraught with evil temptations channeled by the media."[43] The resentment goes back to the Crusaders and later, to the proselytism of Latin missions that left indelible scars in the body of the Greek Orthodox Church. Inevitably, this antagonism toward the West also reflected on the relationship between the Greek Orthodox Church and the Maronite Church, viewed as the spearhead of Western cultural and political influence in the Orient but also as the ones who provided a propitious terrain for the scission of the Greek Catholic Church from its mother church in 1724.

And yet, this relation with the Maronite Church is not without hidden admiration: the Greek Orthodox are aware that only Lebanon provided the climate of freedom that enabled them to achieve their own cultural renaissance since the fifties, through the Orthodox Youth Movement and the founding of monastic communities (Deir el-Harf in Mount-Lebanon), and the University of Balamand (North Lebanon). Although publicly critical of the Maronites' militancy,[44] they privately valued the latter's ability to speak out loud in a repressive regional environment and came to realize that Maronites' waning power in postwar years would have a negative impact on Eastern Christianity. The Greek Orthodox community who did not have a militia during the war had been horrified by the Maronite internecine killings of 1990. As the new order entailed Syria's de facto hegemony over the country as well as the redistribution of power at the expense of the Maronites, and with the subsequent numerical and political decline of the Christians, the Greek Orthodox departed from their reserve. Tenors like the editor in chief of *An-Nahar* newspaper and former ambassador Ghassan Tueni, as well as former Minister of Foreign Affairs Fouad Boutros, adopted more political and militant stands, expressing their concerns about freedom of expression, equal political opportunities for citizens, the future of democracy, independence and sovereignty, the marginalization of the Christians in the institutions of power, and the lack of national entente. "Since the adoption of Ta'if, I have been repeating that pacific coexistence is one thing, and national entente is another thing. Entente is the founding principle on which lays all the rest," wrote Boutros.[45]

Patriarch Hazim himself did not hide his anxiety anymore, and postwar years will witness a significant personal rapprochement and concordance of views with Maronite Patriarch Nasrallah Sfeir. As Eastern Christians, "we have to initiate a constructive process between us," he explains, adding sorrowfully: "We have to realize that we're no longer a majority in this region. We all know that, before Islam, this whole region was overwhelmingly Christian. In the land of the Lord our Christ, we have today become a minority. Therefore, we have an increased responsibility to show the real face of a harmonious Christianity."[46] He did not even hesitate to defend his communities' rights in the sectarian distribution of posts within the administration and in government, which was rather unusual from his part.

This "politization" of the Greek Orthodox discourse was new. In his episcopate of Beirut, Bishop Elias Audeh was raising eyebrows in the official circles, since his televised Sunday sermons were more diatribes against the regime's exclusionist policy, the corruption of the rulers, the arbitrary arrests of young opposition activists, and so on.

Even Mount-Lebanon Bishop George Khodr, one of the sharpest critics of the Maronites' "Westernization" and pugnacity, and the strongest advocate of Greek Orthodox Arabity, became mitigated. Noting the "different theologies" professed by Christianity and Islam and their "divergence as regards women's status and hence, family status," he praised "cultural diversity," "Lebanon as a freedom option," and talked of "our plural society, unified but not homogeneous."[47] As a participant in the Synod, he will also (and unrealistically, though) promote the lost unity of the first millennium.

Khodr viewed that the Greek Orthodox choice was to find a third way "between the nation-in-arms (represented by the Maronites) and resignation." He believed that "the role of the Greek Orthodox should be to attenuate the Maronite rigor," and that the ultimate fate of Christians living in a Muslim environment is "to bear witness" (*chahàda,* in Arabic). But he was nonetheless concerned about the status of the Christians in their Muslim societies. If Christians cannot live by arms, do they have to submit to the status of *dhimmis?* A status the Greek Orthodox Church has known under Islam since the fall of Constantinople (1453), and is unwilling to live again.

"Dhimmitude" was precisely in the back of Christians' minds these days, and the rise of fundamentalism did not help appease their fears. But Muslim leaders were apparently conciliatory. "From sheikh Shamseddine to Ghanoushi in Tunisia, and Tourabi in Sudan, and the Muslim Brothers in Egypt and Jordan and Palestine, the concept of *dhimmi* is obsolete," stated a reassuring Seoud el-Mawla.[48]

AN ISLAMIC STATE?

The issue of establishing an Islamic state was at the heart of Christian-Muslim dialogue. After the 1992 legislative elections, a Hezbollah delegation set a *première* by paying a December visit to the Maronite Patriarch in Bkerké. A few days before, Patriarch Sfeir had taken a sharp-edged public position, warning that "if we are forced to choose between freedom and coexistence, we will choose freedom." Many wondered at that time if Hezbollah's opening to the Maronites was a tactical maneuver or a farsighted approach to Lebanese reality. Soon, then, the Islamic discourse of Hezbollah would gradually shift from a hard-line position to a more realistic discourse. Hezbollah leaders would put forth the concept of *'ahd,* a pact or contract with people of the Book, i.e., the Christians.

Sayyed Fadlallah, their "spiritual guide," was to become one of the main interlocutors for those among Lebanese Christians who were questioning Islamists' intentions in Lebanon. Right after the end of the war, he would pride himself in opening channels with various figures of the Christian clergy (Bishop Audeh would even preface a book on him), and particularly with Apostolic Nuncio Pablo Puente. He would also receive foreign groups (such as World Vision and Protestant ministers), American journalists, and young students. But they would all be baffled by his dialectical skills. His positions are tinted with ambiguity and sometimes with contradiction. He would flatly deny any intention of establishing an Islamic state. "It is a non-realistic goal because Lebanese society is not fit for that right now, but still it would remain a political and cultural goal dependent on future developments in the region," he would say. One of his favorite themes and most telling arguments is that the Christians have no revealed system of social organization, no revealed Shari'ah or rule *(hukm).* So they might just as well be open to discussion about an Islamic state as they are to discussion of a socialist or a liberal state. Only through "conviction," not coercion, can this idea be discussed.

Sheikh Shamseddine's views are no less equivocal. He finds the most palatable tone to say that "Lebanese Muslims cannot exist as Lebanese without the Christians, and Christian Lebanese cannot exist as Lebanese without the Muslims,"[49] and that "Lebanon is not Lebanon without the Christians," it is a joint 'Christian-Muslim project."Yet he writes : "In Islamic society, a non-Christian enjoys full political rights without restrictions, except for the Presidency of the State. We have our own solution. When French society will be mature enough to accept a Muslim President of the Republic, I would be glad to see a Christian as the head of state of any Arab country."[50]

A DIALOGUE OF THE EQUALS OR A MINORITY/MAJORITY ONE?

In view of these theories, the numerical argument has become (has always been) a key element for the Christians to preserve their political rights and their freedom of choice. There is an enhanced conviction that dialogue with the Muslim counterparts can only be true when Christians are dealing on equal basis (demographically and thus, politically). With minorities, there is no dialogue but a relation of power. How long will the Christian-Muslim dialogue in Lebanon remain a dialogue of the equals? Would it become sometime (soon?) a minority/majority dialogue? In that case, one party would be in a position of strength and then the dialogue would turn into negotiation. Was it what Islamic leaders were hoping for, in a political perspective? Were they calming down Christian anxieties in order to gain time, which they thought was on their side?

Wedged between Islam and the West, the Christians of the Levant were feeling more nervous and insecure. They had the disagreeable sensation that Muslim authorities were making things difficult through moral pressure, by contesting their cultural, conceptual, social, and political choices, "so as to make us feel like we're strangers in our own country," said one important Christian figure. Furthermore, individual contacts of Lebanese politicians with Western countries and their trips abroad became carefully scrutinized and sometimes even viewed with wariness. Syria's political calculations and influence were not totally strangers to that scrutiny.

If it went on, the incremental polarization of the two worlds, Islam and the West, would take a heavy toll on the Lebanese pluralistic and open society. Under the paradigm of a clash of civilizations, strenuous work and ingenuity from the Christian and Muslim intelligentsia would be required to formulate Lebanon's contribution to the advancement of Christian-Muslim understanding. Lebanon was, more than ever before indeed, "a state of permanent (material and intellectual) tension," to paraphrase Michel Hayek.

According to many thinkers though, this disturbing polarization between Islam and the West is only transient. It "is not due to the nature of the religions, but to a historical lag of one or two centuries, between them," writes French thinker Edgar Morin.[51] "The Islamic world is going through its own Reformation and counter-Reformation age," analyzes Sayyed Hani Fahs. "It is faced by a rapid pace of changes never witnessed before in history." He adds to his argument that both Catholicism and Protestantism primarily confronted modernity with a wave of fundamentalism and puritanism.[52]

Yes, the evolution is inevitable. Reforming, adapting, modernizing: each religion has had (and still has) its dilemma and its "moment of truth" in the inexorable march of history. In the Islamic world, there is a growing conviction that adapting to the modern world does not necessarily mean adopting the Western terminology of "democracy," "human rights," and so on. After centuries of immobility, the Islamic world initiated a profound mutation in the early twentieth century and, at the onset of the twenty-first, is facing the challenge of a globalized world. At one point, once it has regained its self-confidence and found the answers it is looking for, Islam would reclaim its original opening to pluralism and its traditional tolerance. But when that time comes, will the Christians of the Orient still be there?

PART II

Coexistence in Facts and Figures

Chapter 4

Sharing Exile

In the past decade, Eastern Christians have been counting their numbers with greater anxiety. The statistics gathered from all over the Arab world confirmed what they dreaded most: their physical and geographical presence was shrinking to a level where historians, researchers, and demographers could legitimately wonder if they had reached a point of "no return."

Once again, the liberal Lebanese daily *An-Nahar* (owned by the Greek Orthodox Ghassan Tueni, a close friend to Patriarch Hazim) came out with a special issue, on January 1998, with the blunt title "Halt the Exodus of the *Christians of the Orient!*"[1] It gave a bleak outlook of the situation throughout the Arab world, where Christian communities were leaving in droves, and tolled a bell to warn against their extinction and its effects on Arab civilization itself. With dismay, Christians faced, ink on paper, the crude uttering of their innermost fears and Muslims were abruptly compelled to cast a closer look on what was going wrong in Arab societies.

"Are the Christians of the Orient on the verge of extinction?" I asked Father Tom Siking, professor of theology at St. Joseph University and a spiritual mentor of the Jesuits at the Jamhour College. "If one develops a mere sociopolitical analysis," he replied, "it could lead to a pessimistic conclusion. But from the Christian eschatological angle, the answer is no. Being Christian in the Orient is a mission." His answer mirrors the conviction of most religious orders in Lebanon. But what do facts and figures say?

The overall total estimate of Eastern Christians in the Middle East (the diaspora numbers are excluded) does not exceed 15 million (including Iran and Turkey). Some figures show they amount to between 12 and 14 million. They are distributed (approximately) in the following groups:[2]

- Greek Orthodox: 1.5 million
- Greek Catholics: 400,000 to 425,000
- Syrian Orthodox: 150,000
- Syrian Catholics: 80,000
- Copts (including Orthodox, Catholics, and Protestants): 6.5 million
- Armenian Orthodox: 400,000 to 500,000
- Armenian Catholics: around 50,000
- Maronites: 750,000 to 800,000
- Latins: 80,000
- Protestants: 45,000
- Assyrian (ancient Nestorian) Orthodox: less than 100,000
- Chaldean Catholics: 435,000

Of this total, nearly 1.45 million live in Lebanon, making it the most important concentration of Eastern Christians in one single territory, if one excludes the 6 million Copts in Egypt. Most relevant is the proportional number of Christians as compared to the total number of the population in the Arab countries. Since the Islamic conquest in the seventh century, the demographic patterns of Christians have steadily declined, only to be revamped under the Ottoman rule.

On the eve of the arrival of the Seljuk Turks from Central Asia and their victory over the Byzantine army at the Battle of Manzikert (1071), the Christians were 7 million. From that time on, through the decline of the Byzantine Empire, the Crusades, and then the fall of Constantinople (1453) to the Ottoman Turks, who invaded the Syrian province (*Bilad ash-Sham*) in 1516, the Christians were no more than 400,000, that is, 7 percent of the population in the whole region. They had totally disappeared in North Africa as early as the twelfth century.

The *millet* regime customized by the Ottoman Empire secured a self-rule for Christian minorities by delegating to their religious institutions the administration of their cultural, social, and religious affairs. Furthermore, the 1535 treaty signed by the Ottoman sultan Suleiman II with the French monarch Francis I, and known as the "Capitularies," opened a breach in the Ottoman Empire by entitling France first, and then major European powers as well as Russia, to claim protection over their nationals and then, by extension, over the local Christian minorities (Catholics, Maronites, Greek Orthodox) in the Ottoman Empire. Trade and culture boomed and so did the demographic growth of the Christians during four hundred years of Ottoman rule. On the eve of World War I, Christians represented 20 percent of the total population (except in Egypt, where Copts will always amount to between 8 percent and 10 percent). Under the Moutassarrifiya regime of Mount-Lebanon (1861–1912),

Christians amounted to 81 percent of the population; if one includes the *Wilayet* of Beirut (a stronghold of Muslim Sunni presence), they were still 40 percent.[3]

The demographic slump starts in 1914, with the famine that struck in the Mount-Lebanon due to the Ottoman blockade, exterminating one third of its population, and the Armenian genocide of 1915. After the transfer of population that occurred in 1924 between Greeks and Turks, the number of Christians in Turkey decreased furthermore, and the survivors among the slaughtered Syrian Orthodox of Tour Abdin were forced to leave. What remains today of the many millions of Christians in Turkey amount to 50,000 Armenians, 5,000 Greeks, and 15,000 Syrian Orthodox in the periphery of Istanbul.[4] The Western powers (mainly the French and the British), who distributed false promises of homeland to various minority groups and ended up splitting the Ottoman provinces between themselves (through the Sykes-Picot accord of 1916) and giving birth to the Jewish State (the Balfour Declaration, 1917), also bare a major responsibility in the painful process of eradication that awaited Eastern Christianity as the Arab world scattered into various national states, witnessed revolutionary movements, and engaged in a long and wrecking conflict with the state of Israel.

In Egypt, Syria, Palestine, Iran, and Iraq, the Christian population, which endures the same sufferings as its Muslim counterpart, is yet submitted to petty discrimination that forces it to leave in big numbers. Since the Iranian revolution of 1979, Christians' numbers have shrunk from 200,000 to 97,000 in 1986,[5] in this once vibrant center of Nestorian Christianity (with its seat at Seleucie-Ctesiphon). In places like Syria, the only Arab country (except Lebanon) that officially professes a secular regime, Christians are not subject to direct abuses but their fate and rights lie more in the policy of the regime and its direct protection than in an institutionalized system of democracy and equality. Between 1985 and 1990, 250,000 Christians are said to have left the country, for various reasons.[6] In 1948, the Christian population of the Holy Land was over 18 percent. In 1999, less than 2 percent of Palestinian Christians remained in Palestine. And in Jerusalem, less than 4000 Christians (2 percent) still live there, while they amounted to 51 percent of the population in 1922.[7]

What about Lebanon?

Because of Lebanon's original formula of Christian-Muslim power-sharing, and its reliance on a quota system for the distribution of the higher functions of the State, the ruling class has always avoided dealing with figures. Those would have carried a different meaning to each community, and opposite conclusions could be hastily drawn! This is why, since the last official census of 1932 under French mandate, the Lebanese Republic has not hazarded breaking the "taboo" by conducting a census. It would have been a gamble on the stability of the system, based on a National Pact among two equal partners! The data would have been inevitably dismissed as inaccurate or twisted by those who shuddered at being stripped of their political clout and those who vied in outstripping them. Private associations, political organizations, professional groups, and international institutions have thus assumed the survey task, for their own different purposes and motives of course.

In 1932, the census had showed that Christians represented 51.2 percent (among whom Maronites were 32.4 percent of total population, while Greek Orthodox were 9.8 percent and Greek Catholic 5.9 percent) and Muslims represented 48.8 percent (with a distribution of 22.4 percent of Sunnis and 19.6 percent of Shiites, the Druze sticking to an average of 6.5 percent until 1990). The figures were pretty much the same in the Independence year (1943), with a slight increase of Christian proportion: nearly 53 percent (with the Maronites being the largest minority in Lebanon: 30.4 percent).[8] Until 1975, there would be no change in the demographic balance. After the nationalization of properties by Nasser in Egypt, many Christians fled that country and came to Lebanon. In 1975, at the onset of the troubles, the statistics of the Ministry of Justice displayed an equal split between Christians and Muslims.[9]

In the early eighties, the Shi'a community started conducting its own census. In 1984, Shiites claimed to be 1.1 million, amounting to 30 percent of the Lebanese population.[10] Their data showed that Maronites ranked second, with 900,000, and Sunnis third, with 750,000. Greek Orthodox (250,000), Druze (200,000), Armenians (175,000), and Catholics (150,000) lagged far beyond. At the same period, Maronites were estimated to have fallen to 26.7 percent of the population.[11] The demographic race started hence between the two leading communities, and figures became the invisible raw material meant to shore up each contestant's supremacy and political self-assertion. Soon the Ta'if agreement (October 1989) would seal the new realities on the ground.

In 1989–90, right before the inter-Christians fighting erupted, Christians were estimated at 42.9 percent (26.4 percent Maronites, 7.9 percent Greek Orthodox, and 6.8 percent Greek Catholics) and Muslims at 56.9 percent (28.9 percent Shiites, 24 percent Sunnis, and 4 percent Druze).[12] The violent combats between the Christian militia of the "Lebanese Forces" and the Christian wing of the army led by General Michel Aoun took a heavy toll on Christian demographic as well as economic presence, that was unprecedented even during the darkest years of the war. Their number shrunk to 36.5 percent of the overall population, according to *An-Nahar*.[13]

But the CIA went farther and gave the dim projection of 30 percent for the Christians.[14] Many Christian analysts would resent that assessment, viewing it as a way of supporting the U.S.-sponsored Ta'if accord, by justifying the shift of power from the Maronites to the Muslims. In the next years, the CIA maintained its 30 percent evaluation of Christian presence, out of a total population number of 3,776,317 (as of July 1996).[15] It is rather plausible that the percentage of Christians is roughly 40 percent for a 60 percent of Muslims. (Among Christians, Maronites represent about 65 percent, and the Shiites 51 percent of the Muslims).

EMIGRATION IN FIGURES AND FACTS

The "brain drain" of Christian elites and the steady emigration flow of its working class have undoubtedly weakened the Christians. According to former general director of the Ministry of Foreign Affairs Fouad Turk, 850,000 Lebanese Christians left the country during the fifteen years of war (1975–90), among whom 160,000 emigrated to France. In the nineties, 60,000 would come back, but the rest of the emigrants settled in the United States, Latin America, Canada, and Australia.[16] Many Shiites left South Lebanon for Africa, while Lebanese Sunnis (and a good number of Christians too) worked in the Gulf countries. Those are considered "temporary" emigrants because they tend to come back from the Gulf and Africa, whereas emigrants to the developed countries or immigration countries, most of which are Western, are slow to return.

In his various studies on that subject, researcher and professor Boutros Labaki observes that emigration affected 30 percent of the Lebanese during the war. Instead of slowing down in the postwar years, it has increased after 1994 due to the economic recession and high interest rates, the migratory balance reaching a peak of nearly 190,000 persons in 1996 and 153,000 in 1997. That annual total was never scored between 1975 and 1990, except during the massive flow of the year war broke out, 1975 (which saw 400,000 emigrants, most of whom would come back).[17] Labaki sources are all the more reliable in that they emanate from the "Direction de la Sûreté Générale" (Ministry of Interior), which issues passports and controls departures and arrivals on Lebanese soil. Between 1975 and 1994, 729,000 are estimated to have emigrated, among whom 19.8 percent headed to the United States. Australia, Canada, and France ranked right after. Of the total emigrants, 75.7 percent thus choose to emigrate to Western countries.[18]

More significant are the sectarian profiles of Lebanese emigration. The first figures related to that issue were published in 1978 and mentioned that 75 percent of Lebanese emigrants were Christians.[19] But things have changed rapidly since then. Another study revealed that Muslims represent 64 percent of Lebanese emigrants in the Gulf countries, and 35 percent in the United States. It also showed that 35 percent of the Christians emigrating to the United States were Arab-educated Christians (rather than French-educated) and 23 percent were of Armenian descent.[20]

The same tendency is observed in Australia, where the number of Christian emigrants fell from a percentage of 74.9 percent in 1971 to 59.1 percent in 1981. Starting in 1975, 60 percent of Lebanese emigrants to Australia were Muslims, mostly Sunnis, according to an Australian sociologist and expert.[21]

Muslims have increasingly joined the battalions of emigrants, and as of early 1989, the entourage of Druze leader Walid Joumblatt indicated that 35 percent to 40 percent of Lebanese Druze had left the country since 1975.[22] Western media mentioned that in mid-March 1989 (when General Aoun waged his "war of liberation" against Syrian troops in Lebanon) 75,000 Lebanese left the "Eastern regions" (i.e., the Christian-dominated regions) and 150,000 left the "Western part" (i.e., the Muslim-dominated sector).[23]

Boutros Labaki cites "very well-informed sources" relating to the Lebanese community on the West Coast of the United States, which indicate that there is a clear predominance of Muslims (nearly 80 percent) among the newcomers. The Lebanese community in the United States, once overwhelmingly Christian, is now believed to be 60 percent Christian and 40 percent Muslim.[24] (Lebanese-Americans are estimated to be 1.5 million, that is, 40 percent of the 3.5 million Arab-Americans, according to former Senator Sam Zakhem).[25] The same tendency is observed in Germany, where researchers have established in 1995 the Shiite profile of the majority of Lebanese emigrants who fled from Southern Lebanon.[26]

If Muslim emigration tends to be on a par with Christian emigration, its implications nonetheless are not similar. Christian emigration is more often irreversible, impacts on the social and cultural trends within the country by undermining its cosmopolitan outlook, and jeopardizes the bilateral consensual foundation of the political system. Besides, it is not compensated by the birthrate of those who stay. Although the fertility rate decreased within all communities in Lebanon during the last two decades,[27] due to the sweeping urbanization and to the higher literacy rate among women, the few studies conducted by foreign and Lebanese researchers still show serious differences between Muslims and Christians.

Within the Sunni community, the average rate of children per household decreased from 6.59 to 4.365 in 1971 to 4.2 in 1987. The Shi'a rate at the same period decreased from 7.52 to 5.2 and stabilized at 5.1. The Druze community has today the lowest average rate among the Muslims:

from 8.17 in 1959, it has reached 3.7 in 1971, and 3.9 in 1987. It is believed to have dropped further in the nineties.

On the Christian side, the rate spanned from 5.67 for the Greek Catholics in 1959 to 3.67 in 1971 to 3.3 in 1987; and 4.99 in the Greek Orthodox community in 1959, to 3.3 and then 3.4 in 1971 and 1987.[28] The Maronites witnessed the same decrease, but private surveys conducted by Maronite researchers and sociologists refute the "sectarian" argument to explain the differences in birthrate and privilege the more scientific theory of geographical and economic disparities among the Lebanese, whatever their sectarian affiliation. A comparative study conducted in 1985 showed indeed that Maronites and Shiites had a competing rate of fertility and that theses rates varied according to their standard of living and their rural or urban localization. Thus, both communities shared an average of 8 children per household in South Lebanon; this average oscillated between 5 and 6 in the suburbs of Beirut and is 4.6 (for the Maronites) and 6.8 (for the Shiites) in the mountainous cazas of Kesrouan and Jbeil (Byblos).[29] The nineties have nonetheless witnessed a significant drop in the Christian (and Maronite) birthrate, due to the lack of confidence in the future and economic constraints. In Beirut, the number plunges to 3.2 children per Maronite household.

Furthermore, a new factor appeared, alarming Lebanese, Christians and Muslims alike, and the Vatican itself, along with the local church: it is the selling of Christian lands, especially in Mount-Lebanon. The Christians emerged from war not only weakened and disbanded, but also more impoverished than their fellow Muslims, whose various groups relied one way or another on Iranian or Saudi financial support. The Sunni billionaire Rafik Hariri's rise to power in postwar Lebanon brought about a dynamic commercial and financial revival of the Muslim community in Beirut and Sidon, through his many enterprises. It also sparked a competition with the Shi'a community, represented by Speaker of Parliament Nabih Berri (who demanded a Shiite participation in the reconstruction projects) and by the many social, religious, and cultural activities of Iran-sponsored Hezbollah.

One of the main mottoes of Hariri's government was to attract investment in Lebanon. These investments mainly came from Gulf countries, and were real estate oriented. "Solidere"—the giant joint-stock company entrusted with rebuilding downtown Beirut and Hariri's crown jewel—was a core and profitable "option," but also and especially were the beautifully located lands and properties of the Lebanese, particularly the Christians, in the tourist resorts of Mount-Lebanon, with its enchanting villages and exquisite climate.

Large parcels of land (70 percent belonging to Christians, according to local sources) had already been sold in the Biqaa Valley, and the Metn, the Shouf, and the Kesrouan cazas were yielding their once indomitable spirit, surrendering to the commercial temptations of housing projects, co-owned by Saudi, Koweiti, or Emirati investors. Even the "Lamartine Valley," celebrated by the famous French poet, and stretching between the cazas of the Shouf and the Metn, in Mount-Lebanon, was said to be hosting a huge housing project with cement towers. These transfers of properties (which often occurred by circumventing or outwitting the law that put a limit to foreign purchase of real estate) threatened to inflict an irremediable damage to Lebanon's social, communal and environmental character. Druze leader Walid Joumblatt was appalled and did not hide his fears: the Mount-Lebanon had long been a Christian-Druze "fortress," the spine and the bedrock of Lebanese nationalism and unity. He went on television and in the media, protesting vehemently, "We're going to become strangers and displaced in our fatherland. They're altering the identity of the country!"[30]

Adding up to this apprehension was the naturalization of hundreds of thousands of Arab immigrants, Kurds, Palestinians, Syrians, Iraqis, and others by presidential decree in June 1994. Between 130,000 and 250,000 individuals were granted the Lebanese nationality overnight, more than 85 percent of whom were Muslims. Moreover, the Damocles sword of the settlement of roughly 350,000 Palestinian refugees hangs over Lebanon's fragile balance, since the Oslo accords did not mention the return of the 1948 refugees. Sixty thousand Palestinians were among the newly nationalized people. This concerted policy was dramatically altering Lebanon's demographic landscape, and subsequently its social and cultural features. These were reasons enough to encourage Christian exodus.

THE CONSEQUENCES OF CHRISTIAN EMIGRATION

Beyond its specificity, Christian emigration is the barometer that reveals the health condition of the Arab world. Christian minorities reluctantly leave their historic homeland when the oxygen of freedom necessary for their survival is cut off, and when democracy and civil society break under the heavy grip of dictatorial regimes. The rise of Islamic fundamentalism worsens the situation, removing any possibility of secularization.

One other way Christians migrate is when they choose to retreat from the public sphere into a moral, cultural, and political seclusion. It is a "mental migration," translating into voluntary boycott of public life coupled with their deliberate sidelining by the political authorities. This has been the case of the Christians of Lebanon since the end of the war (see Chapter 9). For the first time in their modern history, they were at a low ebb and that situation did nothing to boost the morale of the Christians in Syria, Iraq, Palestine, or Egypt. Lebanon had been very much present in Eastern Christian consciousness as a place where Arab Christianity had a thriving presence, because it provided the adequate environment allowing Arab Christians to blossom and give their best: religious diversity, cultural tolerance, economic prosperity, and openness to Western civilization. Alexandria and Cairo had harbored this cosmopolitan Levantine spirit until the fifties. When Egypt, Iraq, and Syria were carried away by the winds of Arab radicalism, which would soon be replaced by Islamic mobilization, many Christians and Muslims thought they had found in Lebanon a modern replica of the twelfth-century Andalusia experience of pluralism and tolerance.

Whence, Christian physical emigration or "inward" migration affected Muslims as well as Christians, since it had structural implications on social, cultural, economic, and political levels. But most of all, Christians' departure or abdication unveiled the crisis of identity the Arab world was going through and sent a signal that its civilization was not able to nurture pluralism and conviviality anymore. It made it all the more difficult for the "silent majority" of Muslims who shared Christian aspirations to advance the cause of democracy, civil society, human rights, and cultural diversity.

This is why notable Christian and Muslim figures in Lebanon were convinced that "it is up to the Muslims today to preserve a Christian presence and role if they still hold on to the idea of a pluralistic and consensual society." "The fate of Arab Christians today is the responsibility of Arab Muslims first," wrote one columnist.[31] "Arabs should not turn a blind eye to the exodus of their Christians. We have to recognize there is a problem," comments another.[32]

In a stunning article, Shiite ulema Mohammad Hussein Fadlallah commented on Christian emigration and questioned the changes that have occurred in modern Islam. He wondered why "it went backward" and why it has a problem with religious, cultural, and ethnic minorities living in its bosom. He "certified" that "because of the political and cultural collapse, Islam has been transformed from an open horizon blooming with diversity to a narrow tent that barely opens up to Muslims themselves." Condemning "repressive regimes that confiscated Islam," he called for a "cultural movement to renew Islam, bring out its conceptual and legal ability to accept the other . . . and rid it of its complex toward the West." "Although born in a Western environment, the values of democracy, pluralism, human rights and other political and social values are core values essential for all human beings around the globe, and so are they necessary to Muslims and to Islam," he wrote. Otherwise, "not only the Arab Christians will be leaving but all other minorities too and that will bring about total disintegration of Arab societies."[33]

It is relevant to note that, according to Professor Tarek Mitri, executive secretary of the World Council of Churches (Geneva) and a close adviser of Greek Orthodox Patriarch Hazim, Muslim Egyptians sense that an improvement of the Copts' situation in Egypt would be a good indicator of where the country is heading to, in terms of religious and political freedoms, equality before the law, political participation, and tolerance. Muslims indeed endure the same sufferings Christians complain of, due to the lack of democracy and freedom.

Another argument is that Christian outflow would rescind the traditional Christian-Muslim understanding and turn the Middle East into a region torn between two fundamentalisms: the Islamist and the Zionist. In Lebanon, it would toll the demise of the coexistence and pluralistic experience that challenged the Israeli experiment of a religion-based state.

Political reasons are not the only reasons Christians leave in throngs. Economic hardship and uncertainty are compelling incentives, for them and for their fellow Muslims as well. Although a good number of emigrants came back from Canada, the United States, France, sub-Saharan Africa, and Gulf countries, the significant increase of the candidates for emigration in 1995–96 "at a scale never witnessed before in time of peace," as researcher Boutros Labaki put it,[34] is meaningful. In a survey conducted by the Lebanese daily *As-Safir,* 31.7 percent of resident Lebanese said that the solution to the economic problems they're facing lies in emigrating.[35] But according to Labaki, the study reveals that people at the bottom of the social and financial ladder as well as those with high revenues are willing to emigrate. That can only be explained by the lack of confidence in the future, and that feeling has also a heavy political resonance.

According to the ESCWA figures, unemployment in Lebanon has reached a rate of 30 percent! Other sources in the private sector say it's 13.4 percent out of an active population totaling 1.1 million.[36] Housing is also a crucial problem, especially to young married couples, and so is medical care.

How does the economic plight reflect on the Christians? In the postwar era of reconstruction, Christian businessmen have been reluctant to invest in long-term or even medium-term projects, for the same uncertainty factor besieging the future. Even at the height of the war, Christians did not economically "disengage." Combined with their strong political commitment and military engagement, this fact expressed their visceral attachment to their homeland and most of all their belief in their future and their willingness to fight for it, at that time.

An inventory of the economic institutions established in Lebanon between 1970 and 1983 and officially registered in the "Journal Officiel" and the "Register of Commerce," indicated that Christian-owned companies amounted to 1,153 (491 of whom were Maronite-owned and concentrated in Mount-Lebanon, except for the Armenian-owned companies, based in Beirut), whereas Muslim-owned enterprises amounted to 800 (598 of which were Sunni-owned and concentrated in Beirut), and 29 companies of "unknown" confessional ownership.[37]

Postwar years witnessed the emergence of a new class of Muslim entrepreneurs within the Sunni and Shiite establishment, although the typical "nouveaux-riches" of all the postwar era crossed the sectarian lines. But Christians remained a pivotal element in the dynamic banking sector, and in general in the sector of trade and services that totaled 70 percent of GDP. "Christians are more financially versed than Muslims," Mohammad Sammak was quoted as saying.[38] "They have more experience in banking and they have better connections to and understanding of the free market. When they leave and turn their back on Lebanon, they do great damage to this country. We will need each other to survive."

What are commonly held as being Western economic values, that is, free market economy and capitalism, have been part of Maronite ideology since the socioeconomic transformations that took place in the Mount-Lebanon society at the turn of the nineteenth century. The community integrated democratic bourgeois values, and one of the major theorists of Lebanon's role as a "trading nation," Michel Chiha, a Chaldean Christian, laid the economic vision that reinforced the position of the Christian, and particularly the Maronite, bourgeoisie, in Lebanon's capitalist and service-oriented economy, based on "individual initiative and ingenuity."[39] As such, Lebanese Christians and Maronites have also been the link in economic exchanges between the Arab peninsula and Western markets, before oil States became linked to U.S. strategic interests and developed direct commercial ties with the West.

The cultural role of the Christians of Lebanon was also to be challenged along with their economic influence, since many Christian families could no longer afford private schools and university tuition and the high cost of education. They were either sending their children to study abroad—which, ironically, was more accessible to their purse through scholarship support—or sending them to public schools. Hence, a shift in cultural tendencies with a noticeable decline in the quality level of education among the young generations occurred in the nineties, especially since a substantial number of highly qualified professors had emigrated to Western countries. Between 1975 and 1996, 233,256 university and academic people left the country, that is 24.55 percent of the total number of emigrants during the same period.[40] And since 1990, they amount to 37 percent of the emigrants, according to the Ministry of Social Affairs.[41]

That vital issue would be one of the core subjects raised during the Synod on Lebanon. Cardinal Pio Laghi, the highest authority in the Vatican for Catholic Education, would criticize those in charge of Catholic schools and universities in Lebanon, because they are turning them into "rich people's universities." This could only undermine Lebanon's mission and Christians' role.[42] (See Chapter 7.)

Chapter 5

Broken and Forfeited Bonds to the Land

Nowhere as much as in this tormented Orient, beset with false prophets of earthly kingdoms and martyrs' heavens, has the land been an inseparable part of body and soul. The relation of oriental peoples to the land is an existential one. It is woven with their religious beliefs and spirituality. And yet, nowhere else are these bonds more tried on a daily basis, dismantled, hacked away at by the realities of today and the qualms of tomorrow.

Wars are waged in the name of land and in the name of land peoples are thrown away in packs from their home, and they become labeled as "displaced," and those who leave—forced or by free will—become the "émigrés" who carry fragments of the land in their dreams and are still, for those who stayed, their extension overseas. Displaced people and émigrés keep with their land bonds that are physically broken or distended to the point of engendering forfeited rights.

THE ÉMIGRÉS: A POLITICAL STAKE

Despite its geographical and climatic diversity, tiny Lebanon is a country of emigration. Lebanese have always been a nation of travelers. Once again, estimates vary between 16 million émigrés of Lebanese descent and 4 million. But they all agree on the fact that Christians amount to between 65 percent and 70 percent, among whom Maronites alone represent roughly 48 percent of this diaspora, and are thus the largest "Lebanese" community abroad.

This is one major reason why the Maronite political elite has conferred the emigration "file" to be of inordinate importance. Since figures are the invisible fuel of the Lebanese political engine, one way of tipping the balance would be to outstretch the boundaries of Lebanon and (re-)inject the émigrés into political life! Thus, the Ministry of Foreign Affairs had become the "Ministry of the Emigrants" and in the sixties, the "World Lebanese Cultural Union" was founded in order to create an official link with the Lebanese diaspora. Since the early twenties, the Christian ruling class strongly defended the idea of incorporating the Lebanese émigrés in the national census and giving them the voting rights. Some would go as far as defending the idea of granting them seats in Parliament.

Soon, the Shiite community entered the "contest" and, armed with the same logic, animated a Shiite trend within the Union (evolving mainly around its émigrés in Africa,[1] as opposed to the Maronites who were spread in the Americas). This ultimately led to divisions within the Union, which split to various branches, each one having its own political and confessional agenda. In the early nineties, Maronites created a couple of institutes in the United States, organized the first "World Maronite Conference" in Los Angeles (1994), and animated a set of social and cultural networks. The Druzes decided they, too, should move along and so they established the Young Druze Professionals Association in 1995, in the United States.

In April 1993, and under the impulse of Speaker of Parliament and head of the Shiite movement "Amal," Nabih Berri, the "Ministry of Emigrés" became an autonomous portfolio, although its attributions and the mechanisms of coordination with the Ministry of Foreign Affairs were not clearly defined. Since 1991, the émigrés became pretty much a central theme of Lebanese politics. Secular as well as religious leaders of all levels and affiliations have been visiting various countries where "Lebanese" and their descendants have a strong and active presence, starting with Brazil, to Argentina, Mexico, the United States, Canada, European countries such as France, Germany, and also Australia, without forgetting the African countries. During these visits, which captured wide media coverage, they all stressed the necessity of granting the émigrés Lebanese nationality. This proposition would become a political leitmotiv for Shiites, Druzes, and Maronites, after having been, for decades, an exclusively Maronite tune. Now that the other communities were having large colonies abroad, they were espousing the idea of adding them up to their number and thus gaining more political weight. The "émigrés" theme became a bargaining sectarian card in the local political arena.

But how deep was their relation with their "old country," folklore and emotions put aside? Could they still be considered as Lebanese, especially those of the second and third generations? Was the "emigration dossier" legally valid? Or were the Lebanese leaders engaged in a wild-goose chase around the globe?

When Elias Hrawi paid the first visit to Brazil of a Lebanese President of the Republic (September 1997),[2] he publicly and repeatedly expressed his desire to grant the Lebanese nationality to those who were willing to obtain it. Brazil has the biggest community of Lebanese origin in the whole diaspora: it is estimated to vary between 5 percent and 10 percent of the total 164.4 million Brazilians.[3] Brazilians of Lebanese descent are generally very well integrated, wealthy, and powerful. Many hold important functions in the state (Speaker of Parliament, President of the Senate, deputies, governors, and even presidential candidates) and are successful businessmen. Hraoui and his entourage were very much surprised that one year later, only a handful of Brazilians had applied to get a Lebanese passport.

What Lebanese leaders intentionally ignored during all the decades they spent arguing for and against the "Lebanism" of the émigrés was that the issue of the double nationality was a major obstacle. Most of the "immigration countries" have an integration policy and are thus cautious about allowing double citizenship. South American countries forbid it, while the United States, Canada, and Australia are very much reserved about it. Arab countries, especially Gulf countries, set prohibitive conditions regarding double nationality. Europe and Africa have looser regulations but these cannot be regarded as continents of permanent immigration since Lebanese keep shuttling back and forth to their native land, where they are still active on various levels.

The inconsistency of the Lebanese governments' policy regarding the émigrés showed since day one of Independence. Nothing had been done to help expatriates preserve their Lebanese nationality and passports, for those who wanted it. Generations of emigrants had been lost because their birth certificates were not registered in the Lebanese consulates. Scientific data regarding Lebanese emigration was either unavailable or had been manipulated for political and sectarian purposes, under various administrations (in the late fifties, then again between 1964 and 1983).[4]

Furthermore, émigrés who still had their Lebanese nationality could not cast their ballots in embassies and consulates when elections were held in Lebanon because no legal measures were taken for that purpose. Lebanese laws also did not allow the vote by correspondence or by proxy.

In view of these serious shortages, the political role of the Lebanese émigrés was a myth, entertained by Lebanese leaders for political purposes.

Yet, émigrés' economic role was a reality and the money they sent to their families back home and their private investments in Lebanon kept excess in the balance of payments and covered up the commercial deficit of the State. They contributed to 10 percent of the gross national product.

It was rather this kind of contribution that former Prime Minister Rafik Hariri was seeking when he launched his reconstruction plan for Lebanon, rather than engaging in an overseas sectarian competition.

But as it would turn out, the Christian émigrés were very cautious about investing in postwar Lebanon, as long as Lebanon did not recover its full sovereignty and independence, with the departure of all non-Lebanese troops and the peace process was not back on track and promising. Only the euro-bonds and Solidere shares, which yielded high interest rates, attracted some of the expatriates capital, estimated at $50 billion.

Emigration has also an important role to play on the cultural level, as a bridge between different worlds, if it were only set free from the political web some leaders are snaring it in.

But for that to be possible, identity consciousness had to be preserved. And the situation differed between Muslim and Christian communities abroad. Muslims who emigrated, and particularly the Shiites and to a lesser extent, the Sunnis, kept in touch with their mother country. Those who went to Africa did not cut with their roots and, at one point or another, they came back and built houses and schools in their hometowns. Some of their wealthy entrepreneurs invested in downtown Beirut. Christian emigration was more prone to be a permanent one.

Eminent figures within Christian churches, and especially within the Maronite church, warned against the "dissolution" of the Maronite identity in the emigration societies.[5] The Maronite Patriarch Sfeir echoes this concern. A Catholic environment, such as Latin America, makes it easier to get integrated and abandon Maronite rite and practices to the benefit of the Latin cult. Besides, the Maronite episcopates abroad were linked up to the Congregation of Eastern Churches in the Vatican rather than to the Maronite Patriarchate in Lebanon, and in the case of France, Maronites were attached to the Archbishop of Paris (the present Cardinal Jean-Marie Lustiger).

To prevent a further dilution of the Maronite identity and to reinforce the ties of the church with its diaspora, Maronite dioceses have been established in the United States and Australia. But "the creation of a Maronite diocese in Europe prompts reticence from the local episcopates—of which oriental Catholics are dependent too—, because they fear that it might spur similar demands from the faithful of other oriental Catholic rites living in Europe," reveals Patriarch Sfeir. "In fact, I think they don't understand this need to preserve one's specificity while at the same time belonging to the universal catholicity."[6]

In his treatise on the renewal of the Maronite Church, Yoakim Moubarac distinguishes five migration waves in Lebanese and Maronite history, four of which were intertwined with positive developments: the first one occurred in the wake of the nineteenth-century massacres of Maronites by the Druzes (1860–61) but witnessed the creation of the Mutassarrifiyat regime (1864)—a golden age of political and cultural Maronitism. The second wave took place after World War I and the famine that devastated Mount-Lebanon. It coincided with the creation of Greater Lebanon (1920). The third wave of emigration happened after World War II, simultaneously with the Independence of Lebanon (1943). Independent Lebanon would flourish during the oil boom that sprung in Gulf countries, mainly Saudi Arabia, where the fourth wave of Lebanese emigrants headed and became actively involved in economic development projects. This was the only wave that did not occur under dramatic circumstances, and it contributed to the prosperity of Lebanon in the fifties and the sixties, thanks to the "petro-dollars" that poured into Lebanese banks. The fifth wave—starting in 1975—is, by far, the largest and most violent in Lebanon's history. To Egypt, America, Australia, and Canada, which were the common destinations of all waves, it added Western Europe, where many Christian Lebanese settled. "Will the fifth wave be the last milestone in the trail of Maronite dispersion or will it prod the renewal of the mother Church and the fatherland? " wondered Moubarac.[7]

THE DISPLACED: A SEVERE BLOW TO LEBANON'S COEXISTENCE

Far more tragic than emigration itself is the problem of the displaced families within the boundaries of Lebanon. Two decades before Bosnia, Rwanda, Kosovo, and East Timor, and long before the end of the Cold War, Lebanon experienced "ethno-sectarian cleansing," wide-scale massacres of villagers and transfer of population from one region to another in order to create religiously homogeneous districts. The "Lebanonization" of the Balkans was to take place later on, in the nineties, with the same weapons and armament used by Lebanese militias, which sold their military arsenal to former Yugoslavia when the Lebanese government started dismantling militant groups, according to the Ta'if agreement. Lebanese people had an inkling of the war breaking out soon in the pluri-ethnic Yugoslavian federation. At the end of the twentieth century, the issue of displaced people, turned to refugees in their own country, has become an international one.

Many years after war ended in Lebanon, this issue is still number one on the agenda of the government. The Ta'if agreement clearly stated that "the return of the displaced is the prelude to national entente and the safeguard of social peace and security." The displaced problem was also the leading priority of the church and a central concern of the Vatican curia dealing with Lebanon, which included "Foreign Secretary" Archbishop Jean-Louis Tauran, Cardinal Luigi Gatti (formerly in charge of the "Lebanese file" in the late eighties until the mid-nineties when he was responsible for Middle East policies), Cardinal Achille Silvestrini, head of the Congregation of Eastern Churches, and Apostolic Nuncio in Lebanon Pablo Puente (1989–1997).

The displaced population in Lebanon fits within the category of people who left their home and village because of direct threats to their lives and were prevented from going back because of security concerns. Forced migration and continuous danger are key elements in the definition of the displaced.

Various studies showed that the displaced accounted to nearly one fifth of the total resident population, 81 percent of whom were Christians and 19 percent Muslims. For a total number of 847,000 displaced people (that is 171,000 families on an average scale of five members per family), 680,000 were Christians and 167,000 were Muslims. Most of the displaced originated from Greater Beirut (34.3 percent—115,000 Muslims displaced from East Beirut and 175,000 Christians displaced from West Beirut and its southern suburbs) and Mount-Lebanon (28.9 percent); Southern Lebanon refugees amounted to 19.6 percent, North Lebanon's to 4.1 percent, and the Biqaa's to 13 percent. The bulk of the displaced people were the Christians who were ousted from their villages in the Shouf mountains, Aley, Baabda, and Upper Metn, between 1975 and 1987 (240,000 persons), especially during the Shouf war in 1983–84.[8] If one adds up those displaced after the withdrawal of the Christian militia of the "Lebanese Forces" from the eastern suburbs of Saida and Iqlim el-Kharroub in 1985, the number of Christians displaced from the Shouf and its vicinity reaches 331,000.[9]

An approximate 17.5 percent of the displaced persons emigrated from the country, which means that the number of displaced Lebanese still "residing" in Lebanon varies between 600,000 and 640,000. They are mostly concentrated in the area of Beirut and Mount-Lebanon, and living in a homogeneous religious environment, with people of their own community. The successive flows of displaced throughout the Lebanese war have dislocated the Lebanese plural texture and transformed what was "a federation of communities on an inter-confessional territory" to a "federation of mono-sectarian territories."[10]

In postwar Lebanon, the new picture of sectarian distribution showed that the Sunnis' geographical presence did not witness fundamental changes. An urban community, the Sunnis were still concentrated in the big littoral cities of Beirut, Saida, Tripoli. They also had some bastions in the northern caza of Akkar. As for the Shiites, they were a majority in South Lebanon and in large areas of the Biqaa, and their number was reaching an overwhelming proportion in West Beirut and its southern suburbs.

The postwar "confessional" sketch map also revealed that Christians were basically confined in the regions stretching from East Beirut to Byblos (Jbeil), including the Metn and Kesrouan cazas of Mount-Lebanon, all previously controlled by the "Lebanese Forces" and other Christian groups and parties. Large portions of Christians (Maronites and Greek Orthodox) were present in Batroun, Koura, Akkar, Zghorta, Becharré, in North Lebanon, while in South Lebanon the Christian enclave of Jezzine has been emptied by the ongoing fighting between the SLA (South Lebanon Army), the pro-Israeli militia, and the Hezbollah resistance guerillas.[11] Important Greek Catholic spots remained in the Biqaa valley's "capital," Zahlé, and to a lesser extent in Saida and its suburbs (where some Christians returned after the war). South of what is known as "the Damascus road,"[12] until the Saida-Nabatyeh axis, Christians were sparse.

Here lies the Gordian knot. Through the Christians, who are the main injured party in that process of dismantlement, Lebanon is fatally wounded. Christians were indeed the thread of the Lebanese assorted and mixed fabric that history took four hundred years to knit. Sunnis, Shiites, and Druzes very scarcely lived together in mixed villages. Only Christians lived in the same towns, neighborhoods, and hamlets with Muslims of various confessions, either with the Sunnis in West Beirut, Tripoli, and Saida, or with the Shiites in South Lebanon and the Biqaa, or with the Druzes in the Shouf, Aley, and Upper Metn. The Maronites in particular were the only community disseminated all over Lebanon. At the eve of the war, they represented one quarter of the population in Beirut (22.6 percent) and its suburbs (26.2 percent) as well as in the Biqaa (27.3 percent), 20.4 percent in other cities, one third of the population in North Lebanon(32 percent) and South Lebanon (31.4 percent), and two thirds in Mount-Lebanon (66.5 percent).[13] At the end of the war, the Maronites constituted the majority of the displaced: they amounted to 434,000 persons, i.e., nearly two thirds of the displaced, and almost half of the resident Maronites of Lebanon!

Among the Christians, the Maronites are traditionally the most rural community. It means that they have been literally uprooted from their houses and villages and that they bore the brunt of the war losses in properties and lands. The overall Christian presence on the map receded from 70 percent of the total surface of Lebanon in 1975 to roughly 30 percent today. A mortal blow has been given to the unifying role of the Christians, and the Maronites in particular, translated in their physical presence on the entire territory. Being a ferment of concord was in the core of their original doctrine, even if some of their late-twentieth-century leaders had ignored that fact.

It is thus easy to grasp the scope of the disaster inflicted to Lebanon's centennial coexistence. Without the return of the displaced to their homes and countryside, it is utopian to speak of any such coexistence; those whom we call today "the displaced" are the backbone and the living transcription of that coexistence. For the Assembly of Catholic Patriarchs and Bishops of Lebanon, "the return of the displaced to their villages would be the glaring expression that Lebanese are committed to coexistence and reject partition of the country. We must act quickly, before the feeling of bitterness and deprivation becomes overwhelming and leads to despair and emigration."[14]

Lebanese of all sides and backgrounds agree that the transfer of population that happened during the war was meant to ruin the historical conviviality among Lebanon's various communities. It took place at the behest of the "conspiratorial will" of foreign powers. Israel is the first power associated with such intentions, since its military involvement in Lebanon and the sudden withdrawal of its forces from the Shouf mountain in 1983 led to direct confrontation between the Druzes and the "Lebanese Forces" and to the massacres of the Christians.

The "conspiracy theory" also very likely links the issue of the displaced people in Lebanon to the non-avowed international intent to resettle the Palestinian refugees in the countries where they are dispersed. In Lebanon, the estimated 350,000 Palestinians would therefore fill in the void left by the displaced, particularly south of the "Damascus road," in the Iqlim el-Kharroub, the outskirts of the Christian coastal city of Damour,[15] Saida suburbs, the Shouf environs (such as Qrey'a), and the Jezzine area.

It is precisely to avoid that danger of having his former allies the Palestinians "invade" the underpopulated Druze stronghold, that Walid Joumblatt agreed to cooperate with the government to bring back those who were expelled from their villages.[16] He was also concerned about the economic downturn that hit the Shouf and the devastated Aley-Bhamdoun areas and made it lag behind the rest of the country in the postwar reconstruction era. A return of the population in its villages in the Shouf could only boost the stagnant economy of the region. The successful Beiteddine Festival held in summertime under the patronage of his wife, Nora, was not enough. It was a season attraction, even if it brought the social and cultural elite of Beirut to the nineteenth-century-old palace and former summer residence of the Presidents of the Republic that Joumblatt "expropriated" to the State during the war.[17]

Despite his stated eagerness to restore the Shouf's past coexistence between Christians and Druzes, and despite the government disbursement of more than $500 million for the rebuilding of destroyed villages, schools, and churches in the Shouf, only 15 percent to 20 percent of the displaced had returned to their homes eight years after the end of the war. Notable Maronite figures such as Pierre Helou and Fouad el-Saad[18] had agreed with Joumblatt to run for the 1992 parliamentary elections, braving the wrath of their Christian constituency and mainstream who boycotted the ballot (see Chapter 9), on condition that the displaced would be the full-time job of their mandate and that the Druze leader would be adamant in his support to their efforts. El-Saad had good connections in the Vatican, especially with Archbishop Tauran and Monsignor Gatti, who followed closely the issue of the displaced, since they considered it as the prerequisite to coexistence in Lebanon. Four years later, Helou and el-Saad were openly at odds with Joumblatt and shrugged off the 1996 elections.

What was the problem? After an initial and spontaneous return of villagers in the caza of Saida (1991) under the protection of the Lebanese army and with the cooperation of Shiite movement "Amal," the process stopped. The government decided to take officially in charge the return of the displaced and organized a "national conference" to assess the needs of the displaced and their requirements. Delegates representing the displaced families articulated their priorities: they demanded security and the deployment of the Lebanese Armed Forces, money for the reconstruction of their houses and villages, dialogue and reconciliation with the Druze inhabitants, and the creation of a National Council for the Displaced.

After the 1992 elections, Joumblatt asked and obtained the newly created ministerial portfolio of the Displaced. He wanted to be the sole supervisor of the highly delicate operation and had the support of Prime Minister Rafik Hariri. He also asked, and obtained, the creation of a special National Fund of the Displaced, that would be supplied from government budget. But his style would soon turn to be a contested one.

He wanted his partisans to handle the file exclusively. The appointment of his aides, the choice of his Ministry's headquarters, the use of the money and its distribution to the Druze families who squatted Christian houses, as a compensation "to encourage them to give back the properties to their owners," soon alarmed Christian leaders and the Church. They criticized Joumblatt and he counterattacked by violent charges in which he accused the Maronite Church of sluggishness and even unwillingness to encourage Christians to return to the Shouf. The church would retort that security had to be guaranteed first.

The "displaced issue" was a highly politicized one; political calculations surrounding the whole enterprise were thus inevitable.

Joumblatt was concerned about a "muscled" return of the Christians in the Shouf mountains and so he first put a veto on former members of the

"Lebanese Forces" and the Kataeb party, and their families (only to reverse his attitude a few years later; see Chapter 9). He insisted he should select those allowed to return in what he considered his fief. Many became convinced that he wanted the Christians to return on his own terms: rather weak and low-profile, so that he would keep control on their political orientations and on the whole situation in the Shouf. He was also taking into consideration the deep feeling of his Druze audience, of whom a large portion was still hostile to a Christian comeback. Although badly in need of a fresh economic start, the Druzes feared that Christians would gain strength and take soon a dominant position in the region, if they were encouraged to reestablish in great numbers. Rancors were still very much alive, and the enterprise was like walking on a tight rope without a safety net.

As he was actively working for the return of the Christians in the Shouf, in close cooperation with Fouad el-Saad and George Dib Nehmé, mayor of the Christian outpost and most important town in the Shouf, Deir el-Kamar,[19] Anouar Fatayri, a ranking official in Joumblatt's Progressist Socialist Party (PSP) and one of his key advisers, had been shot dead with his chauffeur in February 1989 while he was on tour in the Shouf. The crime was interpreted as a warning from any party (local or foreign) who was damaged by the rapid healing of the Mount-Lebanon's wounds, and thus the reemergence of a strong and unified Lebanon through the historical Druzo-Maronite alliance. This is why one of the lingering questions in people's minds was whether the "political decision" has been truly taken, and whether the "green light" has been really given to the resolution of the displaced problem.

So the initiative dragged and became mired in controversy. On the practical level, the outcome is modest. The Ministry of the Displaced only recognized the number of 60,000 displaced families that former minister (and former warlord) Elie Hobeika had established in a previous survey largely boycotted by Christian displaced. The Ministry also concentrated its efforts on the displaced in the area of Greater Beirut and Mount-Lebanon, which received 92 percent out of the 450 million U.S.D earmarked for the displaced portfolio. The refugees in these areas represented nearly 93,369 families, 75 percent of whom were Christians (69,369 families) and 25 percent Muslims (23,000 families).[20] Yet grievances were aired regarding the inequality in the payments of indemnities to the families. Muslims allegedly received more than 50 percent of those indemnities. The funds were primarily distributed to the Druze settlers in the Shouf villages to induce them to evacuate the Christian properties they had squatted. Part of the money also helped to start the reconciliation process, which indicates that reconciliation between profoundly torn villages and families was a priority for Walid Joumblatt. He personally oversaw these events, in which poignant embraces brought back together old neighbors and longtime friends, priests, and sheikhs, all eager to forget and forgive, and keys of the abandoned houses were handed to their owners under the spotlight of TV cameras. "Blood tributes" were also paid to the families who had lost members during the 1983 Shouf waves of massacres and reprisals. More than 55 percent of the funds had been allocated to the evacuation of the settlers in Beirut and Mount-Lebanon, a fact that many Christians resented, while 27.3 percent went for the repairing and restoration of houses, mostly in Mount-Lebanon, 10.2 percent for the reconstruction works, 5.1 percent for infrastructure works, and 2 percent for the refection of churches.[21]

That was not enough, and even if 60 percent of the families displaced from Baabda, Aley, and the Shouf had been paid to rebuild their houses, only 33.2 percent had returned to the three cazas of Mount-Lebanon as of July 1997, by the acknowledgment of the Ministry of the Displaced.[22] But according to other sources, only 7.7 percent of the families were able to settle back, because the funds were insufficient to restore their properties.[23]

Money was really a key element to "Operation: return of the displaced," but unfortunately the displaced "file" became a profitable one for many parties. It encouraged political clienteles during the parliamentary elections of 1992 and 1996, when it was used as a political "card" and a campaigning slogan. It also inspired blackmail. Newspapers reported that in Beirut, people and families coming from the South and from the southern suburbs moved in empty buildings downtown in order to receive financial compensation from the Solidere and Elyssar companies (in charge of the reconstruction) when asked to leave.[24]

At one point, the funds were going into extortioners pockets rather than to those who needed to get back their lands and houses and rebuild them. So much so that in summer 1998, Prime Minister Hariri and Minister Joumblatt publicly exchanged accusations of power abuse and electoral use of the displaced persons issue and money. Bursting into angry comments, Hariri revealed that Joumblatt had been "blackmailing" him and had resorted to corrupt practices. He accused him of being the main responsible party for the protracted process of the displaced's return.[25]

THE DILEMMA BETWEEN INTEGRATION AND RETURN

On the other end of the spectrum, and all financial considerations put aside, what did the displaced think of their return? No one ever publicly raised the question of whether they wished to go back to their birthplaces and hometowns. Not even the media. The very thought of pointing out to that matter would mean doubting the Lebanese genuine will of living together. For more than a third of the displaced population, the forced character of their migration had ceased to exist. Yet, deep inside them, people were still concerned about security conditions. What if someday, one "isolated" incident unleashed new episodes of violence and bloodshed? What if, someday, an "invisible hand" killed one prominent figure in an attempt to set the communities one against each other?

Furthermore, social integration into their new environments had worked for a vast majority of the displaced. According to the joint study done by expert teams of the St. Joseph University and the Laval University of Québec, one third of the displaced persons said they were perfectly integrated into their host environment; 49.7 percent said they were fairly well integrated, and 19 percent said they were not integrated.[26] By and large, the displaced had been torn between their desire to adapt to the new reality (find a job, go to school, make new friends) if they did not want to be misfits, and their longing to go home. Many of them lived haunted by the past, which was idealized by their nostalgic feeling. The study posed one crucial question, that applies to all displaced around the world: should we help them adapt and assimilate into their new hosting environment or should we entertain their nostalgia and their yearning to find back their lost Eden? Inasmuch as persons identify with their patrimony, especially persons of rural background, those who had lost their estate, their land, their houses, felt they were deprived of their identity and their dignity as full citizens. "The material foundations of a human being's existence helps consolidate his sense of national adherence."[27] If those foundations are denied or endangered, many would, at the end of the day, choose exile.

After over a decade (two decades for some) of uprooting, the process of return for the Lebanese displaced has officially been launched. Heroic attempts to preserve coexistence in the villages east of Saida and in the surroundings of the Shouf had been made during and after the war by Father Selim Ghazal, Superior of the Monastery of the Savior (St. Sauveur, Deir el-Moukhalles), with the support of Greek Catholic Archbishop of Saida, George Koueyter. The future of coexistence in Lebanon requires that the problem of the displaced cease being used as a political bargaining card and be dealt with as a humanitarian issue by men of goodwill like Ghazal. That coexistence depends very much also on the ability—and the will—of those living pillars of Lebanon's once unique patchwork, the displaced themselves, to overcome their trauma and their fears and to go through a reverse process of adaptation, back in their ancestral villages.

Chapter 6

A Synod for Lebanon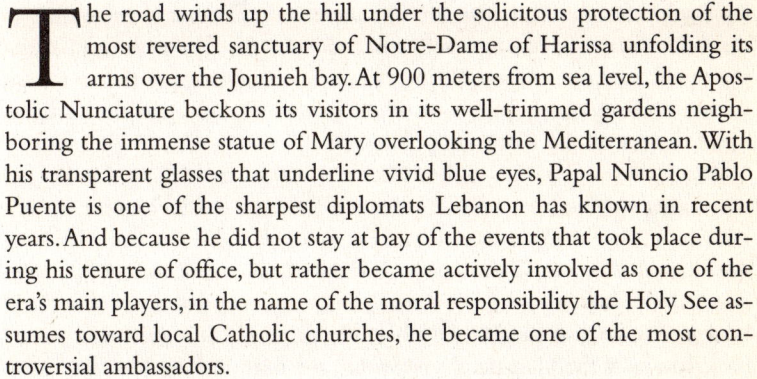

The road winds up the hill under the solicitous protection of the most revered sanctuary of Notre-Dame of Harissa unfolding its arms over the Jounieh bay. At 900 meters from sea level, the Apostolic Nunciature beckons its visitors in its well-trimmed gardens neighboring the immense statue of Mary overlooking the Mediterranean. With his transparent glasses that underline vivid blue eyes, Papal Nuncio Pablo Puente is one of the sharpest diplomats Lebanon has known in recent years. And because he did not stay at bay of the events that took place during his tenure of office, but rather became actively involved as one of the era's main players, in the name of the moral responsibility the Holy See assumes toward local Catholic churches, he became one of the most controversial ambassadors.

A MEDDLESOME PAPAL NUNCIO

During his eight years stay in "the country of the Cedars" (1989–1997), which happened to be a crucial turning point for Lebanon and for the Christians in particular, he left his imprints on many decisive episodes. His pragmatic approach to postwar reality ignited the most fiery comments against him by what he called "Christian extremists."

Since "day one" of his arrival, his mission has proven to be highly delicate. He had already been posted in Lebanon as assistant to the Nuncio from 1973 to 1977, and knew the Lebanese morass quite well, but when he succeeded Luciano Angeloni in April 1989, the Christians were embarked in a reckless "liberation war" waged by General Michel Aoun, head of a military Cabinet, against the Syrian forces in Lebanon. The country was also in the middle of a constitutional crisis due to the vacancy of the

Presidency of the Republic, since no president had been elected to succeed Amine Gemayel in September 1988.

Along with Algerian diplomat and mediator of the Arab tripartite committee Lakhdar Ibrahimi, Puente first tried to secure Aoun's participation to the settlement of the crisis, through the legal institutions and to win him over to the Ta'if accords. His aim was to stop the bloody Christian fights that erupted in 1990 between Aoun's troops and the "Lebanese Forces" in the wake of this disputed agreement.

At a private lunch held in the Pope's apartments in the Vatican, on December 22, 1989, and attended only by the Holy Father and his then secretary of state Agostino Casaroli, his aide Jean-Louis Tauran, Cardinal Angelo Sodano, and Nuncio Pablo Puente, the decision was taken to officially recognize Elias Hrawi as the new President of the Republic. Hrawi was rejected by the majority of the Christians on the ground that he'd been appointed in a military barrack under Syrian control in the Biqaa Valley. Right after the New Year, Puente presented his letter of credentials to the Lebanese president. This act caused him his first rift with the Christian public mainstream supporting Aoun. The Nuncio also did not shun from criticizing the behavior of the "Lebanese Forces," and that antagonized the rest of the Christian public as well.

One mistaken opinion within Christian ranks was to think that Puente was acting on his own behalf. Lebanese Christians did not want to acknowledge that the Vatican cautioned a policy they did not like. Had they read Pope John Paul II's message to Patriarch Sfeir on September 20, 1988, when the presidency succession crisis broke up, they would have realized how important (for the Holy Father) the principle of legality was to the preservation of the Christians' role within the institutions of the state. John Paul II worried that the non-election of a president would "gravely imperil the very future of the nation." He added: "It is primordial that no other consideration matters before the respect of the legality, for the safeguard of the principles that belong to your precious traditions and heritage." Despite the flaws attached to his election, Hrawi represented, in the eyes of the Holy See, "the necessary continuity of the State institutions and of Lebanon's sovereign attributes, which the Christians should herald," as the Papal Nuncio put it.[1]

Although he did not move on his own, Puente did actually have the greatest latitude in his mission and he would induce a subtle shift in the Vatican's stated positions regarding the Christians in Lebanon. Among the main turnabouts initiated by the Papal Nuncio were:

- the overture to the Muslim side of the capital, "West Beirut," in 1991, with a new boost given to Christian-Muslim dialogue, through Puente's personal contacts, and particularly through the cordial rela-

tionship he developed with Shiite ulema Mohammad Hussein Fadlallah, in an attempt to assess the real intentions of Hezbollah fundamentalists in Lebanon;
- the establishment of rational relations with the Ta'if regime;
- a "damage control" policy in the Christian camp after the Syrian military operation of October 13, 1990, that ousted General Aoun from the Baabda presidential palace. This "damage control" aimed at providing a strong Christian protective authority, i.e., the Holy See itself, for the Christian society which was reeling over its losses and facing imminent danger of collapse after the Syrian intervention as well as physical peril for many Christian youth and militants. The Holy See would thus become, through its Nuncio, the first and principal Christian interlocutor of all Lebanese (and non-Lebanese) Muslim parties in the direct postwar years;
- the "Realpolitik" that marked the Vatican's stand towards Syria and the decision to put aside the question of the Syrian presence in Lebanon. It was urgent to set new priorities for the Lebanese Church, which was in critical need of reassessment, of mending, of reflection and contemplation;
- the reinforcement of the church position, and most especially of the Maronite Patriarchate whose role would be propelled after the breakdown of the political leadership of the Christian Maronites. To achieve that purpose, it was vital to keep the Church aloof from daily politics and to prop up its aura lost during the Aoun-Geagea war. On November 26, 1994, the Holy Father presided over a solemn ceremony (broadcast live through satellite) in St. Peter's Basilica, in which he made Patriarch Nasrallah Sfeir a cardinal, in a clear intent to honor the Maronite Church.

Keeping the Maronite clergy out of the political quicksand in which the war had dragged it down would be one of the main focuses of the Papal Nuncio. He would confront a long-established tradition of "militant monks," especially within the Maronite Order of Kaslik. Puente's first outburst happened in November 26, 1989, at the meeting of the Assembly of Catholic Patriarchs and Bishops in Bkerké. He criticized in vehement tones "the interference of clerical persons and institutions in politics without being officially mandated to, by the Church hierarchy." Hammering out his French words in his typical Spanish accent, he added: "You must understand that an end must be put to political visits and declarations that have no clear Church mandate."

The tightening grip of the Holy See, largely embodied in Puente's urge to check what he viewed as the Maronite radical political drive, would be illustrated in the nomination of "visiting bishops" to supervise three "turbulent" orders: the Maronite Order, the Antonine Order, and the Mariamite Order. The opponents of this policy would resent the "direct Vatican tutelage" and consider it as "an intrusive meddling in the internal affairs of the Orders." Although these "exempt Orders," as they are called, were legally under Rome's sway, they claimed more autonomy whenever their political zeal was checked by the Papal Nuncio. The Holy See also formally forbade any selling of the church's lands and real estate properties without its authorization.

Pablo Puente was very much aware of the hostility a reorganization of the church would trigger among the restive clerics, on whom even the patriarch could not exert his jurisdiction. In fact, they frequently challenged Bkerké's national options and the patriarch's authority. Puente, who faced growing opposition to his reformist orientations, had confided to His Holiness that if he wants to work seriously and succeed in his mission, the Nuncio should not look for popularity. Thus, the Nuncio was ready to go through harsh criticism in order to achieve success in what he believed was the best way to revamp the original vocation of the church in Lebanon and bring about a profound spiritual renewal. He would use the word "metanoia" to explain what the Pope was about to call for the Christians of Lebanon.

JOHN PAUL II AND LEBANON

On June 12, 1991, John Paul II announced the convocation of a Synod for Lebanon and asked the Lebanese Catholics to engage in "spiritual mobilization," "an examination of conscience," and a "purification of the heart." The direct cause of the Synod idea was the intra-Maronite war of 1990, with its incalculable consequences: destruction of the infrastructure of the country, acceleration of the emigration, and above all, the breach that occurred between the people and the church. The Nahr el-Mawt massacre (October 2, 1990) is said to have sounded the alarm in the Vatican curia. The Lebanese Forces had reportedly opened fire on a peaceful candlelight procession organized by pro-Aoun forces; twenty-one were killed. At a group funeral for the victims in Antelias, the crowd vented its anger against patriarchs, bishops, and clergymen. The majority of the Christian public opinion, which was pro-Aoun, not only denigrated an imposed government but was also alienated from the church. Something had to be done.

Furthermore, the internal strife within the Maronite community was besetting with difficulties its relations with the other Christian communities, Catholic and Orthodox, who did not condone the Maronites' political and military ventures. It also rattled the very foundations of the

Lebanese entity, based on Christian-Muslim interaction and dialogue. And without that interaction, Lebanon had no meaning. In one of his most revealing addresses, in the midst of the "liberation war" when Christian regions were shelled by Syrian forces, John Paul II had proclaimed "the unique value of Lebanon and of its human and spiritual patrimony." "The Church wishes to make it clear to the world that Lebanon is more than a country: it is a message of freedom and an example of pluralism for the East and the West as well," he said. "This consented and lived pluralism is a fundamental value that presided over Lebanon's long history. This is why if that country disappeared, the cause of liberty itself will suffer a tragic blow" (Papal letter to all Bishops of the Catholic Church, September 7, 1989). The Pope ended his letter warning against the disappearance of Lebanon, which "would be one of the great remorses of the world." "Lebanon's preservation is one of the most urgent and most noble tasks our contemporary world ought to carry," he added. Ultimately, the Holy Father wound up carrying this task alone.

No Pope has ever expressed so much preoccupation and affection for Lebanon as did John Paul II. "This country, so close to the heart of the Church and the Pope" (John Paul II, February 2, 1988), ranked second after his motherland Poland, according to his entourage, and he did not deny that assertion. "I was emotionally Lebanese, now I became effectively Lebanese," he said one evening while he was having dinner with a group of participants in the Synod.[2] He regularly praised "the antique Christian roots of Lebanon" and would find wonderful words during his visit to Lebanon to describe Lebanon's spiritual heritage (see Part III, Chapter 12).

Elected on October 16, 1978, the Pope from Krakow mentioned Lebanon in his first message to the world the very next day, as he expounded his strategy as a new leader of the Catholic Church. He wanted "to say how much (he) took to heart the fate of this beloved land of Lebanon and its people, to whom we ardently wish peace in freedom." When, on October 22, he appeared in St. Peter's Square to celebrate the mass inaugurating his pontificate, the president of Lebanon was on hand, along with the president of Poland, King Juan Carlos of Spain, and the presidents of Austria and of Ireland. Lebanon would be regularly present in his discussions with foreign leaders (such as U.S. president Ronald Reagan), throughout his pontificate, alongside Poland. It would also figure among the range of subjects debated in his meetings with the personal delegates of U.S. president Ronald Reagan, among whom was director of the CIA, William Casey, as revealed in the classified cables Casey reportedly sent to the White House, State Department, or CIA after each visit he made to the Vatican.[3]

This personal kinship also stems from the identical fate of Lebanon and Poland, two Early Christian countries wedged between greedy powerful neighbors and pursuing a dogged struggle to defend their independence and sovereignty. When in 1946, Catholic seminaries were shut down in Poland, Polish seminarists went to Rome and Beirut (where they stayed with the Jesuit community).

As soon as 1986, during the beatification ceremony of Maronite Sister Rafqa (November 17), John Paul II expressed his eagerness to visit Lebanon. He would make more than two hundred public statements during the years of war in Lebanon, all showing deep concern for the national identity, the unity, the freedom, and the dignity of that small nation. He would condemn "the intervention of armed forces from bordering countries" (May 15, 1989), hold "the international community responsible," and send messages of solidarity to the Lebanese people. He would speak out when receiving the diplomatic corps, would appeal to the Muslims around the world "in the name of the same God whom we worship" (September 7, 1989) to help preserve Lebanon's unique and pluralistic society based on coexistence, would announce an "international day of prayer for Lebanon" with 30,000 faithful gathering in St. Peter's Square (October 4, 1989), would pick up the phone and call international leaders, American, European, and Arab presidents, and heads of the Arab League and of the United Nations to urge them to secure Lebanon's territorial sovereignty and independence.

On the practical level, John Paul II assigned the Lebanese dossier to a special work team formed of high-ranking diplomats, cardinals, and bishops of the Vatican curia. Many of them were sent on missions as his personal envoys in Beirut and Damascus. Cardinal Paolo Bertoli came three times to Lebanon at the end of the seventies, as did Cardinal Agostino Casarolli in the early eighties, Cardinal Roger Etchegaray (the first time in 1985 after the downfall of Christian villages in East Sidon and Iqlim el-Kharroub), Cardinals Achille Silvestrini and Luigi Gatti, and Archbishop Jean-Louis Tauran (who had been posted in the Nunciature and became an expert on Lebanon before he was appointed Secretary for Relations with States, i.e., the Vatican's foreign minister).

In the wake of Etchegaray's visit in 1985, the Holy Father also designated a personal delegate in the mountainous Christian burg of Jezzine, Spanish lazarist Celestino Buhigas. This initiative demonstrated his willingness to prevent Christian emigration from Southern Lebanon. Until he died in 1991, Buhigas successfully fulfilled a mission that was human, spiritual, and diplomatic. He gave confidence to the Christians, built schools and churches, granted scholarships, created jobs, and developed a good relationship with Druze leader Walid Joumblatt, which eased the tensions between Druze and Christians. Many Druze children were sent to the schools he established in the region. After Buhigas was gone, Jezzine inhabitants fell back in their solitude and many youngsters left town, especially since the intensification of Hezbollah guerillas' resistance against Israeli occupying forces and their allied militia (the South Lebanon Army, SLA), which controlled Jezzine. Today, and despite the SLA withdrawal from the area, roughly three thousand people remain in Jezzine, most of whom are elderly people.

Officially, diplomatic relations between the Vatican and Lebanon were established in 1947, the same year the last French battalions left Lebanon definitively. Monsignor Marina was the first Apostolic Nuncio and Charles Helou (who would become president of the republic in the sixties), the first ambassador of Lebanon at the Holy See. But in fact, the ties with the "Bishop of Rome" (the Pope's title) date back to the early centuries of Christianity. The Maronites sent their first petition to the Holy Father asking for his help in 517, when 350 monks were massacred by the Jacobites on the Orontes river, in Syria, at the height of the christological quarrels that blazed the Orient. But ongoing relations only developed starting in 1215, when Pope Innocent III sent the pallium to Jeremie Amchiti, recognizing him as "Patriarch of Antioch and all the Levant" for the Maronite nation. After three centuries of interruption due to the Mamlouk occupation, relations resumed with the arrival of Latin missions in the Levant. Two papal delegates exerted influence on the Maronite Church: Jesuit fathers Eliano and Dandini. The latter, who recommended that the Maronite nation be taken under the Pope's protection and that it be the gate to the rest of the Orient, was confirmed as the first Nuncio in the Levant. Soon, the Holy See would extend its relations to other communities, particularly the Druze, as early as 1441, when the Papal delegate Antoine de Troya headed a joint Maronite-Druze delegation visiting Rome.

Even though the Holy See's policy in the Orient depended very much on the personal inclination of the Popes, it has been characterized by a steady tradition of exchanges with Muslim communities and unfailing support to the Arab cause. So much that, among all Western states, the Holy See came to be seen by Arab leaders as their natural ally, especially in matters related to the state of Israel, with which Popes have regularly refused to establish diplomatic relations (until 1993).

Lebanon was considered as the ideal platform for expanding the Vatican's policy regarding Christian-Muslim relations. Its importance as a model of peaceful coexistence was first emphasized by Pope Paul VI when he landed in Beirut airport on his way to Bombay (December 2, 1964). The breakout of violence in Lebanon in 1975 will become a permanent source of worry for the successors of St. Peter. So much that when U.S.

president Jimmy Carter visited the Vatican, he opened the talks with Paul VI by mentioning Lebanon's need to recover its independence and sovereignty. The Pontiff observed how well President Carter had been briefed by his advisers on the Pope's centers of interest. Paul VI had publicly displayed his solicitude in 1977 when he beatified Maronite hermit Charbel, in presence of the Maronite Patriarch. "Your Church," he said, "is the glory of Lebanon."

Under John Paul II, Muslim-Christian dialogue and the openness to Islam became a central theme on the agenda of the Holy See. There is a widespread conviction among the Vatican curia that the future of the world in the next decades will be very much determined by Christian-Muslim relations. This is why Lebanon's experience is meaningful. According to bishop Michael Fitzgerald, member of the Pontifical Council for Interreligious Dialogue, Christian-Muslim relations account for 50 percent of the activities of that Council, presided by Cardinal Francis Arinze. "When John Paul II was elected, there were only 15 embassies representing Muslim countries to the Vatican. Today, most of the Muslim States are represented at the Holy See," he said.[4] John Paul II is the first Pope to travel to Muslim Countries (Morocco, Turkey, Nigeria, Dakar) and to an Arab country in the Middle East (Lebanon). He has also planned a visit to the Holy Land and Jerusalem, and he has challenged the U.S. policy of boycott of Saddam Hussein's Iraq by preparing to go on an Abrahamic pilgrimage to Ur (Ancient Mesopotamia) before renouncing the idea. Gifted with an instinct for the dramatic moment, he has had symbolism-packed meetings at the Vatican with the highest authority in traditional Sunni Islam, the Cairo-based Al-Azhar sheikh Mohammad Tantawi, and with Iran's reform-minded president Mohammed Khatami. Human rights and freedom of religion were inevitably raised by His Holiness as a quintessential pivot of Christian-Muslim dialogue.

"Rome has never wanted Christians to live in ghettos, but on the contrary to establish a symbiotic relationship with Islam," Archbishop Jean-Louis Tauran explained. "The model which the Popes sought to safeguard and to promote is that of the Lebanon."[5] In the vision of the Holy Father, Lebanon should remain a key bridge to the Arab and Muslim world. On the diplomatic level, and in addition to his function as Nuncio in Lebanon, Pablo Puente was appointed in 1994 Apostolic Nuncio in Kuwait and papal delegate in the Arabic Peninsula, based in Harissa (Lebanon).

On the social level, Catholic universities, hospitals, social organizations (such as Caritas) reached out to all Lebanese communities and during the war, pontifical missions stressed on the preservation of coexistence in mixed villages, on the return of the displaced in various zones (like the Harf, in the Shouf, and East Sidon) and some Pontifical Councils such as "Cor Unum" funneled aid to the church in support to the victims of war.

On the political level, John Paul II will be actively involved in the solution of Lebanon's crisis. His first attempt was to be rebuffed by Syria's allies in Lebanon, at the behest of Damascus. In March 1986, the Holy Father had officially charged Archbishop Achille Silvestrini, then secretary of the Council for Public Affairs, to visit Beirut and Damascus and explore the possibility of the Vatican contribution to a "restoration of Lebanese national unity in which all groups—and the Christians first—will be able to gain back their dignity, tranquillity and confidence." Silvestrini was accompanied by Archbishops Tauran and Gatti. In Beirut, where Nuncio Angeloni joined them, they met the main Christian and Muslim leaders of the Maronite, the Sunni, and the Shiite communities. In Damascus, they were received by President Hafez Assad, Abdel-Halim Khaddam, and Farouk el-Chareh. Assad outwitted their virtual intentions by telling them straight off that Syria had been striving in the last twelve years to help Lebanon resolve its internal problems and that it shares the Vatican's concerns in that regard. He thus made it clear to his visitors that Syria was not part of the problem but could be part of the solution.

Not long after, a Vatican blueprint of a "just and adequate" solution was rejected by Muslim Lebanese leaders on the ground that it was biased in favor of the Christians and that it put Syrians and Israelis on the same level. The document was also rejected by the Greek Catholic Patriarch, whose seat is in Damascus, on the ground that the Greek Catholic Church had not been consulted. The relationship between the Holy See and Syria would be a tense one. Long periods of time would elapse before papal nuncios in Damascus presented their letters of credentials, while Syria did not have an appointed ambassador to the Holy See, but was represented by its ambassador to Italy.

The Supreme Pontiff bore in mind this foiled undertaking when the Lebanese deputies convened in Ta'if (October 1989) to put an end to the ravaging "Aounist" war against Syria and to lay out the amendments to the Constitution under the auspices of the tripartite Arab committee. Since 1986, John Paul II had considered that "Lebanon can and must rediscover its identity through a new socio-political equilibrium." As early as December 1979, he had mentioned "the necessary amendments (to the National Pact) imposed by the events" occurring in Lebanon (speech at the United Nations).

The Holy Father wanted to stay attuned to what was going on in Ta'if and was briefed by two Lebanese members of parliament who visited the Vatican to get his opinion on that matter. Whatever reservations to the amendments introduced and the dramatic circumstances that surrounded them, the Pope chose a pragmatic and realistic approach, based on the need to preserve the legal institutions of the Lebanese State, as the embodiment of its *de jure* sovereignty, even if that sovereignty was violated *de facto* and Lebanon was subdued.

Already the first president-elect after Ta'if, René Moawad, had been killed on Independence Day (November 22, 1989) by a bomb placed in his armored car. When the inter-Christian clashes broke up in 1990, weeks only after the Apostolic Nuncio presented his credentials to President Hrawi, John Paul II took it as a personal blow to his endeavors and to the political line followed by the Holy See during the previous years. "During the seventeen long years of the recent civil war, the Holy See always encouraged resistance to the temptation, which certain Lebanese circles harbored, to create a mini-Christian State," explained Tauran. "The rallying cry was to some extent 'Let us save Lebanon to save the Christians,' and not 'Let us save the Christians to save Lebanon.'"[6]

Through his Synod appeal, the Pontiff would launch a programmed exercise in self-criticism and reconciliation, a "time of penance" to "stimulate internal conversion." "The Catholic Churches of Lebanon must, first and foremost, sound their conscience and question their fidelity to the evangelical message," he declared.[7] Once again, the parallel with Poland is irresistible. As a priest, Karol Wojtyla believed that his native Poland in its time of trouble had to be defended not only with the sword but above all through spiritual renewal. Spiritual renewal was also the first condition requested from the Church of Lebanon. In the final analysis, it had fallen because it failed to recognize its spiritual and cultural ideals, which were held high but not realized. And "it could not re-engage into oecumenical cooperation with the Orthodox Church, nor into national dialogue with the Muslim counterparts before this inner reform takes place. It is a prerequisite," said Father Maurice Borrmans, one of the authors of what would become the *Instrumentum Laboris,* the working document of the Synod.[8]

At the end of the twentieth century, the Christians of Lebanon had lost any political importance to the West. For the first time in their history, they were standing alone in the eye of the storm. The Holy See—or rather the Holy Father in person—was their ultimate "Western" resort, after France had been "neutralized" in the wake of the Syrian military intervention in 1990, the subsequent exile of General Aoun in Paris, and the implementation of what has been viewed as the Syrian version of the Ta'if accords.[9]

But the Synod initiative of Pope John Paul II will also be their last-chance bid. This time, it was not what Maronite Patriarch Sfeir believed, "one of the many crisis that trailed our age-old history and we are still here from the dawn of Christianity, deeply entrenched in our historical roots." It was *the* crisis, the turning point that would initiate the irreversible decline or the salutary rise.

The demographic reality of the Christians was on a steep slope and they had lost the sense of their mission in the Levant when they vied for power to the point of killing each other. In order to preserve their presence, they will be asked to stop acting and thinking like an embattled minority obsessed with its survival and to re-immerse themselves in their environment by first going back to their ancient spirituality in order to "rediscover the profound roots of their faith."[10] Who were they? What was their *raison d'être?* Where were they going from here? Where did they belong? What contribution could they still make in what was once the Orient and what is known today as the Middle East?

THE BUMPY ROAD TO THE SYNOD

Cardinal Roger Etchegaray came to Lebanon in July 1991 and was followed in September by Archbishop Jan Schotte, the general Secretary of the Synod, to lay the synodal groundwork and explain its mechanisms and implications. The young and ebullient bishop of Jbeil (Byblos), Beshara Rahi, was invested coordinator of the preparatory works, which included the drafting of a first document called the *Lineamenta,* the general principles or axes of reflection of the Synod. Seventy-two questions were formulated and distributed to all parishes in Lebanon to collect answers at the grass-roots level. The questions were threefold, related to Catholic issues, to the relations with non-Catholic Christians, and to the relations between Christians and Muslims.

After he drew an initial working paper, Rahi called on Greek Orthodox bishop George Khodr and the Mufti's adviser, Mohammad Sammak, for a meeting to sound their opinion. They convened at Bishop Khodr's place in Broummana (Mount-Lebanon) in summer 1992. Sammak expressed strong reserves when he read Rahi's paper. "The paper was based on a logic of 'us' and 'them,' and I did not think that was constructive," he later explained. "So Rahi told me: what are your suggestions? Bishop Khodr also made his own comments. The bishop of Jbeil was more than willing to have a document that would be accepted by both the Greek Orthodox and the Muslims. So at a second meeting, also in Khodr's residence, I submitted a new text that was adopted by both bishops."[11]

John Paul II innovated by involving non-Catholics in the preparation of a Synod, and by inviting both Greek Orthodox and Muslim representatives to attend it and have their say. That way, he made it clear that, although intended first and foremost for the Catholic Church, the Synod was for all Lebanon, and that its scope embraced ecumenism and inter-religion dialogue. He was also implicitly sending a message to the Muslims of Lebanon, by singling them out and endowing them with a special responsibility towards their counterparts in the rest of the Muslim world, through an unprecedented experience in which they would share the church's intimate reflections and would lay down with them the foundations of a Christian-Muslim fraternity and solidarity. "Saying that the Lebanese are doomed to understand one another is not an overstatement. The Synod wants conviviality to be the expression of a conviction rather than a fate," commented the "Black Pope," Jesuit General Kolvenbach.[12]

At the beginning, Lebanese Muslim authorities were lukewarm when the Synod was announced; their reaction reflected suspicion. At best it showed they were not concerned, until the Papal Nuncio in Lebanon and various Catholic bishops transmitted the Pope's invitation. Everything considered, the Shiite, Sunni, and Druze religious authorities decided to send delegates to the Synod rather than attend personally. They did not want to go out on a limb and feel committed to endorse texts or positions they might not agree with. Mohammad Sammak, Seoud el-Mawla, and Abbas Halabi were designated to represent the Sunni, Shiite, and Druze communities, "officially as observers, but practically, as participants."[13] Also, Muslim authorities refused to answer part of the seventy-two questions related to Christian-Muslim relations and preferred to communicate their own vision of national coexistence in Lebanon.

When they read the document that resulted from the wide consultation of the Lebanese Christians in the parishes throughout the country, the cardinals and bishops of the Vatican curia were appalled. They had an inkling of the matter, but they were far from imagining the chasm that separated the church and the people, the people and the state. With dismay, they discovered all the resentment, the despair, and the bitterness that were buried in the invisible recesses of people's minds and souls and that gushed out in the answers to the questionnaire, the distrust among Lebanese themselves and about each sectarian groups' real intentions, the will to emigrate. A bleak outlook was depicted in eight hundred pages, making it a revolutionary text (not to be rendered public), that contrasted with all other presynodal texts.

The Catholics of Lebanon were uttering their grievances against the church and the state, all established authorities whom they felt were untrustworthy. They were critical against the clergy, saying they expected it to be more caring and closer to the poor, the weak, and the displaced during the throes of war, they denounced the violations of the poverty, chastity, and obedience vows of many a priest, and made it clear that they did not want to listen to their pastors and bishops anymore. They also—and wrongly—accused the church of too much political compromise and of accepting Ta'if. They wanted sterner political stands from their religious leaders.[14] It is to be remembered that a vast majority of the Christian public opinion still supported Aoun's ideas and resented the acceptance of Ta'if by the Maronite Church and the Papal Nuncio. In any case, the image of the church was considerably tarnished in the eyes of the faithful, who also rebuked the lack of coordination between Catholics and Orthodox, and the absence of unity as well as the privileges and wealth some members of the religious hierarchies enjoyed.

The text was pruned and its angles rounded off in the Vatican "laboratory," i.e., the council of the General Secretariat of the Synod. Cardinals Silvestrini and Schotte arrived in Beirut in March 1993. In Bkerké, where they met all Catholic patriarchs and bishops, they made public the ninety-six pages of the *Lineamenta,* which were distributed to political and religious leaders in Lebanon and to the media, for further comments and contemplation. The theme of the Synod was: "Christ is our hope: renewed by His Spirit, together, we witness to His Love."

The *Lineamenta* were divided into four parts that touched upon all sensitive issues: the clerical education of the priests, the role of lay people in the church, the parish councils as an important link between the people and the religious hierarchy, the principle of equal opportunities between men and women, the necessity to be attentive to the youth problems, the protection of the family unity, the educational role of the church, the necessity to safeguard freedom of education in Lebanon and to decrease schools and universities' high tuition, social and economic problems (unemployment, poverty, inflation, housing, medical care, drugs, corruption, gambling), solidarity of the church with lower and middle classes through charity work, cooperation between churches of different liturgical traditions, the obstacles facing mixed marriages, political life, freedom and democracy, dialogue with other religions, especially with Islam, the rejection of fanaticism, the need to join efforts to protect the country from foreign interference, and the need to stop the emigration flow.

Silvestrini insisted he wanted to visit Tyre and Sidon in South Lebanon, to encourage the Christians to hold on to their land and villages, and to promote good entente with their Muslim neighbors. Preventing the Christians from disengaging further physically (by leaving the country) and politically (by excluding themselves from political life) had become a priority for the Holy See. In 1992, Christians had boycotted the parliamentary elections and found out they were not genuinely represented anymore in the state institutions. If they kept on that way, they would soon undermine the national foundations of coexistence. "The Synod is meant for reconciliation, not for boycott," Silvestrini bluntly told the Assembly of Patriarchs and Bishops gathered in Bkerké. Eastern Churches "need to stop living in souvenirs and dwelling on their past" and to depart from their nostalgic attitude. "It is important to adapt to the reality of Lebanese society," he added.

The Holy Father wished to see "prophetic gestures." The best way to renew themselves was for the Catholics to reach out to the others, by bridging the gap among Catholics first, among Christian Catholics and Orthodox second, and among Lebanese Christians and Muslims third. The *Lineamenta* confirmed that "coexistence is the only path to Lebanon's resurrection." While Silvestrini and Schotte were still in Lebanon, Pope John Paul II received Greek Orthodox Archbishop of Beirut Elias Audeh, as to confirm that the "synodal march" embraced all Chalcedonian Churches, the Maronite, the "Byzantine" Greek Orthodox, as well as its Catholic offshoot.[15]

Clearly, Lebanese Christians had to be strong enough to take their destiny in their own hands rather than await their decline. This was the real meaning of the Synod. The Roman Catholic Church suddenly realized that the dusk of Eastern Christianity would cut it from its spiritual source and geographical origins. It would break its bond to the land where Jesus was born. "The Mashreq Christianity is the bedrock of world Christianity," said the expurgated version of the *Lineamenta* (which added: "just like Arab Muslims are the essence and nucleus of world Islam").

ROME AND THE ORIENTAL IDENTITY OF THE CHURCH

In one of those ironic twists of history, Rome was now calling those whom it tried to Latinize for centuries to ascertain their liturgical traditions and to "fructify the spiritual richness of the ancient Churches of the Orient, that were the cradle of our faith."[16]

"Your identity is your mission," John Paul II had told the Maronites. In 1988 (February 2), on the Presentation Day of Lord Jesus to the Temple, the Supreme Pontiff had for the first time celebrated mass in St. Peter's Basilica according to the syro-antiochian liturgy, which was the Maronite rite. At the beginning of the ceremony, he was praised by Maronite Patriarch Sfeir: "His Holiness is showing his paternal solicitude and the consideration he always displayed towards the Eastern Churches, among which the Maronite Church is one of the first to use syriac as its liturgical language."

Vatican II had recognized the distinct ritual identity of the Eastern Churches. Those churches, patriarchal in their structures, Antiochian in their spirituality, monastic in their vocation, embodied the initial soul of Christianity. Yet only in 1990 had the canon code for Eastern Churches (*Orientale Lumen*) been promulgated.

Again, the question lingered on: had the Christians of Lebanon and their church, particularly the Maronite Church, identified too much with the West? And was this one of the reasons of their existential crisis? Yet the West did not identify itself with them, although Western powers did not refrain from using them as geopolitical and cultural outposts and the Western churches and missions (both Latin and Protestant) did not balk at "evangelizing" them. And here was Rome confounding them with its insistence to retrieve their oriental heritage before it is too late! What a dramatic historical quid pro quo!

One commanding figure in the Catholic Church with close ties to John Paul II, Cardinal Jean-Marie Lustiger (of Polish origin), grasped all the disarray and dilemma of the Christians of Lebanon when he visited the country three weeks before the Synod. In his capacity as Archbishop of Paris, he was also the Archbishop of all Christian Catholic Lebanese residing in France. This is due to the historic and religious bonds between France and Lebanon.

Like Silvestrini, Lustiger toured the southern harbor cities of Tyre and Sidon, of antique Christian roots, but he also wished to go to Qannoubine, the "sacred Valley" of the Maronites in North Lebanon, which sheltered their Patriarchate during four centuries and helped preserve their existence and identity during the Mamluk invasion. With its churches and monasteries carved in the rock, Qannoubine epitomized the soul of Maronitism and its Syriac spirituality; it was the alma mater of the Maronite nation. The French cardinal was deeply moved by his "pilgrimage" and exclaimed: "How could one loose hope and the power of renewal when living in the proximity of such a vivid fountain of spirituality?"

In a memorable speech given in Notre-Dame of Harissa, Lustiger said: "A few years ago, before the arms became silent, I begged your pardon in the name of my country and in the name of the great nations, because it seems to me that being where you are, where God placed you, in this beautiful country, . . . the ordeal you went through was beyond human limits and you might have thought: 'They all abandoned me.' You might have lacked courage and strength and wondered why God put you here." And he simply and eloquently described what the Catholic Church expected from the Lebanese:

> You're probably the only country in the world where civilization is born and is still bearing fruits. A country where Christians of all confessions are assembled in such a tiny space, and where the great non-Christian religions are also present. . . . Because of your diversity, you can achieve what is impossible to do elsewhere in Europe where the Eastern and the Western lungs of the Church are choking one another instead of breathing together. Because you are a people who has never ceased to pray and to believe, you can advance the unity of the Christians much easier than in Paris, Geneva, Moscow,

or New York. . . . You are probably the only ones in the world to be in a situation one might describe as ambiguous, because you belong to two cultures at the same time. But this is why it is also the only place in the world, here in the Middle East, where a true dialogue can take place and where Christianity, Islam, and Judaism can meet in mutual respect and freedom. You are ascribed to be the bridge between these worlds originating from the same trunk. If you cannot make it, the world won't be able to make it.[17]

Well, "that is a heavy load for such a small country and a small nation," as Cardinal Lustiger did acknowledge in his homily! "None of us chose and would dare choose such a vocation. But it happens that you are here. Through our love and respect to you, and as we try to understand what is befalling to you, we see it as a redeeming path for all. You did not choose it, but you have to," Lustiger concluded in his frank style, leaving his audience with a lump in the throat.

Chapter 7

Three Weeks in Rome

Almost four years of preparation preceded the convocation in Rome of seven patriarchs, eleven cardinals, twenty-two archbishops, seventeen bishops, ten heads and members of religious and monastic orders, seventeen "experts" and special assistants to the Secretary of the Synod, twenty-five priests, nuns and lay "auditors," one representative of the Middle East Council of Churches, and eight "fraternal delegates": five representing the Greek-Orthodox Church and three representing the Lebanese Muslim authorities. The total was 120 participants, coming also from Arab countries such as Syria, Egypt, Iraq, and Palestine. Every Eastern rite of the Catholic family was represented and the Armenian Church as well. The Synod for Lebanon was definitely the Synod of the Eastern Church in its various liturgical branches and historical stripes, all present in Lebanon. The "Synod Fathers" convened on November 27, 1995, in the Vatican City for what would become three momentous weeks in Rome for the participants, and a landmark in Lebanon's modern history.

The working document (*Instrumentum Laboris*) of 122 pages in its original French version was a more elaborate and soothed version of the *Lineamenta*, but it nonetheless underscored themes that would dominate the deliberations. Cardinal Schotte, who prefaced it, said that seventeen dioceses (out of twenty-one) had cooperated in this document, and that the proportion of those who answered the questions reached 80.95 percent and was the highest of all the Synods organized so far. The *Instrumentum Laboris* bore the stamp of the White Fathers (*les Pères Blancs*) Jean Corbon and Maurice Borrmans in its section dealing with inter-religious dialogue. The unity of the church within the diversity of its theological and liturgical traditions and the necessity to further Christian-Muslim cooperation based on the common values of the two great religions were major assignments along with the renewed commitment of the Catholics to evangelical values. "The *Instrumentum Laboris* borrowed important parts of the Christmas 1994 pastoral letter of the Eastern Catholic Patriarchs, who said it all," confides Father Borrmans.[1]

The general message was clear: that Lebanon still provides an open forum where Christians and Muslims of the Arab world can reflect freely on past and present is an achievement worth upholding, and it is incumbent on the Lebanese to preserve that, in the variety of their traditions. This message relieved the Greek Orthodox and the Muslim representatives, who had been hesitant since the publishing of the *Lineamenta*.

The Muslim participation in the Synod did not go without political pressures and backstage lobbying. Many believed that the Synod in Rome was meant to undermine the Ta'if agreement and to come out with a Christian political counter-proposal. The Special Secretariat of the Synod sent an undisclosed letter to the Muslim religious authorities in April 1992, explaining the objectives of the Assembly and asking for their cooperation and suggestions. At first, Syria had been cautious about the active involvement of Muslim authorities in the preparatory phase, but thanks to the information campaign launched by the church and by the national dialogue committee, and also through Lebanese prime minister Rafik Hariri's contacts with the Vatican, its reserves were assuaged. The Iranian-backed Hezbollah watched carefully, with no comments. Their "spiritual guide," Sayyed Fadlallah, had been well briefed by the Apostolic Nuncio in Lebanon. Besides, the Shiites were more familiar with the mystical dimension of religion and their fundamentalism was of a more political kind, so they understood better the spiritual goal of a Christian assembly. Other Sunni fundamentalist movements in the region were less flexible and so Mohammad Sammak received "warnings" from some Islamic fundamentalist groups in Arab countries, who did not understand that a Sunni representative could attend what boiled down to an ecclesiastic reunion in the heartland of the Crusaders' religion.

Although Sammak's two other colleagues, Seoud el-Mawla and Abbas Halaby, did not encounter such problems, Halaby formally required an assurance letter certifying that he represents the Druze community at this unusual event. As a judge, Halaby was close to Walid Joumblatt and had been in Ta'if with his stepfather Sheikh Toufic Assaf, member of the Parliament and a respectable figure of the Druze community. When Nuncio Pablo Puente and Prime Minister Hariri asked him to attend the Synod, he only had four days to prepare his speech before departing to Rome.

Rafik Hariri's support and encouragement to Muslim participation in the Synod was critical. He had enough leverage and high level connections with King Fahd of Saudi Arabia and the Damascus regime to be able to give the political cover needed by the three Muslim delegates.

And he had developed a good relationship with the Holy See, that puzzled and sometimes even rankled his Christian opponents. They deeply disliked the idea of a strong Sunni leader with direct links to St. Peter's successor.

Hariri's first visit to the Vatican took place in 1993. He met with Archbishop Jean-Louis Tauran, with Cardinal Angelo Sodano, Secretary of State, and with the Holy Father. Hariri's reconstruction plans of Beirut and his ambitious vision of Lebanon's role in the Middle East appealed to the Pope's imagination, who saw a bright future for the Christians in that design. The Lebanese prime minister assured the head of the Catholic Church that he would do his utmost to preserve Lebanon's coexistence. He was persuaded that the country would not recover without the indispensable influx of its Christian population. During his tenure in office, Hariri—with his wife and children—would meet John Paul II four times in the Pope's apartments in the Vatican, and when the Pope visited Lebanon.

Through his Christian advisers, the prime minister also kept regularly in touch with the Vatican curia. Daoud Sayegh, a dedicated Greek Catholic (and secretary of the General Council of the Melkite Church) and a firm believer in the crucial role of the Christians in the Middle East, was his chief "negotiator" with the Church in Lebanon and his frequent envoy to Rome. He was also a confidant of Nuncio Puente. He became one of the lay "auditors" at the Synod, along with Boutros Labaki, a Maronite historian also firmly committed to the future of Christians in the region, who occupied the position of vice president of the Council of Development and Reconstruction, the right arm of the Presidency of the Council of Ministers under the tenure of Rafik Hariri. If one adds up those among the clerics who sympathized with the prime minister, it is easy to see that Hariri was well represented in the Synod.

That too became a cause of friction between Puente and his Christian detractors, who denounced his cooperation with the prime minister. Puente had actually been instrumental in the choice of the participants. He picked up people from academic background (professors and university graduates) and members of Christian associations such as the Focolari. He also granted the Jesuits a major role. Their influence was all too obvious, not only among the lay people, but also because the Jesuit Order was represented at the highest level through its General Prefect, Peter-Hans Kolvenbach, and four other members who would occupy key functions in the Synod. Jean Ducruet, honorary rector of the St. Joseph University and director of the preeminent hospital in Beirut, Hôtel-Dieu de France, will be of major contribution in the drafting of the Final Message; John Donohue and Tom Sicking were both among the seventeen assistants of the Special Secretary of the Synod (i.e., Cardinal Jan Schotte), and the Jesuit bishop of Aleppo, Antoine Audo, was the sole representative of the Chaldean community, with Patriarch Raphael I Bidawid, of Iraq.

The Papal Nuncio had imposed young and lay people's participation in the Synod, despite the Lebanese bishops' reluctance. He thus set a precedent, another one, next to the participation of the Muslims. "After all," he pointed out, "40 percent of the Lebanese population is under 20 years old and half of it under 30." Puente was convinced that the renewal of the church was impossible if engaged lay people and young Christians were not associated to it on an equal level with the religious body. Since Vatican II, which recognized the role of the laity in the church, the Eastern churches have had difficulty relinquishing some of their authority. With his characteristic wit, Puente compared the church to a body struck down by arteriosclerosis. It needed fresh blood to engage into reforms, and "only young and lay people could budge things because they do not hold on to their privileges and they have nothing to loose." Besides, and as Puente rightly put it, "the youth in Lebanon still awaits something from the church, while it does not expect anything from it elsewhere in the Western world. This is a real chance for the Church."[2] This policy was in the line of the Holy See and will be pursued by Puente's successor, Italian Nuncio Antonio Maria Veglio.

For the first time, the youth made itself heard at the General Congregation of the Synod, through the addresses of female auditors. Most striking was the speech of young philosophy graduate Emma Gannagé, whose outspoken style captured the attention—and the heart—of His Holiness. Her trembling voice rose—along with the chagrin of several Lebanese prelates—in the big auditorium as she portrayed the malaise of the Lebanese youth and their disappointment with the divisions of their churches and the distrust presiding over the inter-communal relations. She resented the lack of overture of the religious hierarchies, sent them back to back with State authorities, and criticized "the communal bias of the social action of the Church in Lebanon." "Each time charity is denied to a Christian because he is not Maronite, Melkite, Syriac, etc., it is Christ who is killed in the heart of a young," she said. John Paul II labeled her affectionately "my little revolutionary" and remembered her two years later when he visited Lebanon. As she walked out of the auditorium at the end of the plenary debate, she saw the Papal Nuncio hurrying to her, grabbing her arm and whispering feverishly in his inimitable accent: "Congratulations. Don't let anybody beat you down."

Another time, Puente would quip Boutros Labaki's presentation: "Your text about lay people is too clerical." "I will laicize it, Monsignor," replied Labaki, unruffled.

The unflagging Nuncio had pretty much determined one important issue on the agenda of the Synod: the social doctrine of the church, which was his riding subject ever since he arrived in Lebanon. He believed that "a poor Church is a more powerful Church." And he relentlessly honed his speeches and sermons to the Lebanese patriarchs and bishops, pressing them to develop a social policy that would put the *waqfs* (lands owned by the church) at the service of public interest. Under his impulse, Labaki had prepared a study on the use of the *waqfs* of the church to sustain projects of common interest that would stop the emigration of the young and of the middle classes and create jobs (agricultural use and farming lease, housing projects, and so on).

It was a sensitive point to the church, which owned approximately 30 percent of the real estate in Lebanon and was very reluctant to take any risk and venture into some unpredictable enterprise. For the Eastern Church, land ownership is viewed as the physical assurance of its embedded and ever-lasting roots. But what is a land without its people? would retort Puente and those who lobbied for a more productive use of the *waqfs*.

MUSLIM ATTENDANCE: A "PREMIERE"

Under the stern command of Cardinal Schotte, labeled "the Prussian" by some curial bishops and monsignori, everybody split into *carrefours,* or symposiums (working groups), in which the various themes of the Synod were discussed in detail and propositions were advanced. The organizational skills of Schotte, the iron discipline he decreed, and the information blackout he imposed (outside of the occasional press conferences) made more than one member (and journalist!) grumble and most of the participants gasp with deferential admiration. He was a master of efficiency.

Every morning, the "Synod Fathers" gathered in the hall named after Paul VI, with His Holiness in attendance. Each speaker had eight minutes to make his case. Leaning his head forward in a contemplative posture, sometimes gazing at the assembly with his penetrating eyes, the Pontiff was the shepherd of the debates in his white cassock. By his daily presence, he clearly demonstrated his personal commitment to the cause of Lebanon. He was particularly eager to see the church undergo an inner change, a kind of "inner conversion," the same one he called for the Church of Poland in his 1983 trip to his homeland, then under martial law. He hoped the Synod would mark the beginning of a grand turnabout for the Church in Lebanon. Also, John Paul II was keen on establishing personal contact and wanted to learn more about each participant. Every evening, he received at his dinner table a group of ten religious and lay people attending the Synod, and asked them a variety of questions about their life in Lebanon, their traditions, their expectations. He favored open talks, and with the Muslim delegates he was particularly eager to sound what was in the back of their mind. Never before had any representative of Islam shared the Pope's meal in his private dining room. Mohammad Sammak, Seoud el-Mawla, and Abbas Halaby were touched by the special honor made to them and through them to the Muslim communities of Lebanon. Like anybody else, they had been conquered by the Pope's charisma; his profound spirituality commanded respect. Sammak described him as "a fervent of God."

The three representatives of Lebanese Islam did not shy from developing their point of view. Abbas Halaby was unabashed at the Pope's table, when he vented the anger and the frustration of the Druze community towards the Maronites. "I had a message to deliver in the name of the Druze community to the highest Catholic authority in the world and that's what I did," he later explained.[3]

Halaby told the Pope that the Druzes had been forced to spill Christian blood in the 1983–84 Shouf war, out of self-defense. "But the periods of Christian-Druze entente transcend by far the periods of crisis in our history," he added. He complained that some books and publications had spread a culture of hatred and distrust by leading a disinformation campaign against the Druzes and by distorting their core beliefs and the nature of their relations with their fellow Muslims.

He explicitly mentioned "a certain trend within the Order of Kaslik, who, in the past, sowed the seeds of discord." (The Order of Kaslik runs the influential and dynamic University of the Holy Spirit in Kaslik). He also confirmed to the Roman pontiff that the political decision for the return of the displaced has been taken and that the only obstacles were "technical."

The presence of Muslim delegates in the Synod was thrilling for Western media and the "Synod Fathers" alike. On the first Friday of the Synod, Cardinal Schotte interrupted the deliberations and announced to the whole assembly that "our Muslim brethren are leaving us now to attend prayer in the Mosque of Rome." The three "stars" were asked to pray also for the success of the Synod.

And so, Christian-Muslim dialogue and conviviality in Lebanon became a pivotal theme of the Synod from day one. Participants spoke with openness about how it affected the nature of the political system and how compatible were Christian and Muslim concepts of freedom of religion, human rights, equality, democracy, independence, political participation, the rights of the minorities, the status of women, and the importance of the pact between the various communities.

The *Lineamenta* initially mentioned the dialogue of the three great monotheistic religions, Christianity, Judaism, and Islam, and a call had been issued by some Lebanese priests not to forget "the Lebanese Jewish community." But the political implication of dialogue with the Jews and the occupation of South Lebanon by Israeli troops hovered over that issue and relegated it to the attic. "We know there is a major problem that tarnishes this dialogue of religions, and it is the occupation of South Lebanon. Only with the withdrawal of Israeli troops can true dialogue among Lebanese of all religions take place, if however, there are still some Lebanese Jews remaining," explained Bishop Rahi.[4] In fact, the Jewish community of Lebanon had dropped since 1967 to less than twenty families.[5]

In his address to the General Congregation of the Synod, Mohammad Sammak warned that pluralism could not be a goal by itself and become the substitute for unity of the Lebanese society. He advocated a stronger commitment of the Christians to the Arab culture, similar to the role they played in the Arab Renaissance (*Nahda*). He most of all warned against the danger of an Israeli-Islamic dialogue in the context of the peace process, that would exclude Arab Christians and further isolate Islam in the Middle East, depriving it from its historical Arab Christian ally and sibling. He hoped the Synod would lay down a strategy for the Arab Church, through the deeply-rooted Lebanese Church, "to face that fateful challenge."

Seoud el-Mawla reiterated Sheikh Shamseddine's assertions that "Lebanon is our genuine and unique alternative" and that its anchor is "Christian-Muslim partnership," based on justice and equality. He developed a lenient position when he said: "Muslims are aware that there could be no justice, equality, and stability in a country if a portion of its citizens feel deprived of their rights."

Abbas Halaby underlined the "need to rethink the role of the Christians" because "they are a necessity to Lebanon and to the Arab world." He called for "a new Pact between Christians and Druzes," whose "entente is sometimes difficult, but whose divorce is proscribed."

The Synod left a strong impression on the three Muslim emissaries. Mawla and Sammak expressed their admiration for this Christian enterprise of self-criticism and for the depth of the debates they witnessed in the small groups and closed sessions. Halaby went as far as to consider that "unfortunately, the best shortcut to religious dialogue is the Vatican." "My sense is that the Holy See is the indispensable intermediary between Lebanese communities," he stated in his outspoken style. "We have found here a better understanding than among some of the Lebanese participants."[6] They returned to Beirut one week before the conclusion of the Synod. Buoyed by their experience, they were wary, though, because they had noticed tensions rippling the assembly and that did not help ease their feelings.

POLITICS VERSUS SPIRITUAL RENEWAL

The Synod was hemmed in by pointed cleavages. A dividing line cut through the reformist trend, represented, by and large, by the Cardinals of Rome as well as the lay auditors and a number of priests and mother superiors, and the more conservative trend represented by the Lebanese bishops. While the former insisted on the need for "a change of mentality," the latter were more thrifty when it came to the social doctrine of the church and to the role of the lay people, but much more adamant on political issues.

Through Cardinals Achille Silvestrini (Prefect of the Congregation for Eastern Churches), Pio Laghi (Congregation for the Catholic Education), Joseph Ratzinger (Congregation for the Doctrine of the Faith), Francis Arinze (Pontifical Council for Inter-Religious Dialogue), and Eduardo Pironio (Pontifical Council for Laity), the Roman curia subtly dispensed its criticism to the Lebanese episcopate. It painted the Lebanese Churches warts and all, showing that it mastered perfect knowledge of the situation in Lebanon, of the clergy's problems, and of the grass-roots state of mind. The reforms advocated touched all areas, spanning from charity work and solidarity with the poor to cultural opening and coordination between educational institutions, liturgical reform in the respect of Oriental traditions and spirituality, laity's role in pastoral revival, women's participation, and inter-religious cooperation.

Particularly significant was the criticism of Western trends emitted by the curial bishops. They were eager to deter the deleterious influence of the West on Eastern society, culture, and traditions. The Holy See feared "the threat of certain negative aspects of Western culture that are also showing in Lebanon," said Silvestrini. "If we're not able to ward off their effects, the traditional values of the country will be jeopardized." As president of the Congregation for Eastern Churches, he praised the "rich liturgy of the Churches of the Orient," while the guardian of the Catholic dogma, Cardinal Ratzinger, enjoined "the Orient not to follow the wrong steps of standardization of the liturgy, of which the West offer sad examples." The spread and scourges of secularism in Christian society was also one serious concern of His Holiness and of the Vatican Archbishops. It was considered as much a threat as religious fundamentalism and extremism that deny pluralism.

Yet the real polarization occurred when the head of the Pope's "government," Secretary of State Cardinal Angelo Sodano, recommended keeping the church away from state affairs and summoned the clergy to stay out of politics and leave it to lay people. He said the priority must go to inner reflection and renewal of the church, with a focus on social, cultural, and liturgical reforms. His position—based on Vatican II's vision of the church role in the state—clearly challenged the Maronite clergy's traditional stand. In the name of the Maronite episcopate, the bishop of the vibrant Christian port of Jounieh Chucrallah Harb had taken a hard-line position within the Synod, developing political themes: the issue of the displaced, youth emigration, "the selective application of the Ta'if accords," the Palestinian refugees problem, Israeli occupation of South Lebanon, the presence of Syrian troops on Lebanese territory, and the violation of Lebanon's sovereignty. He gave a gloomy picture of the situation in Lebanon: Christians emigrated in throngs, out of despair that their country would ever regain its free national will, and their dynamic business class refrained from investing in a country under occupation. The living standards plummeted and job opportunities were waning.

In its argument with the Roman curia, the Maronite Church defended the idea that it has always stood for the basic rights of freedom, independence, and equality and that it cannot be indifferent to the destiny of its homeland and its people. In the Orient, where politics and religion are intertwined, the Maronite Church has a widely recognized historical and moral responsibility in denouncing injustice, and its Christian and national missions are inseparable. Besides, if it is not able to speak out loud in the name of Lebanon at a watershed event such as the Synod for Lebanon, where and when would that be possible?

In his 1990 Lent letter to his Maronite flock and clergy, Patriarch Sfeir had tackled the delicate issue of "Church and politics" and contended that "the Church does not engage in politics. It is not bound by any temporal limits or linked to any political order. It exerts its moral authority by reaffirming fundamental principles of human dignity and rights."

The Pope had deliberately ruled out the participation of both Archbishop Jean-Louis Tauran, his Secretary for Foreign Relations, and Cardinal Luigi Gatti, officially in charge of the Lebanese and Middle East portfolio for years, in a move clearly intended to withhold any political intention that might be attached to the Synod. Gatti commented: "We're only political technicians. What His Holiness is requiring is the deepening of Christian values. Both Muslims and Christians aspire for a renewal of human, ethical, and moral values to be able to work together. The message of the Pope is moral but it certainly has an impact on the political level. What is wrong in the society and in the country could be repaired if the church initiated an inner reform."[7]

Yet the reasoning of the Maronite Church touched the right chord in the Roman Pontiff and his entourage. How indeed could one separate politics from religion in the Middle East? Besides, "the right of peoples to self-determination is a principle of international law the Holy See has constantly asserted," as Archbishop Tauran later commented.[8]

"The Pope believes in the concept of nation and in nationalism," explained Father Joseph Vandrisse, the correspondent of French daily *Le Figaro* at the Holy See, who has traveled around with John Paul II. "He knows that when the rights of a people are trampled on, catastrophe is waiting at the end of the road. This is why he pleaded for Bosnia and even for Timor. He is convinced that each nation must preserve its identity."[9]

The Maronite position was endorsed by many non-Maronites, such as Greek Catholic bishop of Baalbeck Cyrille Bustros, who wrote the document summing up the Synod debates (*Relatio Ante Disceptationem*), and by other non-Lebanese Eastern prelates. Latin Patriarch of Jerusalem Michel Sabbah also had political concerns, directly related to the issue of human rights and the dignity of the Palestinians in the occupied territory. He worried about the heavy drain of the Christians from the Holy Land due to political turmoil and economic problems. He believed that Christian unity and dialogue with Islam were one way of coping with these grave challenges.[10] Banishing politics from their constant preoccupations was indeed an impossible mission for the Eastern churches, who led a day-to-day struggle for survival.

During the Synod, many among the Vatican curia, including Nuncio Pablo Puente, realized that the Lebanese bishops have the obligation of defending human rights in all the Arab world and, in that respect, the Maronite Church has an important role to play, a role acknowledged even by the Muslim communities in Lebanon.

One other rift was caused by what was viewed as Tauran's line. The "Foreign Minister" of the Pope was known for having a mitigated position regarding the Christians of Lebanon. He considered that the Holy See had already invested too much time and energy by focusing on them, betting on their role, and trying to save them to a point that it somehow neglected the rest of the Christians disseminated in the Arab world. The Roman Church was also responsible to those Arab Christians, and the political gambles of the Maronites in Lebanon could only have negative repercussions on Eastern Christianity. Tauran privileged full insertion of the Lebanese Christians in their Arab environment through the promotion of common cultural and social values in Christian-Muslim dialogue. Pablo Puente aligned on that approach, while he admitted that the Christians of Lebanon were the last bulwark of Eastern Christianity. If they failed to reassess their mission and their relationship with their Muslim countrymen, it could only impact negatively on the rest of the Arab countries, as Patriarch Sabbah observed.

Another keynote of the Synod was the concept of "unity in diversity." It meant complementarity and cooperation of the Eastern Churches within the Universal Church, with respect to each one's specificity. But where did diversity end and unity start?

The Jesuits insisted on the unity of the church. Their influence was evident in the pre-synodal texts. But Eastern Churches are very sensitive to their diversity, i.e., their specificity. "We wanted to avoid the reducing temptation," explains Maronite bishop of Mount-Lebanon, Joseph Bechara, who presided the committee entrusted with the task of drafting the Final Message. "The fact that there are various churches living in one Church is a historic reality. This variety enriches the Church as a universal body. But there was a tendency within the Synod to disincarnate the Church. So it was important to rectify the drift."[11]

"I knew what the Lebanese bishops advocated at the Vatican II Council," tells Jesuit father Jean Ducruet. "I kept in mind that the Maronite priests were holding on to the specificity of their Church. And behind the Lebanese Church, there is the problem of all Eastern Churches, of their personal and territorial jurisdiction and their relation with their émigrés."[12]

At Vatican II, the Lebanese bishops requested that one jurisdiction, the Patriarch's, extend to all the diaspora, through appointed patriarchal vicars. The purpose was to avoid the dilution of the ritual identity and the "latinization" of the Eastern Christians. That claim was rejected. It meant decentralization of the One Catholic and Apostolic Church and raised organizational hurdles.

Having a diaspora larger than its ground basis is the excruciating dilemma of Eastern Churches. And this reality spawns friction points with the Roman Church, which exerts its direct dominion on Eastern Catholic communities overseas.

It is relevant that the diaspora Church has not been formally associated to the Synod, although some of the bishops based overseas attended the assembly. "It is normal to focus on geographical Lebanon because this is where the future of local Churches is at stake," explains Father Borrmans.[13] Yet the disappointment of some Maronite prelates was evident. They needed to define a new evangelical mission and a new organization for their church abroad.

The Greek Orthodox Church had no such problem. It was largely decentralized, and its episcopates were autonomous. The principle of collegiality was its guiding line, in elections as well as in decision-making. These patterns increasingly attracted the Eastern Catholic clergy. The Greek Orthodox also opposed the concept set forth in Vatican I (1870) of the infallibility of the Pope. Metropolitan George Khodr did not miss the opportunity to convey his church's view on that divisive subject, but the

Greek Orthodox were pleased with the Vatican's insistence that Eastern Catholics should return to their oriental and patristic roots of faith. These roots were a shared heritage: Byzantine and Antioch have in common their spirituality, the patriarchal organization of their church, its monasticism, and the typical oriental pattern of married clerics. "Married priests have contributed to the preservation of Christianity for centuries in remote villages and areas," says Khalil Chalfoun, the only married priest who attended the Synod. His presentation raised tremendous interest among the curial bishops and monsignori. He revealed that the Greek Catholic Church has 42 percent of married priests, and the Maronite 33 percent. With the adversities of the present time, there was enough common ground to bolster ecumenism and to bring the Greek Orthodox and Catholic Churches closer together. Cardinal Sodano reminded the audience that a year earlier, the patriarchs of the Middle East had stated: "In the Orient, we will be Christians together or we will not be. Time has come to purify our memory from the sequels of the past, however painful, and to look together towards the future." The Synod would recommend the adoption of a common catechism.

THE OUTBURST OF THE FINAL MESSAGE

The Synod concluded on a vote session in which a list of forty-six recommendations were adopted, to be taken into account by the Holy Father when he would write his Apostolic Exhortation.

Once again, Cardinal Schotte demonstrated his authority. The making of the Final Message was an arduous task and members of the drafting committee were besieged with suggestions from various "lobbying" sides. Should Ta'if be explicitly mentioned? (It was not). How harsh a position could be adopted concerning the occupation/presence of Syrian forces in Lebanon? How severe a judgement should be issued concerning the government's social and economic policy? Clashes occurred with Daoud Sayegh and Boutros Labaki when the two men tried to attenuate the formal condemnation of Hariri's fiscal and customs policy, a policy estimated to widen the gap between rich and poor. No figures and no promises were to be included in the text, decreed the members of the committee.

The subjects of married priests, increased autonomy towards Rome, and the appeal of collegiality in decision-making were also a matter of debate within Maronite ranks. Dialogue and reconciliation between Christians and then between Christians and Muslims, "within the parameters of our dignity," were also the object of intense writing and rewriting.

The Final Message was firm and comprehensive. It underlined the importance of Lebanon's democracy and plural society.

Some said the Final Message lacked piety and spirituality. Some thought it lacked overture toward the Arab world, and others that it lacked vision. Thinkers like Father Michel Hayek, who participated in the draft, wanted a mission statement on Lebanon's role in the Mediterranean area and in the North-South dialogue of civilizations.

The controversy would have never ended if Schotte did not decide it was over. "This text is fine. Nothing needs to be added anymore," he announced. And to the members of the committee who still had observations: "I assume the responsibility of this text vis-à-vis His Holiness." The Final Message was read in evening session and forty-five minutes were given for introducing emendations. The participants voted by a show of hands. "The future depends on our common struggle with the Muslims in favor of democracy, social justice and religious freedom. Liberal Muslims rely on Christians. So if the Christians choose self-defense, the battle is lost," had warned Professor Antoine Messarra, who was the press attaché for the French translation.[14]

Instead of self-defense, the Lebanese Church chose counterattack. The Lebanese regime was pointed at. And the wrongs endured by the Lebanese people, the workers and the youth, the flaws that tainted postwar society, were enumerated one by one. The shortcomings of the Church, although slid over, figured too in that stringent diagnosis. The violation of Lebanon's independence and sovereignty was a cornerstone of the section dealing with national issues. Not only the occupation of Lebanon by foreign forces was condemned, but also the sidelining of Lebanon in the peace talks "as if we were under age and under tutelage." Journalists, intellectuals, politicians, and clergymen had indeed an array of subjects to reflect on for the months and years ahead.

No sooner was the Final Message rendered public than an ominous clamor arose from Beirut. The Muslim leaders were furious. The Message bore the stamp of the Maronite radical camp, they said, and the Pope certainly does not caution it. Three points channeled their fury: the call for the "departure of the Syrian forces from Lebanon," the reference to cultural pluralism, and the reference to consensual democracy.

Yet the three Muslim delegates to the Synod knew perfectly well that the issue of foreign troops (both Israelis and Syrians) was raised in Rome. And pluralism and consensual democracy were at the core of the debates. The *Instrumentum Laboris* had spoken of a "pluri-communal democracy." And during the various meetings at the Synod, Sammak had even suggested to Cardinal Lustiger the term "contractual democracy"(from the Arab word *mithaq*)—which could also be translated to "Covenant Democracy"—although he formally opposed pluralism "as an ultimate objective in itself."

Personally hurt by the virulent criticism of his economic policy, Prime Minister Hariri dispatched to Rome Mohammad Sammak, to convey his chagrin and the protest of both Mufti Kabbani and Sheikh Shamseddine. In his capacity as general secretary of the Islamic committee for dialogue, Sammak carried a verbal message from the Shiite, Sunni, and Druze authorities, in which they expressed their reserves concerning the Final Message, and deplored the fact that it emphasized the negative aspects rather than the achievements of postwar entente and reconstruction.

On February 7, 1996, Sammak met at the Vatican, with Cardinals Schotte and Arinze, as John Paul II was on tour in Latin America. He later said that both prelates were understanding and expressed their anxiety regarding the polemics that the Final Message ignited in Lebanon. He added that Schotte assured him that the Apostolic Exhortation (to be issued by His Holiness) would be the final synodal document with binding effects to the church and that it would be different.

During the next months, Sammak went to Rome three additional times. He briefed the Pope and Cardinals Schotte, Arinze, Silvestrini, and Etchegaray on the malaise of Muslim leaders in Lebanon and he revealed to them that he personally had faced a lot of pressure and had even braved intimidation attempts from fundamentalist sides outside Lebanon when the Muslim participation to the Synodal Assembly had been announced. In the name of the Lebanese Muslim authorities, he expressed the hope that the Holy Father would take into consideration their remarks when he issues his anticipated Apostolic Exhortation. This hope was also expressed by Prime Minister Hariri, who met with John Paul II a few months before the Pope's trip to Lebanon.

Meanwhile, the controversy smoldered in the country for about a year and Catholic bishops multiplied the conferences and talk shows to explain the Message of the Synod. "If those who criticize the Final Message had taken fifteen minutes to read the message, they would have reacted otherwise," commented one non-Catholic bishop who attended the Synod. "The Final Message did not deserve such a bad welcome," deplored Metropolitan George Khodr.

"It is hard to imagine what the critics thought the Synod would produce. Perhaps they were expecting the standard final declaration of any Arab Federation meeting: thank the local president, condemn Israeli atrocities and occupation, and express a hope that decisions taken at last year's meeting would be applied soon," scoffed John Donohue in a conference he gave a few years later.[15]

By and large, the Christian population and intellectuals felt disheartened by the reaction of their Muslim countrymen, and Muslims sensed that the Christians would never get more lenient on certain "national" issues. Seoud el Mawla and Mohammad Sammak contended that Muslims have made more concessions for dialogue than the Christians. Some intellectuals thought the Lebanese Christians failed to induce self-criticism and were not taking the initiative of a deep *aggiornamento* that would resonate all over the region. That was not the opinion of the Christians, who felt uncomfortable with the idea that the Catholic Church of Lebanon was the only party undergoing self-criticism under the scrutiny of all other Lebanese groups, as if it were the sole one to have committed errors.

The climate of concord that reined at the Synod vanished in Beirut. The rift was there, again, caused by words. And also by what many sensed was a different conception of sovereignty and independence. The national committee for dialogue tried to mend fences. Once again, Sisyphus had to roll back his rock to the top of the mountain. Apprehensive questions nagged on everybody's mind: why did public debates have to be different from private meetings? Why does mutual understanding vanish when it hits the ground floor or when political calculations interfere? Does interreligious dialogue have to be plagued by a double-language symptom?

If the Final Message sharpened the differences between Muslim and Christian perceptions, at least the Synod gave a boost to ecumenical dialogue. Maronite, Greek Catholic, and Greek Orthodox priests were coordinating their action and conducting in-depth dialogue.

One of the post-Synod steps was, in 1996, the meeting in Charfé[16] between Catholic and Orthodox Patriarchs, which resulted in the decision to adopt a common catechism.

The Christian Churches of the Orient also closed ranks by activating their cooperation on the regional level within the Middle East Council of Churches and the Assembly of Catholic Patriarchs and Bishops.

Yet, on the intellectual level, some Muslim thinkers drew the lessons of the Synod. Radwan es-Sayyed wrote that "Islam needed to engage into reforms and a renewal process," and citing historian John Meyendorff, he wrote that Islam (like Orthodoxy) was "confronted with two concepts it never experienced: the concept of renewal in the Catholic Church and of Reformation in the Protestant Church."[17] But he regretted that "the only real channels that allow Arab Muslims to get into real dialogue with their fellow Arab Christians are Western channels: the Vatican, the World Council of Churches and the Middle East Council of Churches." "Only Lebanon could have provided the proper environment for Arab Muslims and Christians to interact and build a common State and an adequate political system, but that did not happen," he grimly stated.[18]

Chapter 8

Cloaked in Coexistence

In the buzzing and intricate streets of Ashrafieh, the Christian heartland of Beirut, cars roamed with the same sticker on their windscreen. That sticker spread overnight in the Christian areas of the country. It represented the face of Jesus with the crown of thorns (under the features of actor Robert Powell in *Jesus of Nazareth,* by Franco Zeffirelli) and bore the mention "King of the Kings." This rallying sign was one of the many manifestations of religious zeal that sparked the Christian population in the post-Synod era. People of all ages went on pilgrimages to Marian sanctuaries and to the villages of Maronite saints (Saint Charbel in Annaya, and Saint Hardini-monastery of Kfifane). Churches were full on Sundays and on Christian celebrations.

The Synod and the promised visit of the Holy Father to Lebanon were a catalyst for a new dynamic within the Catholic Church. Religious observances increased, new churches were built, the youth got involved in the activities of their parishes and in "apostolic" movements. "The Holy Spirit is operating. There might not be a change on the political level, but spiritual renewal is visible among the youngsters," confirmed Bishop Rahi.[1] He said the Synod boosted the morale of the Christians. Religious vocations burgeoned. Lebanon numbered twenty times more sacerdotal ordinations than France (relative to the number of Christians in each country).

"In 1995, I have ordained nearly forty priests in one shot," revealed Maronite Patriarch Sfeir.[2]

Forty-five more postulants and novices were preparing for priesthood in the monastic Maronite Order. The same phenomenon was registered in the Greek Catholic diocese of Beirut, which hosted twenty-five seminarists. "We've never seen that through the history of our Church in Lebanon," exclaimed Greek Catholic bishop of Beirut Habib Bacha, who also heads the Post-Synodal Lay Committee.[3]

Six institutions taught theology in Lebanon. Three hundred students were registered in 1996–97, at the Pontifical Faculty of Theology (University of Kaslik), among whom fifty-two prepared for priesthood. The St. John of Damascus Greek Orthodox Institute in Balamand received seventy students, the Greek Catholic Institute of St. Paul in Harissa one hundred, and the Armenian Orthodox Institute in Bickfaya fifty theology students.[4]

On the Muslim side, religious devotion was no less tantamount to the Christians'. A couple of months after the appearance of the "King of the Kings" sticker, bumper stickers bearing the Muslim creed "There is no God but God and Mahomet is the Prophet of God" showed in Muslim neighborhoods. If the beards and the *hijab* (veil), so relished in the eighties, receded, religious practice was more vibrant than ever. Mosques were crowded on Fridays to a point where people prayed on the sidewalk. Sheikhs and ulemas noticed that their flocks complied with Ramadan fasting, paid the *zakat,* and in 1997, 12,000 Lebanese made the pilgrimage to the holy city of Mecca. "There would have been 30,000 if the Saudi regulations allowed it," said one of the ulemas.[5]

Significantly, the Shiite community witnessed an over-ritualization of religious life, largely due to the competition between the Islamic Shi'a Supreme Council headed by Sheikh Shamseddine and the Hezbollah leadership on one side, and to the Sunni-Shiite latent rivalry on the other side. A new "clerical" class emerged from the "*hawzat*" established by Hezbollah. A new religious calendar was set, incorporating the birth of the Prophet, the birth and death of the twelve imams (of duodecimal Shi'ism), the birth of Fatima al-Zahra', Mohammad's daughter, and other events.

With the financial backing of Saudi Arabia and Iran to both Sunni and Shiite communities, new mosques were built and young gathered at *madrasa* and *hawzat* (schools) to learn the *shari'a*. The Hezbollah in the Shiite community and the "Jama'a Islamiya" in the Sunni community competed in social, medical, and educational projects, all coupled with intensive preaching.

On the Christian side, Western movements poured into Lebanon including World Vision, the Beatitudes, and especially the Catholic lay organization of the Opus Dei, to which John Paul II felt particularly close. With 77,000 members around the world, the Opus Dei is conservative in its theology and highly influential. It is directly linked to the Pope, who erected it into a "Personal Prelature" in 1982. The Opus Dei is said to have been John Paul II's right arm in his Catholic *reconquista* of the world, known as the "new evangelization."

It was at the Synod that the Opus Dei officially opened up to the Lebanese Church and signaled its interest in Lebanon. An exploration tour organized a few months earlier had confirmed to the prelate of the Opus

Dei, Archbishop Javier Echevarria, that there was room for social and cultural activities to help improve the situation of the Lebanese middle class and that the Christian communities and especially the Lebanese youth were a fertile ground for the apostolic action of the organization.

Archbishop Echevarria reveals that the founder of the Opus Dei, Josemaria Escriva (who was beatified by John Paul II), wanted to start apostolic work in Lebanon back in the sixties. He insists that the Opus Dei's objective is to back the local church, "who is anxious to communicate hope to its people, while shouldering responsibilities no one else can assume." Using the interrogative form, Echevarria affirms: "What would Lebanon be without the input of religious orders? Would it only exist?" Most of all, the prelate asserts that "the eventual stable settling of Opus Dei in Lebanon could only favor the return of the Lebanese of the diaspora to their homeland, each one bringing back his/her professional knowledge. There are indeed a lot of Lebanese who have known the Opus Dei in Canada, Australia, Mexico, Brazil, and Europe and some of them are members of the organization." Cardinal Echevarria adds that the Opus Dei will carry its mission "in complete harmony with local hierarchies."[6]

A few months later, the Opus Dei opened branches in Beirut with male and female volunteers from different countries, among them young Latin American professionals of Lebanese descent. The organization penetrated academic and business circles and carried out social work among the displaced. But it also raised questions related to its secrecy and its suspected power and proselytism.

This religious activism in both Christian and Muslim societies was confusing. The war and its wretchedness undoubtedly made religion the ultimate popular refuge. But was this a revival of the faith or communal *assabiya* (esprit de corps)? The boundary between the two was slender. Christian and Muslim religious celebrations, namely Christmas, Easter, Ramadan, Adha, and Achoura (among others), became officially non–working days and holidays. But did the religiously bustling almanac intend to create a common national heritage or did it only echo the self-assertiveness of each community's identity in postwar Lebanon?

Many religious leaders on both sides doubted that the external signs of religiosity had anything to do with piety. They were aware that the young of various communities channeled their political deceptions through religion. The failure of political parties and leaders, the absence of national ideals to hold on to, social frustration, and economic hardship have drawn the Lebanese to identify with their community. The return to religion was also a return to confessional identity. Sunni Sheikh Mohammed Kanaan, who preaches in the Mousseytbé mosque of Beirut, gives the example of the Muslims in Bosnia-Herzegovina who, under Tito, had totally forgotten

Islam, but were drawn back to it when they started being massacred for their religious affiliation. "They even became extremists," he adds.[7]

A number of Christian and Muslim religious leaders agree that fanaticism is not totally alien to religious revival in postwar Lebanon. "A certain Christian fundamentalism has emerged lately in an attempt to counter Islamic fundamentalism," says bishop Habib Bacha. "This is due to the fact that Christians fear for their future."[8] One might be tempted to think that a return to religion would drive the young generations toward each other. Unfortunately, that was not the case.

When the war was over and the checkpoints and hurdles separating Christian and Muslim ghettos were removed, Lebanese of different backgrounds rushed to discover their country and their fellow citizens of "the opposite camp." There were stunning images of scarfed women gaping at short-dressed women in Ashrafieh and Christian youth discovering for the first time "West Beirut" and its famous shopping Hamra Street, known before the war as the "Lebanese Champs-Elysées." Travel agencies organized excursion tours throughout Lebanon for the new wave of Lebanese tourists. Soon however, this opening drive was hindered by political mismanagement of Christian uneasiness with postwar Lebanon and by the authoritative tendencies of the regime.

The gap among the young generations widened. Few had struck up lasting friendships on the other side of the invisible fence. "Lebanon's problem does not lie in religion, but in the absence of religion. If we want to suppress confessionalism, we have to deepen real Christian and Muslim values," Sayyed Fadlallah used to say. He was right.

At the concluding press conference of the Synod, Bishop Joseph Beshara had recognized there was "a resurgence of a strong sectarian spirit just like during the war," but, he added, "there is also a common will to transcend that mentality." "We can either achieve that by eliminating any role played by the communities, or together, Christians and Muslims, we can save the Lebanese specificity by finding the political formula that preserves each group and prevents any hegemonic tendency." The Synod spoke of "decloistering the communities." How could that be implemented?

Post-Synod committees and "brainstorm" groups pondered how to translate the Synod's call for change and religious overture on the social level as well as in families, parishes, civil associations, and at the national level. Under the impulse of Bishop Beshara, a reformist movement within the church established in the sixties by Maronite clerics ("a Church for our World") was revived and included young lay people.

These attempts raced with a creeping confessionalization of public life. The technological aspects of modernity went hand in hand with archaic sectarian structures and mentality. Each Lebanese community now had its own media network of radio stations, TV channels (mainly *Télé-Lumière* run by the Catholic Church and *Al-Manar* run by Hezbollah), publishing houses, and printed magazines. Each also supervised a network of charitable organizations, medical centers and hospitals, cultural clubs, and even sports teams. These were the leverages that enabled each community to assert its political claim. Newspapers reflected the political incline of their confessional mainstream, even if they aspired for "objective" and non-sectarian news coverage. The confessional identity of the media ownership was frequently taken into consideration by readers and subscribers and this upset a number of editors in chief and journalists like Talal Selman (*As-Safir*), who aspired to break the sectarian mold in which society and politics had framed him and his colleagues. He was regularly confronted and jolted by reality, while reminded of his confessional "obligations." Yet the most sensitive issue was that of the universities.

CULTURAL GHETTOS

Each community ran its own schools and universities. Cultural polarization increased in the postwar era, and the government did nothing to stop it. It even granted, through ministerial decrees, the right for the consultative bodies of the communities to establish their university. The academic landscape reflected the confessional mosaic of the country. New institutions mushroomed, trying to compete, on the educational level, with the more than a century-old and culturally well-grounded American University of Beirut (AUB) and St. Joseph University. The Islamic Shi'a Supreme Council obtained the right to found its Islamic University, just as the Sunni community had its well-established institution of al-Makassed; the Greek Orthodox administered the Balamand University, Greek Catholic and Maronites, the Universities of Kaslik and Louayzé, the Law School of *La Sagesse,* and the Armenian managed *Haigazian* and *Homenetmen* institutions, to cite only a few. Cultural diversity was certainly a richness and an asset for Lebanon in a mono-cultural environment. But the dark side of the moon was scary. Teenagers and young of the various communities barely related to each other. They lived in isolated cultural islands. The fracture ran through linguistic as well as sectarian lines. The French-speaking students of St. Joseph University viewed their campus as a "cocoon," a serenity haven, the last "sanctuary" of a certain Levantine bourgeoisie and Westernized way of thinking. Before the Synod, students avoided political subjects. They had their baptism of fire during the civil war, when they militated in various Christian parties, and they ultimately went through the horrendous experience of being torn between rival groups within their own community.

The situation was pretty much the same at AUB, with a more cosmopolitan student population, and in all other universities. Just like their Christian counterparts, Muslim students had also been driven to oppose each other within their own sectarian camp, as their various militias struggled for internal power. The realities of war had hacked away at the youths' illusions. But that did not bring them closer to each other.

The postwar generation, who grew up in confessional ghettos, ignored almost everything about "the other." Not only were they reluctant to interact but also skeptical about the efficiency of dialogue such as practiced by the older generation. If Lebanon managed intercommunal living so well, how come it went through such an ugly and destructive war, they wondered. The young preferred to smooth and polite exchanges the sheer bluntness that conveyed their anxieties and their mutual ignorance of other's religion, traditions, and hopes. Sincerity rather than amenity was what they were looking for.

People like bishop Gregoire Haddad suggested that Islam and Christianity be taught at schools and universities to foster mutual knowledge and understanding. Some officials even considered incorporating Islam in schools programs, even in Catholic schools that hosted Muslim students. But Cardinal Pio Laghi, head of the Congregation for Catholic Education at the Vatican, expressed the categorical opposition of the Church "to any sort of State control over the Catholic educational institutions, or to any attempt to impose school programs on us." "There is a difference," he said, "between teaching religion and teaching joint values such as solidarity, human rights, peace, fraternity, non-violence, non-use of drugs. . . . We will never tolerate that the teaching of a religion that is not our religion be imposed in our schools. We don't want to impose our religion on others, and so we want to be free in the practice of our religion. In case there is a Muslim majority in Lebanon and the government's options are affected by this, there is a real danger that the rule of majority be applied, and not only this, but also the religion of the majority. If Lebanon wants to preserve its pluralism, it should promote respect of the other."[9] Likewise, Islamic leaders did not favor the teaching of Christian religion in their schools and universities. One of the propositions voted during the Synod recommended the adoption of a book dealing with shared religious culture to be taught in high school.

The breach between the young Lebanese of various communities was evident during sports games. Basketball and football matches between the Christian team La Sagesse *(Hekmet)* and the Sunni-dominated *Ansar*, between the same *Ansar* and the Shiite *Nejmeh*, often ended up in sectarian clashes and melee and led to the intervention of the police and security forces and to the suspension of the tournament. More worrying were the radical slogans shouted by the players and their supporters during these fights. They expressed political frustration and whetted sectarianism. Shiite spectators went as far as to side with Iran's soccer team playing against Lebanon's, merely because most of the Lebanese players belonged to the Sunni community. The recurrent confrontations and showdown at sports events took such alarming proportions that the President of the Republic, the Prime Minister and the Minister of Interior (who is in charge of the police and the internal security forces) intervened directly to mend fences, and finally canceled the 1997 basketball championship of Lebanon.

Many Lebanese did not hide their anxiety: Lebanon was heading straight toward another bloodshed in one or two generations if the seeds of tolerance and respect of the others were not planted. Hence the vital importance of education. Obviously the sufferings endured in wartime were not enough to preclude future eruption of violence; soon they'd even be forgotten, all the more now that an amnesty law had been adopted in Parliament in a dramatic attempt to substitute national amnesia for accountability and penance.

One institution could live up to the mission of bringing young Lebanese together and helping them forge a common identity and shared goals: it is the Lebanese University (LU), the only public university in the country, also named "the national University." During the war, its various branches were geographically, confessionally, and ideologically divided between "East" and "West" and were the hotbed of political militancy. Once the war was over, the "reunification" of the LU became one of the fundamental priorities of the government, assigned to the Ministry of Higher Education. This "centralization" of the "national university" triggered a lot of controversy and the objection of those who feared political and cultural planning imposed by the state. With 43 sections, 60,000 students and 1,620 professors, the Lebanese University is a giant with clay feet. Financial revenues and restructuring are its two main problems, let alone the political divisions inherited from the war. Prime Minister Hariri took a major decision when his government allocated a land for the building of students' halls of residence in Beirut's suburbs on the LU campus, to unite students of all regions under one roof, literally speaking.

The case of the LU reflects the dramatic situation of public education in Lebanon. While public university and schools are supposed to provide a national mold for younger generations and be at the same time a cultural and social melting pot, these objectives have so far been hampered by the inability of the State to develop a strong public sector able to compete with private schools and universities. On the other hand, the private education sector has been more keen on defending the principle of freedom of education consecrated by the Constitution and the concept of cultural pluralism than on cooperating with the government to help create a decent public education system.

And yet, the champions and persons in charge of private schools in Lebanon, of which the Catholic schools constitute the bulk, claimed more financial support from the State, advocating a French-style state sponsorship of professors' remunerations. "It looks like the State wants to constrict us. It imposes on us regular increase of teachers' salaries but forbids us from augmenting schools' tuition. We have large expenses and many families cannot afford private schools anymore," complains Father Camille Zeidan, general secretary of Catholic Education in Lebanon. "Christians have harder time than Muslims because we have more schools. Besides, the newly founded Muslim schools are generously sponsored by Libya, Iran, Saudi Arabia. The Saudi Kingdom recently granted $96.6 million to a Sunni institution in Beirut."[10]

Nevertheless, Cardinal Laghi did not mince his words when he criticized, during the Synod, those in charge of Catholic schools in Lebanon. He summoned them not to turn "these atheneums into Universities for rich people" and enjoined them "to put the Catholic school at the service of all Lebanese, without religious, social or cultural discrimination." According to the statistics Cardinal Laghi disclosed at the Synod, there were 325 Catholic schools in Lebanon, with 250,000 students (accounting for 34 percent of students in Lebanon-among whom 22 percent were Muslims) and 12,800 professors.

One of the main post-Synod steps is the cooperation initiated between the State and various professors of the private sector to come out together with the reform of education, a stated objective of the Ta'if accords. The building blocks of that reform were the writing of the long-awaited book of civic education, to be taught in all public and private schools, and the homogenization of Lebanon's history teaching. This undertaking was meant to create allegiance to the nation-state rather than to the community.

REWRITING HISTORY

Rewriting a consensus-oriented history as a tool of conflict resolution in postwar eras is one of the most difficult tasks in deeply divided societies. The former Yugoslavia, South Africa, and culturally pluralistic countries such as Belgium and Canada are among the many countries faced with that challenge.

Civic education is a stepping-stone to laying the foundation of a "culture of peace." The book was achieved and entered school programs in 1997. But the history book was like "walking in a minefield," said Professor Mounir Abou-Assly, director of the education center at the Ministry of National Education.[11] The intellectuals and the political class were split: many considered that a unified history book was a heresy and an impossible mission, unless it adopted the dulling "wooden language."

That is why the government-appointed committees entrusted with the layout of a new history blueprint worked behind closed doors, away from the controversy that subject stirred. One of the main Gordian knots they had to untie was: where to start Lebanon's modern history? Would it be on September 1, 1920, with the creation of Greater Lebanon, which Muslims opposed at first? Would it start in 1943 with the joint Christian-Muslim struggle against French mandate, for Independence?[12]

For decades, the historical perception of the Lebanese reflected confessional and cultural biases. More than fifteen books of Lebanese history were listed in the postwar era; communal, regional, and even tribal outlook abounded.[13] "Each community has built up its own collective memory, with its heroes, its anthem and its flag," wrote the *As-Safir* newspaper. "And more alarming is the tone used in these books: they are meant to set people against 'the other.'"[14]

History has served as the ideological platform for the architects of Arab nationalism, Pan-Syrian nationalism, and Lebanese nationalism. And the ideological writing of Lebanon's history remains a major hurdle to the knowledge of others' true aspirations and viewpoint. Lebanese students had a different perspective of their country's history. For some, Lebanon's history started six thousand years ago, in Phoenician times; for others, it really started with the Arab invasion and Muslim conquest.

Some viewed the seventeenth century Emir of Mount-Lebanon Fakhreddine II as the founder of Lebanese nationalism based on a Christian-Druze alliance, and considered him as the most eminent personality of Lebanon's political history. Others dismissed that assertion. Many among the Christian historians also looked at nineteenth century "Grand Emir" Bechir II as a great figure, but his critics called him a tyrant and blamed him for nurturing a sectarian tension that ultimately led to the 1860 massacres between Christians and Druzes. Walid Joumblatt was particularly eager to take a historical revenge against the man who killed his great-grandfather Bechir Joumblatt. So in 1984, he took over the palace of Beiteddine built by Bechir II.[15] The crusades were also perceived according to each community's historical experience with them. Another important milestone was the *amiyat Antelias*, the peasants' uprising against their feudal leaders in Mount-Lebanon: some emphasized the joint Christian-Druze struggle for freedom, while others considered it as the burgeoning of a Maronite democratic thinking as opposed to the conservative and feudal character of the Druze community.

One of the major preoccupations of Lebanese historians has always been to underline the specificity of Lebanon as opposed to its direct environment, i.e., Syria. Geography was the cornerstone of Jesuit father Henri Lammens's book on "Greater Syria," while the "Lebanist" orientation, represented by writers like Jawad Boulos, Bishop Youssef Debs, and Youssef Sawda, advocated the existence of a cultural and national "Lebanese" identity despite geographical promiscuity with Syria. The Mount-Lebanon stood as the bedrock of Lebanese national consciousness and the symbol of resistance to invaders.

Somehow, the writing of history mirrors the balance of power and the dominant position of one party. Since the time of sixteenth-century Patriarch Youssef Doueihy, Maronites have left their fingerprints on the building of the country's historical memory. Historian and writer Ahmad Beydoun shows in detail how Lebanon's history has been assimilated with Mount-Lebanon's.[16]

This is why other communities like the Shi'a, who felt they've been left on the margin of Lebanon's history as well as of political decision-making, wanted to propel Jabal 'Amel into the historical making of Lebanese identity. They contested the "homogenization" of the country's history, that culminated in one community (e.g., the Maronite) and espoused its distinctive traits. Shiite historian Ali al-Zein explained his researches in these terms: "I tried to clarify our political past and to indicate our place (we, Amelites and Metoualis[17]) among the Lebanese people."[18]

Beset by their distant as well as their more recent past, the Lebanese youth oscillated between two different attitudes: they were either detached from reality and sought oblivion in nightlife and social distractions while dreaming of leaving the country once the diploma was obtained, or they were captives of outdated slogans and of a political discourse that had not evolved since the end of the war. Young Christians were either Aounist or pro-Lebanese Forces, Shi'a Muslims were either pro-Amal or pro-Hezbollah, and Sunnis, less engaged in political parties, were either pro-Hariri or opposed to him, albeit not openly because he was perceived as having restored Sunni preeminence in politics.

There was also a gap between the youth, of all communities as a whole, and the state. The postwar generation ignored everything about political participation, the electoral process, and their voting rights, as a survey conducted by *As-Safir* showed in 1992.[19] The "culture of democracy" did not even exist at the university level, where dialogue was fraught with sectarian behavior and discretionary practices.[20] Interestingly enough, young Lebanese were fully aware of their deficiencies, they were able to assess their own weaknesses, their own needs, and to point out to the shortcomings of the state. When he visited Beirut, Cardinal Lustiger met with the university students of St. Joseph, Kaslik, and Balamand, away from the flashbulbs of the media. Forthright exchanges allowed him to grasp the magnitude of the young's disarray, their doubts about their future and the future of their country, of its independence and sovereignty, their concern about freedom, equality, political participation, their feeling of powerlessness to change the gloomy reality, their distrust toward what they considered was a profit-oriented and narrow-minded sectarian establishment, the obstacles that inhibited their relation with traditional authorities: state, religious hierarchies, family. The Archbishop of Paris was bowled over: "Lebanese young have lost hope but they did not reach the point of resignation," he cried out in a press conference before he left. "If they are not part of the rebuilding of their country, they will choose emigration, and this is a mortal threat to Lebanon." That warning applied to Christians and Muslims alike.

SEEKING A COMMON CAUSE

One of the major assets of Lebanon—actually, it is its first and foremost asset—is the dynamism of its civil society and the ingenuity of its people. The post-Synod years witnessed interesting initiatives that made up for the state's lapse from its duties.

An "Observatory of Democracy" was established to gauge Lebanon's democratic recovery, educate people on the role of the institutions in parliamentary regimes, raise awareness on the importance of civil society, of transparency, and of accountability in government, explain what civil rights and political rights are, and set the standards of free and representative elections. Professor Antoine Messarra, who supervised the project, led a wide campaign of information, set a list of 150 "indicators" of democracy, organized seminars on "democracy at the University," conducted studies with his academic colleagues from the Lebanese University on the "New Guard Generation." His goal, he explained, was to foster the "culture of democracy, without which no civil peace can last and no state of law can emerge." He was convinced that "the undermining of the democratic process in Lebanon would produce another war through frustration, fear, hegemony, a winner-loser situation, and an agitated relationship with the Arab environment."[21]

Another group of young professionals—many of whom had graduated from American Universities and were U.S.I.A.'s "international visitors"—established an association to monitor elections and a think tank to sustain their action (the Lebanese Center for Political Studies). Their American-style lobbying and grass-roots campaigning attracted young people from various communities and regions. As they gained support from deputies, they ultimately showed their efficiency when they launched a media campaign and even engaged in a showdown with the Beirut police, to force a reluctant government to organize municipal elections (those had not been held for thirty-five years). The elections finally took place in spring 1998.

Young Lebanese were very much frustrated by their divisions; they aspired for unity. They were looking for a unifying discourse and shared goals that neither the education system nor the postwar regime—mired as it was in sectarian competition at the highest level, in corruption, and in undemocratic practices—were able to provide them with.

On various occasions, university students surprised the whole political spectrum when they successfully mobilized in defense of fundamental principles such as freedom of expression and the country's sovereignty. When the government banned a programmed TV interview with exiled General Aoun in December 1997, hundreds of Christian students gathered in front of the TV station to protest. Pictures of youngsters beaten and arrested by policemen and security forces made the headline news, and prompted a national student strike in major Lebanese universities. Christian and Muslim students of all political affiliations, including anti-Aounist, organized a sit-in in front of the Parliament building to defend the sacrosanct principles of freedom of expression, of association, and of gathering. They ultimately registered a frank success and the interview was aired two weeks later.

The Israeli occupation of Southern Lebanon was also a determinant catalyst of national unity. Not only Hezbollah's resistance in the South and its heroic military deeds were capturing the imagination of all Lebanese, but when the Israeli army launched its April 1996 "Operation Grapes of Wrath" (which ended with the terrifying Cana massacres), Lebanese of all sides spontaneously came together and showed solidarity with the people of the South. Young Christians who lived in Byblos and had never developed relations with their Muslim countrymen risked their lives braving the Israeli blockade and shelling of the coast, to provide food and medical support to the Southerners. Three years later (February 1999), when Israeli troops barricaded the village of Arnoun in an attempt to expand the "occupation zone," students of St. Joseph University as well as of AUB and other places descended on Arnoun and challenged Israeli troops. The youngsters dismantled the barricades and roadblocks erected by the Israeli soldiers in Arnoun and "liberated" the village, in a dazzling move that was lauded by local politicians—who were again outstripped by the young—and left American diplomats and Israeli officials puzzled.

The Lebanese youth had shown once more its ability and willingness to rally around a national cause. Syria's tight hold on Lebanon and the presence of roughly one million Syrian workers in a country bogged in unemployment were also motives of popular resentment often echoed by the press. If Christian youth was more overt in its opposition to Syrian military forces in Lebanon (which brought more arrests in its ranks), young Shiites vented their anger on occasions such as a football game between Lebanon's team and Syria's.[22]

RELIGIOUS PREACHING POLITICS

Yet, whatever tenets they advocated, whatever their age, Lebanese of all communities remained trapped in the web of their sectarian affiliation. With the collapse of political leadership on the Christian side and the emergence of fundamentalist leaders on the Muslim side—that only the power of capitalism represented by Rafik Hariri could counterbalance—religious and spiritual authorities have gained more political leverage. To paraphrase Ahmad Beydoun, "communities have become political bodies." This situation where the religious shepherd of a minority group turns into the spokesperson of his community and becomes vested with temporal powers is typical of the Middle East. All Eastern groups have, at some point of their history, endured persecution, feared for their future, and strove to preserve their identity. They have turned to their Patriarch or their Sheikh, who embodied the collective memory and the continuity of his people. As their political role was further declining, the Copts in Egypt were going through the same process, leaving it to their Patriarch and clerics.

The role of the Lebanese religious authorities in the postwar years has been formally recognized:

- on the media level, the preachings of Friday (for Muslim imams) and the sermons of Sunday (for Christian bishops and patriarchs) absorb a substantial spot in broadcast news as well as in newspapers, with follow-ups and additional "clarifications" from the religious authorities themselves when needed;
- on the substance level, religious authorities have a "censorship right" in the elaboration of audiovisual and TV programs, and also in the official approval of books and printed materials (entry and release) by the General Security (Sûreté Générale) office at the Ministry of Interior;
- on the constitutional level, the document of national accord (Ta'if) granted religious authorities the right to appeal before the Constitutional Court (the highest jurisdiction) regarding any law or regulation that they perceive as infringing upon the personal status of their communities, freedom of religion and conscience, and freedom of education and religious teaching.

Furthermore, the heads of the communities have their say whenever the future of the country is at stake and whenever crucial decisions have to be taken by the government that involve the nation's destiny or the consensual foundations of the political system.

The political leadership of religious authorities was eloquently illustrated—and consecrated—by former Prime Minister Hariri when, in March 1998, he initiated consultations with religious leaders of all Muslim and Christian communities regarding the economic and financial policy of his Cabinet. In an unprecedented move (that stirred ironic comments in the press), he personally visited each and every spiritual leader, seeking advice and remarks on his budget platform!

His most striking visit was his eight-hour-long "marathon day" in Bkerké, where he met in close session with the Maronite Patriarch and the assembly of Maronite bishops. Superiors of Religious Orders attended the meeting, at the end of which the Maronite Church submitted a lengthy memorandum touching on political, economic, judicial, and social issues and criticizing the government's overall policy (see Chapter 9).[23]

Many Lebanese contested the fact that their religious leaders were getting increasingly involved in politics and less so in religion. No sermon escaped from political allusions when it was not an outright political speech. The more Lebanese people saw and heard the men in robes, the less they detected the echoes of a living spiritual thinking and religious meditation that would give a sense to what they had gone through.

Chapter 9

The Swings of the Pendulum

In the immediate aftermath of the civil war, as Lebanon's Second Republic was formally established on the basis of the 1989 Ta'if agreement, a brand-new concept poked through the political lexicon: *al Ihbat al Masihi,* Christian disenchantment. This disenchantment stemmed from the broad feeling of the Christian population that, despite the no-winner-no-loser formula adopted in Ta'if, in terms of a confessionalist group logic, there was no doubt about who the winners and losers are.

The constitutional changes introduced in Ta'if, Saudi Arabia, in October 1989, by the Lebanese deputies, were meant to balance what the Muslims considered as the exceeding powers of the Christian Maronites in Lebanon's constitution and political system.

In an attempt to boost his weak popularity, President Hrawi occasionally called for constitutional changes that would return some prerogatives to the Maronite President of the Republic. By doing so, he suggested that the problem lay with the formal distribution of power. Among the preeminent positions still held by Maronites in the Ta'if Republic were the high command of the Lebanese Armed Forces and the post of governor of the Central Bank.

But Christian uneasiness with postwar Lebanon resulted from the fact that, whatever their formal representation, the leadership of the country was in the hands of Muslim politicians. The first evidence of that came with the 1992 legislative elections. These were fraught with irregularities and tailored to thwart any successful participation of the opposition, especially the Christian opposition groups (Aounists, Lebanese Forces, Chamounists of the National Liberal Party). Christians estimated that these elections represented a continuation of the war by nonmilitary means and they massively boycotted the ballot, which took place with a sparse 13 percent of total Lebanese electors.

Furthermore, a general amnesty for all but a few of the crimes and atrocities of the civil war has been denied for those who refused to cooperate with the regime. Samir Geagea, leader of the Lebanese Forces, who blatantly refused to be part of the first postwar government (although he was represented in it), has been jailed and on trial since 1994, for various postwar and wartime murders, and his party dismantled and banned.[1]

THE MARONITE PATRIARCH AS A SUBSTITUTE LEADER

Maronite *Ihbat* increased as a generation of Maronite leaders—former President Amine Gemayel, Michel Aoun, and Samir Geagea—has been defeated or ousted, either in the last stages of the war or thereafter. Since Maronite identity is primarily a religious identity, in which the Patriarch is the central and unifying figure, the only Maronite leader left was thus the Patriarch himself.

A man of modest demeanor, Nasrallah Boutros Sfeir was courageous and he combined the piety of the Maronite monk with the crafty obstinacy of the Kesrouan highlander. These highly appraised virtues would be invaluable resources that would allow the Patriarch to uphold, time and again, the principles of freedom, independence, and democracy and to fend off various attempts to bring him to adopt more lenient stands or even to pay a visit to Damascus.

Sfeir had the acute consciousness of the responsibility that rested on his shoulder at that decisive moment of Maronite history. His was a dramatic time, as he watched the military disasters and political twilight that befell his community. He has been the powerless and forlorn witness of Maronites turning against each other in a senseless wrestle, while being stripped from their political sway in Ta'if and shunted toward the margins. He has seen their leaders divided, exiled, killed, arrested, most often as a result of their own short-sightedness and suicidal behavior. And his confusion was no less acute than that of his flock. But he was invigorated by the Synod for Lebanon initiative of John Paul II and gathered his strength.

Like his predecessors in periods of crisis, he stood as the point of reference of his community. Among all public figures, he was the only one indeed to ask overtly for "the withdrawal of all occupation forces from Lebanon," meaning by that Israeli as well as Syrian troops. He also regularly denounced human rights abuses by security forces, the arrest of young supporters of opposition groups, social injustice, unequal distribution of economic resources, the rise of sectarianism in public life, corruption of the political class, and all flagrant distortions to democracy and public freedoms, the violation of Lebanon's sovereignty and of the "integrity of our national decision." He could do so because Bkerké was, in the collective cognition of the Lebanese, the "conscience of Lebanon," the pulpit that was bestowed with "the glory of Lebanon," as is written on the fronton of the patriarchal seat and on the armorial bearings of the Maronite Church. ("Gloria Libani Data Est" is the motto of the Maronite Church of Antioch.)

Not only the Maronite Patriarch was listened to, but he even set the tone of politics in the postwar era. In the vast hall of his patriarchal residence, Sfeir received people of all social and political backgrounds and listened to their claims. Many came from remote villages in the North, the Biqaa, or the South, looking for support and asking for his mediation with official authorities to help solve a problem. For many Christians, he was their only resort. To gain credibility, Christian politicians sought his advice or assent, Muslim politicians came to see him as their main interlocutor and as the spokesperson of the Christian mainstream.

Patriarch Sfeir had accepted Ta'if to stop the fighting. But he considered that the "national entente" accord has been distorted. He had a list of grievances he relentlessly aired and conveyed to the regime.

They included:

- a fair implementation of the Ta'if accords, which provided for the redeployment of Syrian troops in the Biqaa Valley;
- the formation of a genuine "national entente" government, as laid down in the Ta'if agreement;
- the return of the displaced in their villages;
- a fair and balanced electoral law that guarantees real representability for the Christians and adopts one standard electoral district for all on equal level (either at the *caza* level or the *mohafazat* level);[2]
- the disarmament of all Lebanese militias, as stated by the Ta'if accords, and not only of Christian militias (this implied that the Hezbollah should be disarmed, but that claim became politically

moot when the State recognized Hezbollah as a national resistance group against Israeli occupation);
- the settling of Geagea's case, which Sfeir considered as the *summum* of unfair treatment since many of the former warlords not only benefitted from the amnesty law, but some (such as Elie Hobeika and Walid Joumblatt, who became "permanent" government ministers of the new republic under Hrawi's mandate, and Nabih Berri, who became Speaker of Parliament) also held eminent positions;
- the rescinding of the decree of naturalization that granted arbitrarily and overnight the Lebanese citizenship to approximately 200,000 foreign workers and emigrants (nobody knows exactly how many, not even the Lebanese authorities), about 90 percent of whom were Muslims, thus seriously jeopardizing Lebanon's fragile internal balance;[3]
- the opposition to any resettling of the 367,610 Palestinian refugees in Lebanon,[4] which would irremediably affect Lebanon's demographic composition and its consensual system;
- the release of Lebanese detainees in Syrian prisons; and
- the restoration of some of the President's prerogatives, in order to reestablish a constitutional balance of powers.

Those grievances—privately shared by a fair number of Muslim leaders—were echoed by the bishops in their parishes, especially bishop Bechara Rahi of Byblos. Sfeir's concerns were also relayed by the Greek Orthodox bishop of Beirut Elias Audeh, especially since Patriarch Hazim, who was based in Damascus and was more circumspect in his public comments, seemed to tacitly agree on his Maronite counterpart's stands.

The church thus became the political mentor of the Christians. This was illustrated by the weekly press release of the Council of Maronite Bishops in Bkerké, dealing with current national issues. With the encouragement of Patriarch Sfeir, the Christians reacted differently during the 1996 legislative elections, registering a higher rate of participation. The Assembly of Catholic Patriarchs and Bishops of Lebanon also issued a communiqué at the eve of the 1998 municipal elections, the first ever held in Lebanon since 1962, calling for participation "because it is a fundamental right and a duty of the citizen," and asking the State to ensure that those elections will be held in a climate of freedom and democracy. The communiqué summoned the voters to choose candidates known for their competence and their commitment to public interest.[5]

Soon, the Maronite patriarch became a central piece of the Lebanese chessboard. In such a confessional mosaic like Lebanon, there could be no monolithic Muslim majority and Christian minority. Lebanon is a country of eighteen minority groups, based on a consociational plural system. No matter how big the largest one of its communities (yesterday the Maronites, today the Shiites, reached a peak of nearly 30 percent of the overall population), it is not able to impose its will on the others. Within the Muslim "camp," Sunni, Shi'a, and Druzes have divergent and often competing political agendas and interests, and so do the Christians on the other side. Striking alliances that cross sectarian lines is the name of the game and determines the political weight of each group.

In postwar Lebanon, Sunnis and Shiites vied for political as well as economic power. To tip the balance in their favor, within Parliament or on the political arena, both sides needed to woo the Christians, who were still essential players. Shiite fundamentalists of Hezbollah, Sunni Premier Rafik Hariri, and Druze leader Walid Joumblatt will successively open up to the Maronites. Those had still to learn how to take advantage of their being an indispensable link and "soothing agent" among rivaling groups.

DECEIVED BY TA'IF

Sectarian tactics set aside, many Muslim opposition leaders and politicians realized that inequality of treatment and undemocratic practices, like a spreading disease, reached all categories and could not be confined to one segment of the population. The main approach of Lebanon's ruling class was to produce what Volker Perthes called an "authoritarian integration."[6] It was meant to force the acceptance of the new order, beyond the simple restoration of state functions. So the Hrawi regime undertook a series of actions intended to intimidate potential and real political opposition to the regime itself, to the current distribution of power as a whole, and to Syria's involvement in Lebanon.

Public freedoms came under considerable strains: public demonstrations were banned in 1996[7] and numerous people suspected of connection to opposition groups, mainly pro-Aounist Christians and Islamist militants, were arrested. Furthermore, the Hariri government interfered in labor union affairs to undermine the independence of the powerful Lebanese General Confederation of Workers and circumvent its ability to launch general strikes. It exerted so much pressure and resorted to security forces to enforce the general ban on demonstration and ultimately succeeded in splitting the union during its general elections.

Freedom of the media was also under heavy threat when the government passed a decree seen by many as an onslaught on pluralism and as an attempt by the prime minister and his partners to protect their own business interests, which lay in their shares of the audiovisual advertising business. The audiovisual landscape had been characterized since the war by the proliferation of more than one hundred radio stations and fifty television networks. The decree stipulated that only a number of private radio and television stations would be licensed. Only four private television networks and three private radio stations were allowed to send news and political programs, all of them owned by Lebanese officials (Hariri, Speaker of Parliament Nabih Berri, and Vice Premier and Minister of Interior Michel Murr).[8]

Freedom of association (guaranteed by article 13 of the Constitution) also receded. Nongovernmental organizations accused the Interior Ministry of intimidation and of placing constant obstacles to their activity. One of the main complaints was that Ministry officials were turning the right of association into a kind of "licensing" process, in clear violation of the law.[9] The presidential election was also tainted when, in 1995, the Constitution was manipulated to allow an unprecedented extension of Hrawi's term for three additional years.[10]

On the other hand, political institutions such as parties, that illustrated a vibrant democratic society, were going through a major crisis, as they emerged from war scattered and facing ideological bankruptcy. Political parties in Lebanon have always relied on personal leadership, and reflected familial or tribal interests. Besides, they were sectarian in their orientation and in their militant base. The only nonsectarian groupings were the trans-nationalist parties, mainly the pan-arabist Baath, the Syrian Nationalist Party, and the Communist Party. The immediate postwar years failed to inspire the emergence of a genuine national party or trend that would draw lessons from the past and develop the ideological framework of coexistence and nation-building, parallel to the physical reconstruction of the country launched by the Hariri Cabinet.

How could this take place anyway when sectarian and confessional maneuvers have plagued Lebanon's politics since the end of the war? Administrative reform had been a priority goal of the first Hariri Cabinet, but this attempt failed. Patronage and nepotism became the hallmarks of the designation of civil servants, each community striving to add as many posts as it could to its postwar "trophies." Hariri and Berri were the top contestants in that bout, while Christians saw their shares shrink in the administration because they had no strong champions defending their "rights," and because Christian masses were reluctant to enroll in the public sector (be it the civil administration or the security forces and army). Patriarchs and bishops increasingly voiced their communities' claims regarding the distribution of senior charges, while Shiite and Sunni clerics bitterly vied in defense of their communities' self-assertion in the government apparatus and the administration.

Ta'if was supposed to pave the way for the phasing out of the sectarian order, under the provision of "the abolition of political confessionalism." Instead, it was deepening sectarian division lines. The political system was distorted through the *troika,* in which the three heads of state, of government, and of Parliament, monopolized decision-making, in flagrant violation of the parliamentary regime and of the checks-and-balances system. Furthermore, each one of them used his Syrian connections to neutralize his political rivals, check opposition, curtail public freedoms, and even get significant shares in some infrastructure and business projects. Syrians became more directly involved in Lebanese politics and exerted total hegemony on Lebanon's internal and foreign policy.

Muslim and Christian elites were disgruntled by the regime's practices. "The 'Ihbat' is no more a Christian illness, it has become Lebanese," said Seoud el-Mawla, in a roundtable organized by French-speaking daily *l'Orient LE-JOUR*. "Muslims feel uncomfortable because Sunni money and Shiite militias are in power. This is why Muslim middle class and intellectuals are as much frustrated as the Christians are."[11]

Pillars of the Ta'if accord, such as former speaker of Parliament Hussein Husseini, joined the opposition ranks. He had expected a better share in the postwar order and also resented the divisions occasioned by the bad implementation of the "national entente" agreement, the violations of many of its provisions, and the twists occurred at the institutional level. Besides, Husseini had been a persistent advocate of Christian-Muslim cooperation and he was concerned about the Christian malaise. Ta'if had deceived many of its early knights. Whether the Ta'if accord was good but unfairly implemented or whether its flaws were inherent was a matter of extensive debate.

Albert Mansour, former deputy and minister in the postwar Cabinet, and a Greek Catholic who opposed General Aoun and had close ties with the Syrian regime, denounced the Coup against Ta'if in an insightful book.[12] He warned that "the regime's practices are reviving and sharpening the divisions, and inducing the outbreak of another civil war." He also commented that "the way relations with Syria are handled stimulates the isolationist tendency among the Christians and regenerates the causes of hostility against Syria and against Arabity among all Lebanese of various political and sectarian affiliations."[13]

No one illustrates better the dramatic dilemma of Christian leaders with regard to Ta'if than the late president of the Maronite Kataeb (Phalangist) Party, Georges Saadeh. As the head of this mythical and militant Maronite stronghold, founded by charismatic leader Pierre Gemayel to become "the military shield of the Christians of Lebanon," Saadeh had been, with Speaker Hussein Husseini, one of the pillars of Ta'if. There, and in the line of the Kataeb's traditional policy of unfailing support to the Presidency of the Republic, he sought to preserve the Maronites' constitutional prerogatives. He was instrumental in the bailing out of the Ta'if document by Christian deputies, and later on, in "selling" it to the Christian public opinion as the only pragmatic solution in the wake of Aoun's "war of liberation" against Syria. If nothing else, Ta'if had stopped the language of the canons and vowed to restore Lebanon's sovereignty under the auspices of the Arab tripartite committee and the international community.

Everybody knew there could be no peace in Lebanon without the Kataeb party.[14] And yet, Saadeh was sidelined by the Ta'if regime, his party became the only party that participated in the war but not in government, although it played a key role in the making of peace. The Socialist Progressist Party of Druze Walid Joumblatt, the Shiite Amal movement of Nabih Berri, and the pro-Syrian parties were all represented in both government and Parliament.

While rejected by the regime, Saadeh was not popular among the Christians, either. They blamed him for all the Ta'if mismanagement and the deviations that downsized Christians' powers. They simply forgot that Ta'if was the result of Aoun's highly risky military gambit against Syria, that it could have been Aoun's diplomatic victory, and that the Aoun-Geagea bloody strife after Ta'if turned it instead into a disaster by irrevocably blowing up the balance of power between Christians and Muslims. This balance of power would have guaranteed a fair implementation of the Ta'if agreement. In an attempt to bridge the gap with his Christian constituency, Saadeh followed the mainstream and boycotted the 1992 elections. He thus ruined his last chances with the regime, but did not find grace in Christians' eyes.

Georges Saadeh had also sought to transform the Kataeb from a "family-owned" party, the Gemayel's, to "an institution party," as he said. He wanted to rejuvenate a party that many associated with the war. He thus alienated the Gemayel supporters within the party and former president Amin Gemayel.

Like a misunderstood hero of a tragic tale, Saadeh carried the wound of his political fate with resilience. But he still felt the need to leave his testimony behind. *My Story with Ta'if* was released a few weeks before he died.[15] And as it often happens in these cases, by an irony of fate, all those who opposed him, castigated him, and turned him into a political pariah (representatives of the *troika,* Lebanese and Syrian officials, and Christian figures, including the Gemayel camp) attended his funeral, praised him, and acknowledged the injustice done to him. The hero was no longer misunderstood . . . once he was gone.

THE POSTWAR AGENDA OF HEZBOLLAH

Ta'if certainly introduced an internal balance in favor of the Shiite community. Hussein Husseini, who presided over the Parliament in Ta'if, had made it sure that the prerogatives of the Speaker be enhanced in a way that he could not only counter the executive body represented by the President and the Council of Ministers but also neutralize it. In the *troika* system, Speaker Nabih Berri would use his clout to claim more posts for his community, both in the diplomatic corps and in the central administration. The Shiites even infringed upon Christian quotas in the administration, particularly upon the smaller Christian communities, prompting the protests of Greek Catholic and Greek Orthodox leaders. Like communicating vessels, the Shiites have been gaining more confidence in their future as they gained more power, while Christians have been losing theirs.

In December 1992, a Hezbollah delegation effected a groundbreaking visit to the Maronite seat of Bkerké and met with Patriarch Nasrallah Sfeir. A couple of months before, the "Party of God" had managed to get eight of its candidates elected to Parliament, taking the Lebanese by surprise. The '92 elections represented a major shift in Hezbollah's political discourse and behavior. The radical militant phase (1983–92) was gone, when "political maronitism" was assimilated with "zionist and American interests" and when Hezbollah leaders called for "the advent of an Islamic Republic in Lebanon, on the ruins of the Maronite regime."[16] The "Lebanonization" process of Hezbollah started the day they abided by the rules of the confessional system that they once castigated and accommodated themselves with the country's plural nature and consociational formula of coexistence.

"We believe in Islam but we will not impose Islam on anybody else," said Sheikh Naim Kassem, vice general secretary of the Hezbollah. "We do not consider that there is a fundamental conflict between Muslims and Christians in Lebanon. We want to build bridges of understanding and cooperation with the Christians."[17]

And he added: "Maronites have to stop hinting to the Arabs that the Shiite wave represents a terrorist and fundamentalist threat. They are wrong and it is in their interest to open a dialogue (with us) if they want to have their say in the solution rather than let it be imposed on them, as it happened during the parliamentary elections and the formation of the government."[18]

Throughout the years, Hezbollah refined its political speech, and grasped the subtleties of Lebanon's politics, that are dominated by "confessional alliances, compromises and minority coalitions against any emerging majority."[19]

Hezbollah members were the most efficient group in Parliament. They also managed to build a network of relations with various parties, playing perfectly well the loyalists/opposition game of democracy. They progressively merged into the system, and, with the blessing of Iran, the direction of Hezbollah under the command of its charismatic leader Sayyed Hassan Nasrallah, pushed the forces of radicalism represented by sheikh Sobhi Toufayli to the fringes. Toufayli did not understand the changes occurring not only in Lebanon but in Iran and Syria as well. He initiated a rebellion in the Biqaa Valley but was defeated by the Lebanese Armed Forces in summer 1997. The president of the Iranian Parliament, Ayatollah Nateq Nouri, came to Beirut to reiterate the support of the Iranian regime to the Lebanese government.

The "parliamentarian phase" of Hezbollah turned out to be a meaningful lesson on the impact democracy, political participation, capitalism, and free market have on extremism and on the ideological impulse of the Islamists. In return, it allowed the party to reap the benefits of its moderation—its "political maturity," according to Fadlallah, its pragmatism, simply put.

As Sayyed Nasrallah confirmed the "Lebanonization of the Party,"[20] the main payoff for Hezbollah has been the "Lebanonization" of its resistance against the Israeli occupation of the South. After an initial period of hesitation, Hezbollah guerilla fighters were recognized by the State as "Lebanon's legitimate resistance," and as such, it has remained the only authorized armed group. It was even allowed to place ads in the papers to collect money that would enable the resistance to buy weapons. "Associate yourself with the resistance," said the ad, "contribute with the price of a bullet."²¹ As a symbolic gesture and to assert its "national" character rather than its exclusively "Islamic" one, Hezbollah announced in 1998 that it was enrolling in its guerilla ranks members of other communities.

The situation in Southern Lebanon was precisely one bone of contention with Bkerké. "Why is it that Lebanon alone has to pay the high cost of resistance against Israel, among all other Arab nations?" wondered Patriarch Sfeir when he discussed the tragic fate of the South with the Hezbollah delegates. "Because this is the only place where we find real men," they replied, proudly.²² Sfeir was not opposed to the principle of resistance against Israel, who violated Lebanon's sovereignty. But he worried that whole towns were emptied of their inhabitants, and that very few Christians remained in that area. This could only alter Lebanon's social fabric and facilitate the mostly dreaded resettlement of the Palestinian refugees in the deserted villages. He was especially alarmed by the situation in the Christian burg of Jezzine, on the fringes of the "buffer zone" established by the Israelis. The remaining residents there were harassed by the Israeli proxy militia, the South Lebanon Army (SLA), who controlled the village, and at the same time they suffered regular losses due to Hezbollah's attacks against the SLA. When the pro-Israeli militia withdrew from Jezzine in June 1999, then one year later, when the Israeli troops withdrew from South Lebanon (May 2000), more than 5,000 Lebanese, with their families, a great number of them Christians, left their villages and sought refuge in Israel, for fear of reprisals from the Hezbollah against "collaborators." Meanwhile, and despite the insistence of the United Nations and countries such as France and the United States, the Lebanese government refused to deploy the army in Southern Lebanon, on the ground that the Chebaa farms, on the slopes of Mount Hermon, were still under occupation.

Whether these farms, long considered as part of occupied Syrian land on the Golan Heights, fell under the 425 resolution or the 242, was a matter that divided the Lebanese political class. Druze leader Walid Joumblatt wondered if Lebanon would be "Hanoi or Hong-Kong," meaning that Lebanon could not engage into reconstruction efforts while having instability at its southern borders.

For Christians in the Middle East, and especially in a country like Lebanon, which remained the last Arab battleground against Israel, the deadlock in the peace process was an additional motive of *Ihbat*. The success of the peace process would bring an end to the sufferings of the population and to the uncertainty linked to the future. It could result in the withdrawal of the Israeli troops from Lebanon, followed by the Syrian troops, the restoration of Lebanese sovereignty, the revival of the country's economy and of Christians' leading role in business and political affairs. It would also reduce the radicalization of Muslim societies. According to some analysts, there appears to be a growing connection between the degree of Islamic fervor and negative attitudes toward peace with Israel. In a research paper on popular attitudes toward peace with Israel among Lebanese, Syrians, and Jordanians, Hilal Khashan, an associate professor of political science at the American University of Beirut, indicated that in early 1995, "highly religious Muslims—both fundamentalists and non-fundamentalists—are the primary opponents of the peace process among the surveyed segments of the three Levantine Arab societies. Depending on the demographic category, large majorities (between 72 percent and 83 percent) of highly religious respondents oppose peace, as compared to a total of 38 percent for moderately religious and irreligious Muslims and 15 percent for Lebanese Maronite Christians."[23] But he also noted an increase in support for peace among the Lebanese Shi'a and the Muslim Syrian professional class at the height of peace talks in 1993 and 1995.

More conceivably, the 1996 "Operation Grapes of Wrath" against Lebanon has increased the level of distrust and negative perception of Israel's intentions among Christian and Muslim Lebanese as well. There is a broader conviction that Israel is "a vicious enemy aiming to destroy our faith, culture and identity," as Lebanon's Sunni Mufti declared.[24] And Patriarch Sfeir proclaimed when he received Hariri in Bkerké: "We Christians are still suffering from the wound inflicted to us by Israel" (in 1983, when Israeli troops suddenly withdrew from the Shouf, triggering the massacres of Christians and their exodus). "No one will squander our unity and our willingness to see resolution 425 implemented and Israeli forces withdraw from Lebanon. 425 is a guarantee for all."[25] Yet many Lebanese feared that, although Lebanese blood was spilled in the raids and bombardments that were conducted on a routine basis by the Israelis in the South, the Biqaa, and the Iqlim al-Tuffah, Lebanon might not be a full and equal partner in the peace negotiations but a mere "bargaining card" with Israel and with the United States. After the election of Ehud Barak in Israel and the stated intentions of the U.S. administration to push for the resumption of the Syrian-Israeli talks, anxiety spread among Lebanese people that their country might be sitting *on* the table of negotiations rather than *at* the table.[26]

The election of Ariel Sharon as the head of the Israeli government, coupled with the disengagement of the Bush administration from the peace process in the Middle East, gave a serious blow to any prospect of peace in that region. The undeclared daily war between the Palestinians and the Israelis in the occupied territories, increases the feeling of insecurity and volatility in the whole region and especially in Lebanon, and keeps that country firmly under the Syrian grip, despite the repeated protests of the Maronite Patriarch and a number of Lebanese politicians and parties.

Interestingly enough, one Lebanese editorialist wondered what would happen on the internal level in case the Israelis withdrew from the South. "Would the old cleavages reappear within the Lebanese society, with the Christians asking for a withdrawal of the Syrian forces, the Muslims opposing that demand and the demons of a Palestinian resettlement awakened?" wrote Faysal Selman. "Have we fought a twenty-year-old war only to find ourselves back to square one?"[27] In some way, this scenario almost took place . . . except that many Muslim leaders were now sharing the concerns of their Christian counterparts and expressing them out loud, through democratic forums and movements that were established in winter 2001.

Islamist groups such as Hezbollah remained at bay of the internal political game. Their main focus had been, in the previous years, the liberation of Southern Lebanon. Once that goal was reached (except for the Chebaa farms), they became a kind of model to the Palestinians in the West Bank. When, in 1999, before the Israeli withdrawal from Southern Lebanon, Hezbollah leader Sayyed Hassan Nasrallah declared that "the United States remains our number one enemy,"[28] he surprised those who thought the winds of change in Khatami's Iran would affect Hezbollah's positions. It is true that the pragmatic approach of Hezbollah to Lebanon's political and confessional reality was inspired by Khamenei's call to halt the "export of the Islamic revolution." Besides, Iran's overture to Saudi Arabia also had a moderating effect on Hezbollah's relationship with Hariri.[29]

But even if Hezbollah recognizes *wilayat al-faqih* and the supreme authority of Iran's Guide Ayatollah Khamenei, it has increasingly become autonomous and has set its own Lebanese agenda and priorities,[30] especially since Lebanon and Iran agreed that "Iranian officials should establish relations with the Lebanese State, not with a Lebanese group."[31]

The bridges built by Hezbollah with Christian religious leaders multiplied, according to their interests. Sometimes, to counter the financial power of Prime Minister Rafik Hariri, they would resort to some political alliance with ideologically opposed parties, such as the Kata'ib party. They would also develop good relations with one of the major TV networks in Lebanon, the Lebanese Broadcasting Corporation International

(LBCI), previously owned by the "Lebanese Forces." Hezbollah leaders were more often interviewed on LBCI than on their own private channel, *Al-Manar*.

All these overtures dwindled after the celebration of the victory of the Resistance and the withdrawal of the Israeli troops from the South. In winning the laurels of its achievement, the Hezbollah lost the measured tone that characterized its rhetoric on the internal level. Observers agreed on the fact that it was now becoming kind of an arbiter of the State and, very much aware that it has become a predominant political force, it determined important decisions. The Lebanese government decided that the Armed Forces would not be deployed in the South before the Chebaa farms were liberated, and even when Prime Minister Rafik Hariri contested some "untimely" military attacks of Hezbollah in that region, for fear that investments would run away from the country if tensions raised, he had to back off.

Parallel to that, when the maronite Patriarch asked for the withdrawal of the Syrian troops from Lebanon, the Hezbollah claimed it represented a "majority" that was favorable to the Syrian presence in Lebanon.

TUGGED BETWEEN JOUMBLATT AND HARIRI

Despite his sporadic blasts against Bkerké and "those isolationist Maronites," and despite his (jagged) alliance with Hariri, Walid Joumblatt needed an opening to the Christians. In various TV interviews, he expressed his willingness to have candid discussions with young Christian students of the St.-Joseph University or Kaslik University. His political *volte-faces* showed how pulled he was between his reluctance to let the Christians regain political strength once they return to their Shouf villages, and his fear to see them too weakened and unable to face the two Sunni and Shiite heavyweights on the local arena.

The Druze community had also emerged weakened by nearly two decades of war. It faced its own demographic and political crisis. But the leadership of Walid Joumblatt was intact. In winter 1998, Joumblatt held out his hand to all Christian political parties, including his longtime adversaries: he met with representatives of the Aounist trend; he visited the headquarters of the Kataeb party, and had a closed session with its Central Committee; he convened with his Maronite "traditional ally" in the Shouf, Dory Chamoun; he met with the National Bloc of exiled Maronite leader

Raymond Eddé, and with the president of the Maronite League, his former electoral ally Pierre Helou.

Officially, these meetings were meant to coordinate and set alliances in the coming municipal elections. They also dealt with the displaced issue and the reconciliation process in the Shouf. But the Lebanese media wondered if Joumblatt's move was "inspired" by his Syrian mentor and if he had a "green light" to go further ahead in this opening and start a new page of political cooperation between Druzes and Christians. A few months later, "the Beiteddine Conference" (July 1998) confirmed the Christian-Druze rapprochement. It was attended by various religious leaders and sealed the reconciliation between the two former enemies: the Socialist Progressist Party of Joumblatt and the Maronite Kataeb Party.

But the real turning point occurred during the legislative elections of summer 2000. Walid Joumblatt operated a complete political turnabout by echoing the claims and demands of the Maronites, criticizing the State for its failures and lapses, condemning the arrests of young Christian opponents, asking for the redeployment of the Syrian army, and for a relation based on equal footing between Lebanon and Syria. He reinforced his alliance with the Christian camp by putting together a cohesive and representative electoral list, that was all propelled into the Parliament. He perfected his political "come-back" by imposing three ministers, two druzes and one maronite, in the new Rafik Hariri government that was formed in the wake of the 2000 elections.

Suddenly, Joumblatt was reviving a Mount Lebanon that was historically grounded in a Maronite-Druze cooperation, as the bedrock of Lebanese nationalism. While brutal alterations of demography threatened the Lebanese identity, Joumblatt embodied the awakening of the national conscience of a Mountain where he reigned as one of the last feudal leaders. His attitude rallied around him a large fringe of the Christian public opinion and his visit to the Maronite patriarch, in spring 2001, reinforced his popularity with his Druze and Christian constituency. The rapprochement of these two major communities, founders of historic Lebanon, culminated in August 2001, with the historical visit that Patriarch Nasrallah Sfeir paid to the Chouf Mountain, sealing the reconciliation between these two groups who underwent horrible massacres during the war, in what was known as "the mountain war" in 1983.

Rafik Hariri was alarmed: under his first mandate (1992–98), the Maronite discontent was spreading to all levels of society and opposition to his authoritarian tendencies grew and strengthened through alliance-building. It is true that major reconstruction works were achieved in downtown Beirut, but the living standards continued to plummet. Lebanon staggered to its feet and its workers seethed. The country found itself mired in debt. Deterioration of the human rights record (regularly reported by Amnesty International, Human Rights Watch, and the State Department's annual report on human rights), the non-application of some Ta'if provisions such as the formation of an Economic and Social Council, as well as social and economic problems gave a common ground for Christians and Muslims to join in a disparate front made of liberals, Christian hard-liners, Islamists, trade unionists, and outspoken leftists. Whether right or wrong, the bold "reconstruction plan" of Hariri was perceived as being exclusive, not inclusive: socially excluding the middle classes, confessionally excluding all other communities than the Sunnis, and excluding other regions than Beirut.

In his ongoing institutional wrestle with the Shiite community represented by Speaker Nabih Berri, Hariri needed the Christians more as allies than as equal partners in power. He did not understand their malaise concerning his overwhelming dominance of the political arena. He was also worried that his reconstruction program was not fully adopted and supported by the Christians: he needed their investments as well as their economic and cultural edge and technological know-how. In September 1997, bank deposits of nonresidents represented only 12.9 percent of the total bank deposits in Lebanon.[32]

Although Ta'if has transferred the powers of the Presidency of the Republic to the Council of ministers as a body and not to the prime minister per se, Hariri has come to incarnate the attributions of the government, by his stature, his financial clout, and his Arab and international connections. This personalization of power highly displeased his opponents and particularly the Christians. Yet part of their irritation was due to the fact that they lacked the sort of leader the Sunnis had in the person of Rafik Hariri. But if that man existed, would he be allowed to emerge on the local scene?

Hariri intensified his contacts with Bkerké and visited Patriarch Sfeir on various occasions. He had better ties with the Maronite Church and bishops than the Maronite president Elias Hrawi did. But Hariri did not hide from Sfeir that he reproved his continual criticism and the pessimistic tone of his Sunday sermons. He felt this had a negative impact on Christians' morale and triggered one aspiration among the youth: to pack and leave the country.

The prime minister believed that only the Holy See could soothe the

Patriarch's positions and bring him to instill hope to his Christian flock. So he remained in touch with Cardinal Sodano and Archbishop Tauran in the Vatican.

During his eight-hour discussions in Bkerké on March 6, 1998, with the Patriarch, bishops, and superiors of the Maronite Church, Hariri took note of all the grievances and reproaches to his policy expressed by his interlocutors. They included national complaints concerning the fiscal and economic policy as well as the judiciary shortcomings, the corruption of the political class, and the social problems. In that regard, the Maronite Church said it was speaking in the name of all Lebanese. But it did also reflect the central concern of the Maronites in postwar Lebanon: "Maronites will no longer accept that their role be minimized and that their participation to political decisions be null," warned the exhaustive memorandum handed to Hariri. And it went on: "Until when some of those people in power will keep relying on the foreigner and ignoring Lebanon's structure and the red lines that should not be transgressed when it comes to one essential partner in the Lebanese equation, that is the Christians? Why aren't the so-called privileged relations with Syria based on respect and allegiance to the Lebanese nation and in accordance with our national interests on equal basis? Why this rush to sign unbalanced treaties with Syria?"[33]

Both parties, the Maronite religious hierarchy and the Sunni Premier, knew that the answers to these questions lay outside the Lebanese borders, in the capital where ultimately decisions involving Lebanon as well as Syria were made, Damascus.

WHAT DOES SYRIA WANT FROM THE CHRISTIANS ?

Syria had been intermittently sending signals to the Christians, especially since the holding of the Synod, which gave a boost to their morale. Those signals reached a peak in winter and spring 1997, and the news that Syria desired a dialogue with the Christians came a few weeks before the official announcement that Pope John Paul II would be visiting Beirut on May 10–11. The official announcement of the visit followed a meeting between the Pope and Prime Minister Rafik Hariri, at the Vatican, where Patriarch Sfeir was also staying.

Since its military operation against the Baabda palace to oust General Aoun, Syria has tightened its grip over Lebanon. On the international level, it has become the inevitable "guardian" of the Lebanese gate, filtering the foreign relations of its small neighbor. France realized that in order to preserve its age-old bonds with Lebanon, it had no other choice but to develop a good relationship with the Syrian regime. "Lebanese-French relations could only prosper if French-Syrian relations are built on the factor of trust," acknowledged French ambassador in Beirut Daniel Jouanneau, on the eve of Jacques Chirac's visit to Lebanon.[34] Thanks to his close friendship with the French President, Hariri was instrumental in bringing French-Syrian relations to a level of coordination and cooperation never witnessed before. Saudia Arabia, which backed Hariri, coordinated its policy with Syria in Lebanon as well, Iran's support to Hezbollah and to its military actions in South Lebanon also needed coordination with Syria. Even the Holy See realized it could not avoid the reality of the Syrian presence and authority in Lebanon, and so the Pope's visit to Lebanon was preceded by a formal visit of Archbishop Tauran in Damascus to explain the objectives of the visit (see Part III, Chapter 12).

The Syrians have been wary of Prime Minister Hariri's international connections, even if Hariri has used these relations in order to foster international cooperation with Syria. Damascus has particularly been nervous about Hariri's cordial relations with the United States. This was particularly evident after the "Friends of Lebanon" forum in December 1996, held in Washington under the auspices of President Bill Clinton, to pledge support to Lebanon's reconstruction after the Israeli military operation "Grapes of Wrath" in spring 1996. The Syrian regime eventually showed its distaste for the closer ties between Washington and Beirut. It was particularly fearful that Hariri would decide to bolt from the Syrian sphere of influence, under U.S. aegis and with the aim of concluding a settlement with Israel. In this analytical perspective, his natural allies in such an endeavor would probably be the Christians, who might consider such a step necessary to water down Syrian influence in Lebanon.

The Maronites were the most outspoken group in Lebanon and overtly critical of Syria's influence. Besides, their active and highly connected diaspora was an asset that the Damascus regime preferred to bring round to its positive role rather than have it lobby on the international arena against the presence of Syria in Lebanon.

According to analysts, the Syrians, who felt vulnerable regionally, knew that a dissatisfied Christian community may be a source of unwanted instability in Lebanon. They also wanted to show that they are supportive of, and indispensable to, national reconciliation in Lebanon. "More ominously, the flip side of this proposition is that unless Syria is allowed to act freely in Lebanon, reconciliation can be blocked," wrote *The Lebanon Report*.[35]

In supervising internal dialogue in Lebanon and Lebanese-Syrian dialogue, Syria was also seeking to preclude unilateral Christian initiatives that might weaken its control over Lebanon. Christian demands were becoming more forceful and pushed for a greater equilibrium in relations between Christians and Muslims in Lebanon, and in relations between Lebanon and Syria, especially in the signing of bilateral treaties and economic accords.

Syrian overtures to the Maronites took multiple avenues. But they all converged to one point: Bkerké. They happened in two phases: before and after the death of Syrian president Hafez Assad. Many Christian political figures contributed.

The first aim of the interventions was to convince Patriarch Sfeir he should visit Syria. This would be a highly symbolic move. The head of the Maronite Church was the only public figure in Lebanon who had not hit the Damascus road yet. Every Lebanese knew that going to Damascus meant paying allegiance to the Syrian tutor. The mediators said the Maronite Patriarch would be welcomed by President Assad in person, with all the honors due to a head of state. They added that he could take advantage of this visit and tour the Maronite community living in Syria's big cities.

Rumors that President Assad's son, Bachar, would be visiting Bkerké filled the Lebanese papers. The pressures on Bkerké increased. Some Maronite politicians (ministers and deputies) with close ties to the Syrian regime lobbied in favor of the idea. But the Christian public opinion was wary and hostile to it. Symbolically, Bkerké was the last bastion of the Maronite's untamed spirit of independence.

Sfeir stood steadfast in his political requests. He wanted the complete list of grievances (concerning Ta'if implementation and fair political participation and representation) reviewed by the Syrians and relations between the two countries established on equal footing. The Syrians were hesitant. Was the Maronite Patriarch too demanding? "I have never received a formal invitation [from the Syrians]," Sfeir made it clear in an interview to a French magazine. "Some Lebanese with close ties to the Syrian regime try to prompt me to go to Damascus. But I will not go there before the relations between our two countries are clarified and before Lebanon regains its sovereignty and independence."[36]

The Apostolic Nuncio in Lebanon and the Roman curia in the Vatican were uncomfortable with what was going on. Questions were raised, fueling doubts. Was this a dialogue between a State, Syria, and one community in Lebanon, to the exclusion of other groups ? If yes, there was an imbalance among the two dialoguing parties, and besides, this could arise suspicion and malaise among other Lebanese communities, particularly the Muslims. Besides, any confessional maneuvering could trigger tensions. The only possible and effective dialogue was a State-to-State dialogue. This is why all communities should feel equitably represented in the State institutions.

The Vatican was not the only side to be reserved about these non-official contacts. President Hrawi was getting nervous about a Syro-Christian dialogue and he overtly expressed his displeasure about it. He denounced the fact that the State was excluded from that dialogue. He also knew that one of the issues at stake was the election of a new president that would be accepted by the Maronite community and not imposed on it.

The ongoing negotiations came to a halt when Syrian vice president Abdel-Halim Khaddam acceded to Hrawi (and Hariri)'s request. "Dialogue can only take place between States and we only deal with the Lebanese State," he said in June 1997, one month after the Pope's visit to Lebanon. Bachar Assad, who was preparing for the succession of his father and was incrementally taking over the Lebanese portfolio from the hands of Abdel-Halim Khaddam, assured his Lebanese visitors that Syria was willing to have good relations with all Lebanese parties, and that it had no intention of gobbling up Lebanon.

One basic demand of the Maronites—and of the Lebanese people in general—was that there would be no second extension of Hrawi's unpopular mandate. They wanted the democratic process to get back on track and a new president elected, who would truly represent his community, be accepted by all other Lebanese communities and especially the Muslims, would have a national agenda and stature, and would have the required credibility and integrity to carry on his supreme functions and fight the corruption that was creeping at all levels.

One Maronite figure enjoyed the required qualifications and broad respect of the Lebanese; the polls indicated he was their favorite "candidate" to the presidency, although the constitution did not allow him to run for the higher post of the state: he was the commander in chief of the Lebanese Armed Forces.

On October 15, 1998, General Emile Lahoud was elected by the Parliament, after clause three of article 49 in the Constitution (barring high-ranking civil servants from running for president) was amended. He was the eleventh President of the Lebanese Republic and the second army commander in the modern history of Lebanon to become head of the

State, since General Fouad Chehab ruled the country following 1958's first civil clash.

Chapter 10

Coexistence in Uniform

In the Middle East, the military has long been a central element in the functioning and maintenance of virtually every state. It has played a decisive role in domestic and foreign affairs and is certain to play a key role in the political transformations many countries in the region are experiencing or likely to experience over the next several years. The military and society in the Middle East have a close relationship and its effects on internal peace and stability are undeniable.

The election of an army commander in chief at the head of the only Arab state with democratic traditions such as Lebanon is a sign that priority has been given to Lebanon's stability in an increasingly volatile environment, where most Arab regimes are or would be soon confronted by the difficult equation of their succession. But General Emile Lahoud's election was also the expression of a genuine need of the Lebanese people for a leadership committed to institution-building as well as nation-building.

The Lebanese army was the first among the state institutions to be struck by war and its security mission was impeded by internal divisions along sectarian lines. In postwar Lebanon, it is the first institution to emerge as a reunited and nonsectarian body and is referred to as a typical model of postwar integration.

The experience of the Lebanese army during and after the Lebanese civil war illustrates both the international dimension of ethno-religious conflicts and their sectarian aspect. The international dimension of ethnic and religious conflicts starts by neutralizing the armed forces of a country or shattering them. Security of the social body is then assumed by militias. This is what happened in Lebanon, and later on in former Yugoslavia. The traditional weakness of the Lebanese central power and the feeble legitimacy of the territorial nation-state associated with feudal structures, familial, and confessional allegiances made this enterprise all the more easier.

If the internal fighting can be stopped by external intervention in an international conference such as in Ta'if (which confirms the international character of the Lebanese civil war), civil peace can only be secured by the national authorities themselves. In Lebanon's case, the Lebanese Armed Forces under the command of General Emile Lahoud have been the engine and guarantor of this peace. How was this achievement possible, since the army was the microcosm of a deeply divided society such as Lebanon's?

General Lahoud accomplished this primary objective of army reunification by restructuring the brigades to include both Christian and Muslim elements. He felt it was incumbent on him to rehabilitate the army as the bulwark and the pith of a united nation. With U.S. military assistance and Syrian cooperation and support, he has been able to rebuild the 60,000-strong Lebanese Armed Forces (LAF), including five brigades deployed along the zone Israel occupied in Southern Lebanon. The LAF also disarmed and dissolved the former militias and restored order around Palestinian refugee camps. With strong backing from a neighboring Syria put under pressure by the U.S. administration, which accused it of harboring drug trafficking and terrorism, the LAF also took part in a vast campaign to eradicate drug cultivation in the Biqaa Valley.[1]

The central role played by the LAF in bringing about postwar order owes first and foremost to the "policy of global integration" pursued by its determined commander in chief. The insights of that policy are still unknown to the public, yet they are of invaluable contribution to: (1) the understanding of the ominous mechanisms of civil conflict within a national army; (2) the resolution of any comparative case in deeply torn countries, because in many ways, the Lebanese performance in rebuilding a scattered army in post-civil conflict is an unmatched experience.

An inestimable account of that experience has been given by one of the key senior officers who assumed a most sensitive task in postwar Lebanon. General Jamil Sayyed was assistant director of the military intelligence, the famous "Second Bureau," and a close adviser to General Lahoud. He is today general director of the General Security ("Sûreté Générale"). In the most revealing and first of its kind thesis on the integrationist policy within the Lebanese Armed Forces, he has described the situation of the army during the war, its sectarian divisions, and explained the objectives of postwar integration, its philosophy, the obstacles it encountered, and the new structure of the LAF. The subtitle of his dissertation is meaningful: "The Integration in the Lebanese Armed Forces, a Transitory Experience or a Permanent Policy?"[2]

In this somehow unique document, General Sayyed gives two examples of plural countries, the United States and Belgium, which built a national army despite strong ethnic cleavages (in the case of Belgium) and a civil war (in the case of the Unites States). But Sayyed warns that it is not possible to draw a parallel between the Lebanese case and the United States' or Belgium's. And the reason is that the U.S. civil war ended with a winner and a loser, and the reunification of the U.S. army was based on that paradigm. Some Southern officers were court-martialed, others joined the ranks, and others were dismissed.

As for the Belgium army, explains Sayyed, its troops are divided like its society, along ethnic and cultural lines, and so the Belgian army is structured within fragmented units that are either Flemish or Walloon. Joint commands coordinate their actions. "Although united, this is not an integrated army," comments Sayyed. Given the specificity of the Lebanese reality, "integration by itself is a country's formula more than it is a set of conditions imposed by a winner on a loser, or a mere artificial formula of coexistence between different ethnic groups," he writes.[3]

Significantly, the high-ranking officer contests, in his introduction, the "pluralistic" character of the Lebanese society, and prefers the denomination of "confessionalist society." Breaking with the traditional duty of reserve of the military, he blames the "sectarianist system" of the state and the "distribution of confessional portions at power level" for having failed to promote a national unity spirit. This ultimately affected the military institution, he added. Sayyed's attitude could only be explained by a widespread tenet among officers that the army is the institution that took the lead in postwar Lebanon and shed the sectarian traditions of the Lebanese system.

General Sayyed explains that the aim of the central command was to make the army the backbone of national unity, so as to prevent any collapse of political institutions, keep political antagonisms within the limits of the democratic game, and preclude any tension from reaching street level, which would reactivate civil war.

Sayyed first describes the "trenchant split of the army between two big blocks, Christian and Muslim," between 1975 and 1990. These blocks splintered to smaller groups as military troops joined their regions or their confessions of origin. The twelve brigades of the army were hence respectively known as "the Shiite brigade of the Biqaa," "the Sunni brigade of the North," "the Christian brigade of Mount-Lebanon," "the Druze brigade of the mountain," etc., with sparsely dispersed "minorities" in each brigade for familial or residential circumstances. This situation had extended to the navy, air force, military academies, and had reached all levels of command. Many military and civilians considered it natural for soldiers to fulfill their military duties clustered within their own geographical and sectarian environment.

Interestingly enough, General Sayyed admits that "domestic insecurity and political turmoil resulted from external, regional and international polarization, which hampered any attempt of reunification of the army, because it would have changed the balance of power on the ground."[4]

As Ta'if provided the propitious "regional and international" environment to initiate such an endeavor, the reunification of the army became the first goal to attain. Yet the commander in chief of the army did not want to secure mere coexistence and sectarian balance within the army, he wanted to provide the troops with a factor of cohesion and unification, a national doctrine that would create an "esprit de corps" and would bring together the multiple components of the army, which mirrors the diversity of the society. "This doctrine clearly articulated that Israel was the enemy and Arabs in general, and Syria in particular, were our friends, and that Lebanon's strategic and permanent interests as well as its security and stability were linked to Syria's, whatever the regional circumstances are"[5] wrote Sayyed. The national role of the army in confronting Israeli occupation in the South and in western Biqaa was thus reinforced.

Once the doctrinal foundation of the army was established, the policy of integration relied on the practical strategy of structuring sectarian diversity within the armed forces and mixing the brigades. An initial trial in spring 1991 failed. It consisted of transplanting five small units from their homogeneous brigades into other brigades, which meant positioning them in a different regional and sectarian context. But psychological, social, and geographical barriers were still deeply entrenched and the objectives of that first operation had not been explained enough nor sufficiently publicized at the various levels of the army. Those who went through that experiment were just a few and they felt odd with the rest of the troops.

"Operation Global Integration" really started in 1992. All brigades were mixed in a way that they no longer bore sectarian labels or fell under one predominant political influence. Soldiers were sent out of the regions they were confined to during the war, so that they could get a better knowledge of their country. Brigades were supposed to fulfill any military mission in any region without triggering moral or psychological strains between the citizens and the troops stationed in their area. Competence and productivity became the criteria of selection and promotion rather than sectarian quotas and political clientelism. This undertaking was coupled with intensive education and information sessions to break psychological barriers and to explain the objectives of the operation. In that regard, the army training camps provided a school of civic education, before civic education books were completed and distributed in schools.

Yet the main obstacles came from the political class and the militias, who looked at that daring enterprise as a threat to their interests and to their clout. Many complained directly to the Syrian authorities, asking them to intervene and stop the process launched by General Lahoud. But the Syrians remained at bay, as the commander in chief clearly expressed his resolve to carry on his national duty of reunification of the Lebanese Armed Forces. This bold undertaking was further complicated by the decision of Lebanese political authorities to absorb former militiamen in the army and other security forces. Their number reached 4,000, 85 percent of whom were Muslims, because Christian "Lebanese Forces," who were still skeptical about the whole operation and did not believe in its final outcome, boycotted it and refused to join the army. This created an imbalance at the ground level, and when the commander in chief applied the compulsory military service, the "flag service," which enlisted between 8,000 and 10,000 recruits a year, the proportion of Muslim conscripts reached 60 percent to 70 percent, as opposed to 30 percent to 40 percent of Christians. In 1996, the difference sharpened and reached 77.5 percent and 22.5 percent. As to the army volunteers, Christians amounted to 41.8 percent and Muslims to 58.2 percent.

This inequality was compensated by an ingenious communal distribution among the various brigades and divisions. The central command also adopted a consistent policy of an evenhanded blend of "affirmative action" and of encouragement to enroll in the brigades and units of preference, since it noticed that Christians preferred to enroll in some specific units (such as the Republican Guard, the Military Police, and the highly trained special unit of the navy forces, created by General Lahoud, a navy officer himself) while Muslims were dominant in combat units and regional commands.

From its inception, the Lebanese army has been confronted with the problem of unequal army enrollment between Christian and Muslim communities. This was due to the disparity of social and education levels as well as variances in birth rates, rather than to political attitudes. Still, one of the main breeding grounds of the army was the Maronite enclaves of Kobeyate and Andakt in the Northern caza of Akkar, a region as poor and "disinherited" as the Shiite regions of the South.

Since national allegiance and discipline were restored, the LAF were able to carry their twofold mission. It consisted in (1) preserving internal security and stability (the LAF were the real guarantor of the legislative and municipal elections held in 1996 and 1998 with no major incidents reported on the ground), and (2) facing Israeli occupation in the South, while providing the Southerners with rapid relief and care during brutal attacks. In his final evaluation of the army integration, General Sayyed considers that "confessional balance in the army is secured but it is established on the basis of competence, not on the old criteria of quota attributions and religious and political patronage."[6]

He confirms that "integration" will remain the permanent policy within the army, but he pointedly stresses on the responsibility of the state to carry out that national mission too.

Jamil Sayyed's conclusion is highly pertinent and speaks for itself. The senior officer observes: "The big lacunas that still hinder the complete cohesion of Lebanese society are in the education field, where students and teachers are most often from one religious confession, starting in the primary level all through high school, and later in the university." This is why, he says, "integration should not be a task solely assumed by one of the state institutions, such as the army. For whatever the efforts deployed, the army cannot be an integrated island within a non-integrated social body, or within a state that does not put school integration at the forefront of its priorities. This is all the more important that the army opens its ranks to the citizens after they have reached 18 years old, which is relatively late to assimilate the basic rules of a solid civic education."[7] Still, in the modern history of Lebanon, there is no doubt that the challenge carried out by General Emile Lahoud in the postwar era has been a unique and pioneering action.

PART III

The Leaven in the Dough

Chapter 11

The Democracy of the National Pact

Bringing the subject of "political confessionalism" to the table is like opening Pandora's box in Lebanon. No sooner is it mentioned than religious leaders, politicians, intellectuals, and journalists join in a cacophony of comments aimed at picturing the darkest side of the system or defending it. They would usually enhance their point of view with arguments based on sociology, history, geography, psychology, or constitutional law. They all claim objectivity, although they are strong about their standpoint, and if you take a close look at their arguments, you will be able to find out the communal identity of each one of the polemicists, depending on what is being advocated. Is it abolition of confessionalism at the political level? Then you know you're dealing with a Muslim side. Abolition of confessionalism in all aspects of society, i.e., secularism? Then it is a Christian defense. "Let's erase confessionalism from the texts," would say the Shiites. "No, let's suppress it from minds first," would retort the Maronites.

The dispute has become a fulcrum for lingering sectarian mistrust. Yet, the positions of the parties are mitigated, since many Sunni politicians and intellectuals have toned down their demand for de-confessionalization as Shi'ites have strongly advocated it, on the ground that they've become the largest minority group in Lebanon. The position of Druze leader Walid Joumblatt has also been a hodgepodge of contradictions: he publicly says he favors de-confessionalisation although he knows that the small Druze minority can only keep on playing a significant role under the current system.

Political confessionalism means the distribution of power on confessional or sectarian basis. Its founding idea is that the requisite equilibrium among the eighteen official communities in Lebanon can only be achieved through a meticulous system of quotas.

Political confessionalism is not the favored child of the Lebanese people, but it is certainly their bond, the architecture of their "house of many mansions,"[1] the institutional form of their unity. They have also come to view it as their "registered trademark," as they looked around and discovered the international turmoil of the post–Cold War era. Since the end of their internationalized civil strife, Lebanese share one common conviction, paraphrasing Churchill on democracy: "It is the worst system I know, but I cannot find a better one." That conviction has been translated in Ta'if.

Still, Lebanese are looking for a better political and constitutional shell.

THE HISTORICAL AND EXISTENTIAL BASIS OF CONFESSIONALISM

Lebanon emerged from its war while the rest of the world headed right towards the same kind of conflict the Lebanese inaugurated seventeen years earlier. Suddenly, the problem of fragmented and pluralistic societies imposed itself to the international community. The era of conventional wars between states has given place to substitute wars in pluralistic countries where the minorities syndrome is often exploited in regional and international stakes. Africa, Bosnia, and Kosovo, after Lebanon, typically illustrated that new era in world politics. But the aspiration of minorities for participation, if not autonomy, challenged the traditional Westminster-style majoritarian democracy.

In a region such as the Middle East, where governments have failed to deal with their minorities, and have built social and political integration on repression and de facto discrimination, the Lebanese consensual formula attracts as a way of alleviating conflict in deeply divided societies and reducing insecurities. The founding fathers of independent Lebanon created a (non-written) formula of distribution of the State's charges among the main communities, called the "National Pact of 1943." Most writers on contemporary Lebanese affairs point to it as a political invention of the highest order that produced relative stability in a highly unstable environment, until 1975.[2]

Although it left the Maronites as the most powerful community, for their demographic superiority as well as their historic responsibility in the birth of Greater Lebanon, it brought the non-Christian groups, especially the Sunnis, into a more prominent position. It stipulated that the powerful President of the Republic would be a Maronite Christian, the prime minister a Sunni Muslim, the Speaker of Parliament a Shiite Muslim, and his deputy chairman a Greek Orthodox Christian. Parliamentary seats and government portfolios were allocated on the basis of sectarian proportionality, with an overall Christian-to-Muslim ratio of six to five, turned six to six in Ta'if. One of the most important parts of the National Pact was the understanding that each community would not appeal to its particular foreign patron for support. This provision clearly meant that Muslims would not seek alliances with Syria and the Arab-Muslim world, and Christians would not rely on the backing of the West, meaning France and the Christian powers.

This simultaneous "no" (to the West and to the Arabs) prompted at that time the ironic comment of famous Lebanese journalist Alfred Naccache and owner of the influential French-speaking daily L'Orient, who wrote: "Two negations do not build up a nation." A sentence that passed through history but led its author to jail.

It is impossible to grasp the full significance of Lebanon's power-sharing formula if one does not keep in mind its existential bearing for all Lebanese communities. What holds the Lebanese society together is not the law, as is the case in the Unites States, where law has even become the supreme conscience of society. It is not even a centralized authority (although Lebanon has a very centralized form of government). It is the Pact. Lebanon is a "Covenant democracy' based on the consensus of its religious communities.

Historically, these communities came to Mount-Lebanon, seeking refuge in its rugged terrain and natural "fortress," fleeing persecution, in order to protect their freedom of religion and their specific traditions. In Mount-Lebanon, they were able to secure their legal existence as well as the political rights they did not enjoy anywhere else in the Ottoman Empire.

Except for the Maronite community whose entrenchment in Mount-Lebanon contributed to its autonomy and nurtured its perpetual resistance to any domination, all other Christian communities were *dhimmi,* and as such benefited from Arab-Muslim protection. The *millet* regime secured a form of self-rule for religious minorities in the Ottoman Empire by delegating to religious institutions the administration of their social, religious, legal, and cultural affairs.

Christians were better off than the non-Sunni Muslims (such as Shiites, Druzes, Alaouites, Ismailites, and Yezidis) under the Ottoman rule. Those were forced to abide by the hanafite law (the official law in the Ottoman empire). They had no legal autonomy in the Muslim Sunni state. Being the core of the nation, of the *umma,* "real believers (i.e., the Sunnis) did not conceive themselves as a mere community in the legal sense accepted by the Shari'a," explained the late Edmond Rabbath, the prominent Lebanese Constitution expert and historian.[3] So the non-Sunni Muslims were not viewed as "communities" as well, but part of the whole body.

It was in Mount-Lebanon, first under the Mutassarrifiyat regime (the Organic Rule of 1861 and then of 1864 stated civic equality and political representation in Mount-Lebanon's Assembly for Christians and Muslims), then under French mandate, and finally in independent Lebanon, that the "communal regime" and legal recognition was extended to all communities that did not benefit from it, and particularly the Muslim communities. On January 27, 1926, the French governor (Haut-Commissaire) of Greater Lebanon, Leon Cayla, recognized by official decree "the right of the Shiite Muslims to submit their personal status to the prescriptions of the jaafari rite." He created the Shiite jaafari tribunal and formally declared in the first article that "Shiite Muslims constitute an independent religious community in Greater Lebanon." Later, the law of December 19, 1967, organized "the affairs of the Shiite Muslim community in Lebanon," and granted it complete autonomy regarding its religious matters, its *waqfs* (real estate properties) and its legal institutions. It also recognized that its legal jaafari dispositions (*shari'a*) would conform to "the supreme Shiite authority in the world," that is the supreme imam in Najaf (Iraq).

The organic law that presides over the legal destiny of the Sunni community was voted on January 13, 1955 (legal decree number 18, modified in March 1965). It also granted the Sunnis "total independence in their internal and religious affairs" and it specifically mentioned that the supreme authority of the community lies in the hands of the Grand Mufti of the Republic. The legislators also gave the Sunni community the legislative power to amend the dispositions of its founding law; that is, it granted it legislative sovereignty.

The irony of fate is such that the Druze community, whose emirs ruled Mount-Lebanon, was officially recognized only in 1842, when Mount-Lebanon was divided in two separate Maronite and Druze entities, *caimacamats,* imposed by Europe after the collapse of the *Emirate.* Like other Muslim communities, its courts and tribunals will be formally recognized under French mandate, and like all Muslim courts, they will be administratively and financially linked up to the Ministry of Justice. Yet, the communal status of the Druzes is legislated and promulgated on July 13, 1962. Its laws grant it full autonomy and provides for the election of its "sheikh akl," the religious head of the community.

As for the Christians and the Jewish communities, the organic (or fundamental) law of April 2, 1951, erected them as political entities, with full legal autonomy. It is easy to see how the Lebanese state has thus projected in its constitution this multi-communal reality. "It is in Lebanon that the communal regime has found its constitutional foundations and flourished in the form of a political system," comments Edmond Rabbath. "Each community has developed an ancestral vocation to become a specific nation."[4]

The system is grounded in the idea of Lebanon being "an asylum for minorities" in the Orient, "a project of freedom and modernity" and "a privileged place for conviviality." This philosophy has been extensively developed by Maronite thinkers and writers, and has been confirmed by the tumultuous modern history of the Middle East. Under the pressure of Arab nationalist regimes and the successive coups that left them dispossessed in countries such as Iraq, Egypt, and Syria, Eastern Christian communities have transferred their seats to Lebanon and consolidated their presence in that country, where all Eastern Patriarchates have their residence. It has even become a tradition to grant Lebanese citizenship to the head of a community if he chooses to reside in Lebanon.

Initially intended to secure political participation for all minorities, the power-sharing formula was based on the quota system. But article 95 of the Lebanese Constitution stressed the "transitory" aspect of political confessionalism. Yet the quota system was formally endorsed by article 96 of a 1959 law on the status of civil servants. The imperatives of sectarian balance overruled the competence criteria in the designation of civil servants. Ta'if amended that provision but kept the imperative of Christian-Muslim balance for "the civil servants of first category," that is, the general directors in the administration.

Political representation based on confessionalism has given birth to a strongly sectarian mentality that impregnated all aspects of public life as well as the mentalities. "Lebanon has erected that system to a reason of state,"[5] wrote Rabbath, who was very critical about it and was an advocate of secularism. Even city councils, union labors, bar associations, and medical orders spontaneously ensured a sectarian balance in their internal elections.

Soon the limits of the quota system were apparent. The formula turned to be a trap as it became rigid to the point of incoherence. "Confessional representation in public functions, which aimed at establishing a modus vivendi among communities, became a source of permanent conflict and put the various sectarian groups at odds with each other, because it infused a hierarchy of rights," wrote Nawaf Salam, a professor at AUB.[6] Besides, politicians and traditional notables have unabashedly exploited that system and turned it into a profitable business, building a political clientele and a constituency for themselves by dispensing patronage through a system of intermediation known as *wasta*.

Michael Hudson, who has written broadly on Lebanon politics, notes that, at one point, "power-sharing impedes what might be the transition to a more inclusive political order that would provide not just for sectarian participation but the growth and integration of a larger, more complex civil society into the body politic."[7]

In a way, communities have become the necessary intermediaries between state and citizens. "Public liberties in Lebanon were granted to communities before being secured to the citizens," remarked Rabbath, who compared Lebanon to a sort of federation of communities. Rabbath resented the fact that "those who do not belong to a specific community do not enjoy civic rights."[8] Religion, he said, governs all aspects of social and public life: birth, baptism, marriage, work, education, inheritance. Even the identity cards bear the mention of the citizen's sectarian affiliation. The post-Ta'if regime only recently took the decision to remove that mention from ID cards. In any case, it would be fair enough to wonder whether Lebanon is a nation of communities or of individuals.

Lebanese of all sides have not failed to criticize their system, as they were aware of its flaws. It has been viewed as a system aimed at securing domination of one group, the Christian Maronites, over the others, particularly the Muslims, through a set of presidential prerogatives considered as "privileges." Christians would rather speak about "guarantees" destined to offset the Arab unionist tendencies of their Muslim countrymen, until they formally acknowledged in Ta'if the "final" character of the Lebanese homeland. The exclusive and unique relationship of the Maronite community and Lebanon—the geographic and national entity—granted the Maronites a special position in the formation of the Lebanese state. This is why the dominant Maronite thinking considered Lebanon as a model of coexistence between religious communities, as a bridge between East and West, and as a "center for enlightenment" in the region, whose very existence depended upon preserving political preeminence of the Maronites within the state. Ultimately, then, any challenge to Maronite dominance was a challenge to the Lebanese entity itself.[9] And without the existence of Lebanon, in which the Maronites assumed a leading role, the whole Arab East would fall back into cultural ossification.

Another critical look at the Lebanese confessionalist system is the "merchant Republic" thesis. Those who favor that approach assert that the system that bore the generic (and dubious) name of "political maronitism" was actually ruled by an elite of Christian and Muslim landowners and merchants who stood at the top of a segmented, quasi-feudal socioeconomic structure with a highly skewed distribution of wealth and prestige. Lebanese presidents relied on key notables from each of the country's provinces (Beirut, Mount-Lebanon, North Lebanon, South Lebanon, and the Biqaa) to share in the running of the country and provide a winning coalition. These political coalitions were multi-sectarian, as were the opposition coalitions.[10] Within that distribution of power, regional antagonisms were exacerbated, sometimes inside the same community.

This bourgeois order made of Beirut Sunnis, southern Shiite feudal leaders, and Christian landlords, bankers, and merchant classes stemmed from Michel Chiha's economic vision of "Lebanon as a trading nation." This Christian thinker who was personally associated with the banking sector conceived a Lebanese entity based on confessional "equilibrium" and dominated by a Christian bourgeoisie that played the chief role in the country's capitalist service economy.

Shiite spiritual leader Sheikh Mohammed Mehdi Shamseddine is among those who scold the mercantile contract that laid the basis of the current system. "The [Lebanese] formula was laid down by the Christians for pragmatic reasons: they viewed that Christian Mount-Lebanon needed an economic vital space and so they annexed the other provinces to have a market for their products. The implementation of the formula was assumed by a set of politicians who had the mentality of contractors and entrepreneurs and thought in terms of profits and losses," he commented.[11] "Of course, some of the founders of the Lebanese state enjoyed high moral and spiritual standing and so they prevented Lebanon from turning to a total bidding project," he added.

Liberal Christian intellectuals have had some difficulties justifying or defending "political confessionalism." They viewed it as a stifling order that inhibited the plain development of citizenship. Many embraced the "contractual" theory of a cross-sectarian feudal and trading establishment that dominated Lebanon and shared the Lebanese "cake." Professor Hassan Saab[12] and writer George Corm[13] adopted the term "sectocracy" to describe the Lebanese quota system. The "National Pact" (*As-Sigha*) was discredited during the war and overtly contested by both Muslim and Christian militias. War unleashed not only a language of violence but also a range of disturbing questions regarding the coexistence formula.

Was war, for the Muslims, a means to change the rules of the game or was it an attempt to reverse the equation of power and tip the balance in their favor? The answer lay in Ta'if: tipping the balance was the issue, on the short and medium term. The outcome of Ta'if seems ambivalent anyway: does it re-establish the sectarian order or does it pave the way for its phasing out?

On the Christian side, war unveiled atavistic Christian fears underlying the "National Pact" philosophy: Christians dominated to avoid being dominated. But they did it through liberal institutions of a democratic parliamentary regime that also benefited the Muslims, since the president of the republic needed the countersignature of the prime minister at the bottom of the presidential decrees. However, in their eagerness to preserve their political edge, Maronite leaders have displayed a shortsightedness that led to fatal errors. One of these errors was to oppose the reformist orientations of General Fouad Chehab, the only Maronite president who embarked on a social program destined to bridge the gap between various Lebanese groups by providing social justice and equity to all.

When the Muslims challenged the whole system based on Christian dominance, a certain Maronite intelligentsia conceived a national project based on a federalist organization. The "Lebanese Forces" led by Samir Geagea strongly favored that option, as they thought that the Covenant failed to guarantee the political future of the Christians in a Muslim-Arab environment.

THE MEANING OF TA'IF

Interestingly enough, the post—Ta'if period has been a mind—stirring phase for all Lebanese. It has been said that the Ta'if accords have two dimensions: one internal, revolving around reforms, and one external, concerning sovereignty.[14] Most of the Christians feel it brought peace at the price of independence. And this peace was brokered by regional and international powers.

As Michael Hudson pointedly observed,[15] the Ta'if process was actually the only successful international mediation that worked in the protracted Lebanese crisis, after years of hostility to any form of "internationalization" of the solution. "Successful international interventions require indeed a minimum of acceptance on the part of the principal antagonists, domestic and external." But more important is the fact that, on the internal level, Ta'if brought an end to the war by involving the militias in the political process: warlords were offered seats in government and parliament, and militiamen were incorporated in the national army. In so doing, Ta'if went through the supreme stage of the sectarianist system.

In his essay on military integration in postwar Lebanon, General Jamil Sayyed acknowledged that "the Lebanese war ended with a political settlement between the conflicting parties, at the behest of regional and international forces. Warlords thus became the Statelords. In other words, the Ta'if settlement obligated the chiefs of militias to give up their weapons in exchange for a seat in State offices."[16]

In that regard, Ta'if was what many called it "a necessary evil." This conviction reveals an implicit and shared admission that Ta'if is only a process rather than a durable solution. Which necessarily brings up the question: does the long-appraised Lebanese formula still have any realistic prospects for the future? Or is Lebanon—and other multi-ethnic and multi-religious places like the Balkans—doomed to a fateful cycle of wars every two or three generations? Do pluralistic societies carry within their weave the seeds of their implosion?

"Not if they choose the democratic path of consensus and of national loyalty rather than particularism," replies Jesuit general prefect Kolvenbach. "This is why the Synod insisted on the de-cloistering [not the suppression] of the communities."[17] "Our democracy must lie on our National Pact, for we are essentially a Covenant State [*mîthaq*]. The post-[French] mandate State was grounded on the 1943 Pact, and the post-civil war State was built on the 1989 Pact [Ta'if]," wrote Mohammad Sammak. "We want the utmost of democracy, yet its limits are only defined by the National Pact."[18] Noticeably, Sammak points to the fact that "Muslims accepted in Ta'if a democratic formula based on [demographic] inequality,"[19] and he insists that Christian-Muslim political equality was consecrated under the auspices of the Muslim Wahabite Kingdom of Saudi Arabia itself, despite the numerical inequality of both parties.

One of the founding tenets of the Lebanese state has been engraved in the introduction of the Ta'if constitution as its fundamental principle: "There is no legitimacy to a power that violates the Pact of national co-existence." All is said in these few and measured words. Ta'if is a major achievement in that it has formally proclaimed that power in Lebanon draws its legitimacy from its ability to maintain the "vouloir vivre en commun," the will of living together, and that conviviality between all the Lebanese is the "raison d'être" of this country. Behind that profession of faith, Ta'if intended to defuse the frustration of the Muslims who estimated they were under-represented in political and administrative posts, and the qualms of the Christians who worried for the future of the Lebanese entity if Muslims took power. In that respect, "the Ta'if accord represents, much better than all the military ventures in which both camps have engaged since 1975, the first real step of the Lebanese to regain possession of their own common destiny," as a group of Maronite intellectuals put it in an outstanding self-critical "reflection on the crisis of the Maronite community" triggered by the Synod phase.[20] And their document goes on: "While the Ta'if accord granted the Muslims their legitimate rights, it has forced them to change their attitude. By becoming equal partners, they are bound to assume their responsibilities in a system in which they are no longer victims but actors." Indeed, the Ta'if agreement was meant to compel each group to assume its share in the shaping of the future and to get rid of the "victim syndrome" or the "conspiracy theory" entrenched in Lebanese mentality.

At the same time, Ta'if explicitly states a procedure for ending "political confessionalism." But it does not rule out sectarian representation, since the Ta'if agreement provides for creating a bicameral Parliament made up of a lower house elected on a non-sectarian basis and a Senate representing "all of Lebanon's religious families." But the new system is to be introduced once sectarianism in politics (known as "political confessionalism") is abolished.

WHO WANTS TO ABOLISH CONFESSIONALISM?

Abolition of political confessionalism has always been a stated objective of the Lebanese Constitution, ever since day one of Independence. But Ta'if in practice has deepened sectarian segmentation, especially in the top executive institutions. This is why there is a common perception among the Christians (shared by various Sunni and Druze leaders and intellectuals) that those who call for desectarianizing the political system are actually seeking to replace it with the rule of majority. Druze deputy and former minister Marwan Hamadé queried the government in a Parliament session: "Which de-confessionalisation is the government talking about? Political, religious, administrative? If it is all this together, why not speak of secularism? Is it to hide the real objective or to set an unrealistic goal so that sectarianism keeps corroding Lebanon and its institutions?"[21]

In that fiery bout over the future of political sectarianism in Lebanon, the Shiite community is the worrying factor for the other Lebanese communities. Sheikh Shamseddine had advocated, on various occasions, the advent of what he called a "numeric democracy," spreading the malaise among the various minority groups that form the Lebanese mosaic. But his adviser Seoud el-Mawla affirmed that the Shiite religious leader discarded that idea "because it frightens the Christians."[22] "We want to find another system that would be accepted by the Christians," he added. "Those have a great responsibility in that process: even if they don't trust their Muslim counterpart, they must do their best to engage him into a shared reflection on the elaboration of a new political system. Together, we can face Muslim and Christian fundamentalism." These enlightened words were uttered during a roundtable destined to evaluate the visit of John Paul II to Lebanon in May 1997. The Apostolic Exhortation had been welcomed by all Lebanese and inspired a general meditation that was not devoid of self-criticism.

"Abolition of political confessionalism" as stated in the Ta'if constitution could only be, in the view of many constitutionalists, a "transitory phase to something else." One cannot set loose a society that looks more like an ethno-religious kaleidoscope, and hand it over to the rule of majority after decades of communal and proportionate representation. This is a recipe for a renewed war. In a pluralistic society, the rule of majority becomes a factor of inequality and injustice, not of democracy.

There is a temptation in the West to mix up political desectarianization and secularism. For many Western scholars, it is all too natural that sectarianism should be banned from politics on the way to further democratization and political inclusiveness. "Salvation for Lebanon requires movement toward non-sectarian politics and lessening of class barriers," writes Charles Winslow.[23] "Because religious leaders cannot deliver the goods in a global economic and political system, the religion disease will run its course once outsiders stop subsidizing it."

A big misunderstanding on the Western side and a religious obstacle on the Muslim side are underpinning the dialectics on political sectarianism: secularism or laicism is a concept Muslim clerics say it is incompatible with Islam. It has been staunchly rejected by Muslims every time Christians have advocated it. It has even become an automated process for the Christian intelligentsia to oppose secularism to the Muslim demand of political deconfessionalisation, on the ground that one cannot stop halfway in the process of desectarianisation.

In postwar Lebanon, fear of the unknown and of "the other" has nourished both the attachment of the Lebanese to their traditional *za'amat* (leaderships) and the vested interests of the ruling classes and of religious hierarchies of all sides. It is thus easy to explain the huge uproar that accompanied a project of civil marriage championed by former President Elias Hrawi in February 1998. For once, Christian and Muslim religious leaders were united in a common "holy war" against the scourges of secularism and opposed the civil marriage proposal, which was not even a compulsory project but an optional one! Only a few Christian and Muslim intellectuals showed public support for the project, alongside university students. This concerted opposition revealed (if needed be!) the ingrained sectarianism that entangles the Lebanese society like an inescapable web.

Whatever their sectarian affiliation, Lebanese know that abolition of confessionalism would induce irreversible and drastic changes in the Lebanese system and society. It would scuttle the establishment of power-sharing. It also threatened to alter the Lebanese identity itself.

A CONSENSUAL DEMOCRACY

"Lebanon stands out in the region thanks to its legacy of democratic management of pluralism, consensus and conflict, and a dogged struggle for liberties," says Professor Antoine Messarra.[24]

Messarra has been for years the unrelenting advocate of consensual democracy, or what he calls the "consociative democracy," in which no community has immutable rights to the detriment of other groups but where mechanisms of governance rely on a consensus and a customary organization of power (including coalition governments, veto right, and proportionality) based on equal opportunities in power-sharing. He is convinced that the consensual type of democracy will extend to various countries witnessing a resurgence of cultural identities and claims of participation from minority groups.

In a multi-communal country such as Lebanon, "consensus," "participation," "dialogue," but also "compromise" (translated from the Arabic *tassouya*, meaning settlement), and even "concession" are key words of the political vocabulary. In a plural society, no one can get it all. The irrevocable fate of living together makes it necessary to negotiate and compromise; it transforms mediation and moderation into national virtues.

Former majority leader in the U.S. Senate George Mitchell, who brokered the historic Northern Ireland agreement in April 1998, established a parallel between the Middle East and Northern Ireland. He stressed that one of the main needs to achieve resolution of conflicts "is a willingness to compromise. Peace and political stability are not achievable between sharply divided societies unless there is a genuine willingness to understand the other point of view and to enter into principled compromise."[25]

One of the Ta'if provisions underlines the consensual aspect of decision-making. The constitution explicitly mentions that "the executive body [i.e., the Council of Ministers] takes its decisions on a consensual basis, and would resort to voting in case consensus is impossible to reach" (article 65).

Antoine Messarra is also aware that a confessional system undermines the accountability system. By identifying each community with one official charge (the Maronites with the presidency of the republic, the Sunnis with the presidency of government, and the Shi'ites with the presidency of Parliament), it personalizes the institutions. Holding politicians accountable equates with penalizing their respective community, or so it is perceived. But Messarra observes that "political development does not consist in shifting from a consensual model—although rigid at times—to a competitive one, but to respect the natural evolution of each system."[26] Even a secular society like the American society somehow could not rely only on the competitive system. Americans had to take into consideration the pluralistic features of their society. Affirmative action, implemented thirty years ago, has been a deliberate commitment for inclusion of minority groups in universities and other areas.

Most delicate is the balancing act between the promotion of citizens' rights and equality and the preservation of communities' rights and equality. How is it possible to promote these without infringing on those and vice versa? Sometimes, the dilemma could translate into having to choose between a weak state, unable to enforce a public policy but securing participation for all its minority groups, and a strong and efficient state that ignores communal representability but secures equality for all its citizens.

THE NUMERIC FACTOR

The challenge posed to all Lebanese by the issue of "political confessionalism" is big. John Paul II specifically urged them to come out with a "model of coexistence" applicable not only in Lebanon but in all countries where Christians and Muslims live together.

Father Michel Hayek differentiates between the Pact (*mîthaq*) and the formula (*sîgha*). "The former, which pertains to the symbol, is inalienable and non-negotiable. It is the guarantor of coexistence. The latter is adaptable because it reflects a legal and social order, always perfectible."[27] In Hayek's view, Lebanon is a spiritual Pact among its various religious families before being a political or an economic one.

In that perspective, would the founding Pact of the Lebanese entity still be preserved if political confessionalism was abolished? Would the Pact transcend the very formal and numeric aspects of the formula? In other words, would it guarantee political participation and equality for minorities in the governing process and respect of their religious and cultural rights regardless of their demographic size?

How crucial is the demographic issue in defining the role of Oriental Christians in the Arab world? With no hefty counterpart (i.e., the Christian one) translated into a significant demographic balance justifying power-sharing, does the Pact hold on? Would Muslims share power with a demographically non-equal partner?

The numeric argument is undoubtedly a determinant factor, for both Christians and Muslims. It has been first used by bishop Nicolas Murad (1796–1862) in his writings, to justify Christian rule over the Emirate.[28] Still, from the birth of democratic thinking in Mount-Lebanon (early nineteenth century), Christians have pondered how to sway between confessionalism and democracy. In Lebanon's twenty-first century, this dilemma is more acute than ever, and many believe it is up to the Muslims to contribute to an adequate solution, since the numeric equation has been reversed.

Liberal thinkers and advocates of dialogue like Seoud el-Mawla are aware that "Christian youth think it is incumbent on the Muslims to bear a greater responsibility since they are the ones who wield more political power. So Muslims must take up the challenge, they should not yield to the rapture of power and think they are stronger because they are more numerous."[29]

For the two visionaries and high priests of Maronity, Michel Hayek and Yoakim Moubarac, Christians can only compensate their demographic decline by the quality of their presence. It is the essence of their mission.

"We should not stress on the numeric aspect," says Father Michel Hayek. "What counts is our moral, intellectual, and spiritual assets. We ought to be an elite in the Orient, the leaven in the dough. But are we forging an elite today?" To Father Yoakim Moubarac, human rights and civil citizenship ought to be the anthem of the Christians. He breaks a taboo by asking for "the substitution of communities rights in Lebanon with human rights, under the banner of civil citizenship."[30] Moubarac summons the Christians to give more importance to social and economic reforms, in order to promote social justice and development in their environment and thus eliminate the causes of frustration and extremism. He also sees Christians' role in the advancement of a public education that would foster integration.

Building a vibrant civil society is certainly the best bet for national harmony. Christians and Muslims are increasingly engaged in common fights for democracy, public freedoms, and economic development. Union labors, professional associations, and business deals are probably the most effective tools of a natural evolution toward integration.

On the political level, Antoine Messarra recommends a change in the ideology of the Presidency of the Republic. "To safeguard their presence and their participation, the Maronites, and by and large all Christians, should bet on their Cabinet ministers, their deputies and their parties, rather than identify with the Presidency of the Republic and force it to become partisan," he wrote.[31] "The logics of a consensual system require that the head of State be left outside the stakes in power-sharing. He should be the supreme arbiter, exerting a moral magistrature that goes beyond its small attributions, overseeing the State of law and preserving the public interest. He is the guardian of the principles of legality, national unity and independence."

WHOSE DECISION IS IT ANYWAY?

"Political deconfessionalisation will be the ultimate battle of the Christians of Lebanon," said a Roman prelate in a private meeting during the Synod. While arguing over it, the Lebanese have been convinced however that neither its initiative nor its timing was in their hands. Which meant it could be decided any time when they are not psychologically and institutionally prepared for this giant leap. Thus the pressure has been great, living under the Damocles sword.

A few weeks before the Lebanese parliamentary elections of summer 1992, U.S. Secretary of State James Baker and his Assistant Secretary for NEA, Edward Djerejian, met in Damascus with President Hafez Assad. Vice president Abdel-Halim Khaddam attended the meeting. When Secretary Baker raised the issue of Syrian troops redeployment in Lebanon according to the Ta'if agreement, he was told that this would only happen after the organization of the ballot in Lebanon. "But this is not the interpretation agreed upon in Ta'if, when the document was drafted under the auspices of Saudi Arabia, Algeria and Morocco (the Arab tripartite committee)," Baker insisted.

"What's important is our interpretation. Lebanon is our turf," replied the Syrian president, placidly.

The U.S. Secretary of State stood up and turned to Djerejian: "Why don't you explain to Mr. President our position on that subject," he said, and he left the room. At this point, Khaddam intervened: "The Ta'if accords state that our troops will redeploy after the constitutional reforms have been implemented in Lebanon."

"They have been achieved," retorted Djerejian.

"Not all of them. There is still the issue of political deconfessionalization."

The next day, the Syrian vice president publicly declared that Syrian troops will redeploy only once the abolition of political confessionalism has been voted in Parliament.[32]

The message did not fall on deaf ears: for Lebanese, it meant the "choice" was either Syrian presence or the termination of the constitutional guarantee of power-sharing and the unleashing of some fundamentalist claims for a majority rule. Between a rock and a hard place....

Yet, the Maronite Patriarch had been adamant when he reaffirmed the unflagging commitment of the Christians to freedom. "If Lebanese are put in the difficult situation of having to choose between conviviality and freedom, History taught us that the Lebanese people, and the Christians first, will not hesitate, they will choose freedom."[33] The premise of that position is that without freedom anyway, would there be coexistence?

Chapter 12

John Paul II in Lebanon

The Pope's visit to Lebanon was scheduled for the weekend of May 10–11, 1997. His journey was endowed with political meaning, no matter how hard his Nuncio in Beirut tried to portray it as a "pastoral visit." This was the first trip of the Roman Pontiff to the region. Monsignor Pablo Puente and John Paul II's advisers in the Vatican were indeed vigilant not to fan any political susceptibility or controversy and to avoid any political exploitation of the visit in a tinderbox such as the Middle East.

"Lebanon is the mailbox of the region, but the messages are usually bombs," Puente had once remarked when the newly appointed French ambassador to Beirut visited him in Harissa. According to the BBC, the Italian intelligence services were concerned about a possible criminal attempt against the Pope's life in Beirut. An earlier visit of John Paul II in 1994 had been canceled after the bombing of the Zouk Church, in the Christian suburbs of Beirut, which killed twelve worshipers and wounded over sixty, and the subsequent indictment of Samir Geagea.[1]

While Nuncio Puente toured the political and religious establishment in Beirut to "test the waters" and explain the purpose and the formalities of the Pontiff's trip, Archbishop Jean-Louis Tauran went to Damascus. This visit sparked off mixed feelings among the Christians. It was an explicit recognition by the Holy See of Syria's influence in Lebanon. Christian opposition leaders feared the Pope's visit to Lebanon would consecrate a *fait accompli* and give credit to a government viewed as "a mere puppet." But then, the Lebanese had to be realistic and even Bishop Bechara Rahi took a moderate stand: "Monsignor Tauran's visit to Damascus was justified," he said. "The Vatican cannot ignore the pivotal role of Syrian officials in the settlement of the Lebanese crisis."[2]

One of the most noticeable results of Tauran's discussions in Damascus was the accreditation of a Syrian ambassador to the Holy See. Although Syria established diplomatic relations with the Holy See in 1966, its ambassador to Italy was also its representative to the Vatican. As of July 30, 1996, the post to the Holy See was vacant. On April 24, 1997, over two weeks before the Pope's visit to Lebanon, Syria's newly appointed ambassador to the Vatican, Greek Catholic Elias Najmeh, presented his letters of credentials, but he resided in Paris.[3] Through Tauran, the Syrian officials also extended an invitation to the Pope to visit Damascus. They were told that the Pope would eventually do so when he initiates his Abrahamic tour in the region, as he was planning to.

One of the main concerns of the Syrians was that the Pope's visit and the mass he was planning to celebrate wouldn't turn into a political rally. It was thus important to emphasize the "pastoral" aspect of the visit. So Damascus was reassured that the Pope wouldn't take political stands and that, in his speeches, he wouldn't directly mention its military presence in Lebanon. Since the release of the Final Message of the Synod in 1995, the Holy See had indeed adopted a more lenient position regarding Syria, in the line of Realpolitik.

In Lebanon, Christian expectations of John Paul II's historic trip were high. The parallel with Karol Wojtyla's first trip to Poland was irresistible. People had in mind the changes it brought about and the demise of the Soviet empire a few years later. Once again, prominent figures such as former Foreign Minister Fouad Boutros preached a realistic outlook: "Lebanon is not Poland," he observed, "even if the Pope told me in 1979 when I met him: 'Your country reminds me of Poland'. In Poland, the Americans and the CIA were involved in the transformation process and the Pope's visit was a catalyst that accelerated the process at the popular level. This is not the case in Lebanon."[4]

Still, at the minimum, John Paul II's visit was expected to reinvigorate the Christians and invite them to remain attached to their land. It would be, at least, "a blast of fresh air," as many a journalist wrote.

By and large, the visit prompted an outpouring of goodwill across the broad spectrum of society: from Prime Minister Rafik Hariri, who traveled to the Vatican to help arrange the trip, to such Muslim leaders as Sheikh Mohammed Mehdi Shamseddine and Sheikh Mohammad Hussein Fadlallah. Former Speaker of Parliament Hussein Husseini observed that the Holy See had always been supportive of Lebanon's unity and coexistence. He said the Synod actually confirmed the principles laid down in Tai'f. The "national entente" document, Husseini added, started maturing in 1985, after a visit he personally accomplished to the Vatican, while he was in office.[5]

Even Hezbollah militants did not want to be seen as opponents of reconciliation. On May 6, four days before the Pope's arrival to Lebanon, a Hezbollah delegation went to the Nuncio's residence in Harissa to deliver a message to the Supreme Pontiff. They hoped he would mention the plight of the South under Israeli occupation and that Vatican statements would favor Israeli withdrawal from Southern Lebanon. They also insisted they are not a fundamentalist threat to coexistence and to the Christians, highlighting instead their resistance goal.

The issues of the peace process and of Jerusalem, and the recognition of Israel by the Vatican, were very much on the mind of Muslim clerics such as Fadlallah. Extremists such as the late leader of the Sunni Islamic Unification Movement in Tripoli (close to the Muslim Brothers), Sheikh Shaaban, said the Pope should present "excuses" for his "support" to Israel. The general secretary of Hezbollah, Sheikh Nasrallah, said "a disciple of Christ cannot but condemn the injustice incarnated by Israel."[6] Most of all, religious leaders in the Middle East had been mostly sensitive to the statement of the Holy Father about the "Judaism of Christ," when he had received Israeli Prime Minister Benyamin Netanyahu in the Vatican. This declaration provoked an outcry of indignation among Muslim and Christian Arabs as well, to which Pope Chenouda III of the Copts associated himself.

From Damascus, where he participated in the meeting of the Middle East Council of Churches held only a few days before the Pope's trip to Lebanon,[7] he stated that "the orientations of the Pope of Rome are different from the orientations of all Eastern Christians." "Eastern Churches," he added, "share the sufferings of that region, while the Western Church does not know anything about it."[8]

This hodgepodge of reactions destined to curtail or minimize the Roman Pontiff's visit to the Levant were soon eclipsed by the momentous event of John Paul II's landing on the soil of Lebanon, "on the footsteps of Christ," as he said. Gifted with an instinct for communication, the Holy Father captured the spirits and the hearts of the people, during his thirty-six hour stay (the episodes of which were transmitted live on major TV networks).

The Lebanese authorities feverishly prepared for the event, but they were apprehensive. The consequences of the whirlwind tours of John Paul II have always been unpredictable. What if the Pontiff dropped a word criticizing the regime for shunting the Christians toward the margins or trampling on human rights and public freedoms? Banderoles bearing the mentions "sovereignty," "independence," and "liberty," were banned. Yet they would appear along the avenues taken by the Popemobile. Security measures were tight. The Lebanese Armed Forces were in charge of the

Pope's safety as well as the good organization of his visit. Some 20,000 soldiers and police were placed along the Pope's route.

On the Alitalia flight that carried him to Lebanon, the Pope was asked by foreign journalists if he thought his visit might give credit to the Syrian occupation of the country. "I am going to Lebanon, a sovereign Lebanon," John Paul II replied, tersely.[9]

AN UNFORGETTABLE ENCOUNTER

In this sunny afternoon of May, "the month of Mary" in Lebanon, the illustrious silhouette of the man in his white cassock appeared on the steps of the plane. When he waved his hand in greeting and blessing, sweeping with his penetrating eyes the land of Lebanon, its sea and its mountains stretching across the horizon, there was a whiff of emotion in the air. All bells throughout Lebanon pealed over and over. The official Republic was lined up on the tarmac to welcome him.

The whole population was riveted to its TV screens, as the Pope was handed a lump of earth to kiss, like he always did on every soil he landed. The main boulevards were bedecked with signs and flags, and banners welcoming him adorned the streets of the capital. Rows of young Muslim boys and girls awaited him in the southern suburbs of Beirut and cheered him with the Vatican flags, on his way from the airport to the Baabda palace, where he met with the officials but also with the spiritual leaders of the three Muslim communities.

Jostled by the crowd of politicians who wanted a picture with him, the ailing Pope looked sad and ruffled at times, his mind somewhere else, his posture more stooped than ever. It is a totally different man who met later in the evening with the Lebanese youth, in what turned to be the climax of his visit to Lebanon.

The encounter took place under the beatific gaze of "Our Lady of Harissa," who stands as an emblem of the special bond that has long linked the Catholics of Lebanon to Rome. The Marian sanctuary was erected by common accord of the Apostolic Delegate, Monsignor Duval, and the Maronite Patriarchate. It was inaugurated on May 3, 1908. In the basilica of Harissa, John Paul II met with over 50,000 young Christians from all regions of Lebanon, who were waving colored handkerchiefs and singing "El-Baba," as he is known in Lebanon. It is there that the Holy Father signed and promulgated his 194-page "Apostolic Exhortation" on Lebanon, entitled: "A New Hope for Lebanon." As he told them, he wanted the youths to be "the recipient of the message of renewal your Church and your country need." The words that were said in Harissa that evening were of utmost importance.

Overwhelmed with the heat and the raucous atmosphere within the walls of the cathedral, John Paul II changed the program: surrounded with the crimson and violet birettas of his cardinals, he stood outdoors, where he oversaw the throngs of youths gathered at the feet of Our Lady's statue. "What a beautiful horizon !" he said as he watched the sun setting in the Mediterranean. It was a minute of closeness. His communicative talents operated. The whole world knows that John Paul II loves young people. In their presence, he uncorks all his charm. He was rejuvenated by the contact with the youth chanting their love to him. But he was also aware of the sheer dramatic power of this moment. How could the Slavic Pope ignore that the hands and faces of these young were raised to him as their ultimate hope and support? Several of them held up their wrists handcuffed and their mouths muffled with their handkerchiefs.

The Pope spoke in a strong, clear voice. "Dear young, do not fear to let Christ walk by your side like the disciples of Emmaus. You are the treasure of Lebanon.... Bring down the walls erected in the painful past, don't raise new barricades in your country. Build new bridges of communication among people, families and communities. Make gestures of reconciliation that will turn distrust into trust. The changes you are aspiring for in your country start with a transformation of the hearts. Don't forget your Christian identity. It is your glory, it is your hope, it is your mission. . . . May the Virgin Mary, Our Lady of Lebanon, assist you in flowering Lebanon again, this piece of the Holy Lands God cherishes."

Cries of "freedom" and "peace" flashed across the cathedral.

John Paul II sent another message of hope: "There are times when God is silent like on Holy Thursday, times of distress like on Good Friday, when we think God has abandoned those He loves. But Easter Day always comes, representing the final victory of Life over Death. Trust in God like Jesus did." A clamor of approval rose to him.

"I see that you have listened well to me and that you applauded when you ought to," the Holy Father remarked. "And I must tell you that I have also paid attention to you. I understand your aspirations and your impatience." By these words, he established a bond of complicity with his audience. The Pope was buoyed by the wild enthusiasm of these young, who were even clutching at the trees like clusters of human grapes. When they chanted "John Paul II, we love you," he calmly observed: "Why don't you say it in Arabic?" The remark was clearly allusive. It did not go unnoticed. The Roman Pontiff called the Christian youth of Lebanon to identify with its Arabic culture.

Although his language was circumspect and he steered clear of internal political issues, he gave room to the young for their freedom of speech. Two delegates spoke in the Basilica, in the name of the Lebanese youth. Their words had not been previewed or censored by any clerical or official authority, so the surprise was complete as the nation watched them live on TV voicing their frustration and asking the Pope to "speak out loud what we dare not say." The call was poignant. "Holy Father, be our courage and call the things by their name. Be our cry of grief and bring our voice to the world," asked student Pierre Najm. "The pacification they insist on calling peace did not heal the souls. It rebuilt cities but not the society, which is hemmed in a lack of real intercommunal dialogue, disguised violence, injustice and absence of sovereignty and independence. Our very existence of Christians seems imperiled to us as well as this Lebanon-message, like you call it."

The Maronite patriarch Sfeir echoed the young, in his speech in front of the Roman Pontiff: "Our youth is deprived from its right to assume political responsibilities and to build a society based on democracy, human rights, justice and equality, although it has shown generosity on the social level in defending just and noble causes."

The moving and intimate evening with His Holiness came to an end after the Pope received gifts, among them a silver sculpture representing him, carved by a young Muslim. He also showed great tenderness to the handicapped, victims of the war, whom he embraced and kissed on their foreheads, holding their hands in his for minutes.

Lebanon's "coup de foudre" for John Paul II would prove unfailing the next day. The open-air mass on Sunday morning was to take place by the seaside, on a landfill created with the debris of buildings destroyed in the war, next to the port of Beirut and a few blocks from the place of Martyrs, the devastated heart of the capital now under reconstruction. The emplacement had been chosen by the Holy See, it had a symbolic significance: downtown Beirut was once the thriving center where Lebanese of all communities interconnected in work and recreation.

Local organizers—including the Church and Hariri's staff in Solidere—created an elaborate construction surmounting the altar. The canopy above the tabernacle was shaped like a Cedar of Lebanon and yellow lights filtered behind each "branch," steeping the platform on which the Pope would celebrate the mass in a celestial ambiance. The snow-capped mountain range serving as a backdrop, the blue glittering sea lying ahead, and the dense buildings of the capital on the western flank could be no better setting for the historic triumph that awaited the Pope.

In the few weeks before John Paul II's arrival, the church had increased efforts in schools and parishes to mobilize its flocks and encourage them to go down to the streets and welcome the Pope. Christian TV networks were put into contribution through video-clips and special programs to shake up the blue mood of the Christians. Organizers expected no more than 150,000 people to attend the mass.

Neither the Pope himself nor the Maronite patriarch who stood next to him in the glass-walled Popemobile, neither the officials of the country nor its people, Christians and Muslims alike, expected to see the human ocean that inundated the streets, as the special car of the Roman Pontiff crawled through the waves of yellow and white flags brandished by the people. From Jounieh, fifteen kilometers north of the capital, to the port of Beirut, over 100,000 faithful lined up both sides of the roads. As the Popemobile approached Beirut's harbor, the stupefaction had seized international and national media as well: over half a million people chanted "Viva el Papa," waving the Vatican and the Lebanese flags, under a burning sun. Many had spent the night there, a good number had come from abroad to witness that historic moment. The cardinals and bishops were stunned as they watched the gigantic throng acclaiming the Pope. "Lebanon has welcomed the Pope like Poland did," confided a member of the Pontiff's delegation.[10] Patriarch Sfeir could not believe his eyes. He was stirred: so the Church really wasn't on the decline and the Christians of Lebanon were still able to mobilize in great numbers. They were present and alive! The figures could not lie.

To draw 550,000 people[11] in a country of 3.5 million was incredible. It was something of a revelation. "It is the first time since the end of the war that we see the Christians wake up, gather in the streets and express themselves. We have regained hope," commented one eminent journalist.[12] Lebanese officials who came to attend the mass with their wives were dazzled. Authorities said it was the largest crowd ever assembled in Lebanese history.

The Popemobile dived into the bubbling cauldron of the jubilant crowd. It was strewn with rose petals and rice. His face turned red by the sweltering heat of May and by the emotion, the Supreme Pontiff scanned with tenderness and attention the faces and the hands lifted toward him. He opened the window and reached out to a child. He spent thirty minutes in his Popemobile riding through the lanes separating the sections into which the crowd had been subdivided. A few portraits of Samir Geagea and Michel Aoun made a brief appearance in the multitude. When the Supreme Pontiff reached the altar, the Syriac and Byzantine choirs of Christian Orient sent their "Kyrie" and "Alleluia" to the sky.

All Eastern Catholic and Orthodox Patriarchs and bishops were gathered around the altar, in the diversity of their rites and history: Armenians, Chaldeans, Maronites, Syriac, Copts, Melkites. One by one, they welcomed the "bishop of Rome," the patriarch of Western Christendom, who was holding his staff. These representatives of early Christianity were the living chain that linked Rome to the geographical and spiritual sources of its faith.

"As salam lakoum," said John Paul II to the crowd.[13]

Then, in the name of Eastern Christianity and the Church of Lebanon, the Maronite patriarch stood up. "This visit that we have long been waiting for is a balm on our wounds," he said in French and in a loud voice that resonated. "I want to repeat the words of Polish cardinal Wyszynski when he welcomed you during your first visit to your fatherland:[14] 'Our hearts are dancing of joy in your hands, and so is the soul of Lebanon, with all its nobleness and loyalty.'" Sfeir compared the Holy Father's visit to "the Lord's visit to Sidon, two thousand years ago." He evoked the marks of solicitude of John Paul II during the Lebanese war, his personal endeavors to draw the international community's attention to the Lebanese tragedy, and finally his ultimate effort represented by the Synod for Lebanon. "This Synod has given the Christians the opportunity to think, to get closer to each other, to forgive and to reconcile. It has also allowed all the Lebanese to discuss certain aspects of their common life together."

When the Pope delivered his speech, all the Lebanese held their breath. He reiterated "the love of the Church and of the Holy See for Lebanon and all the Lebanese, Christians and Muslims." He sent "a special greeting to Muslim and Druze leaders." "We want the world to know the importance of Lebanon, its historical mission. For centuries, this country has demonstrated that multiple communities can live together in peace, fraternity and cooperation, that freedom of religion for each person can be respected, and that all are united in their common devotion to their homeland and in the preservation of the spiritual heritage of their fathers, especially the monk Saint Maron." He stressed on the antique roots of Christianity in Lebanon: "Lord Jesus himself was the first preacher of your ancestors. What an extraordinary privilege! Your country is a biblical land." Speaking of Tyre and Sidon, he mentioned the sufferings of Southern Lebanon and prayed for "a just and lasting peace in the Middle East." Then his voice was slurred, a symptom of his Parkinson's disease. Yet, the silence was so complete in the crowd, a gentle breeze rustled the small yellow and white flags.

Suddenly his voice rose. "I say it with confidence: the Holy Spirit will renew the face of your land." So strong was his power of communication and prayer that when he uttered these words, tears of joy welled in people's eyes. Muslim and Christian presidents and politicians seated on the first row were all moved, as was the crowd. He pursued: "The sufferings of past years are not vain; they will strengthen your freedom and unity." It was one of those moments where all were united in a common prayer and a sudden consciousness of their common destiny. It was no doubt a moment of reconciliation for Christians and Muslims alike, with themselves, with each other, with the one God in which they all believed.

The man who presided over this moment ended on a prayer: "Spirit of God, pour your light and your love into human hearts to achieve reconciliation between individuals, within families, between neighbors, in cities and villages, and within the institutions of civil society."

Later that day, John Paul II said Lebanon should become "ever more democratic, in the full independence of its institutions and in recognition of its borders, which are indispensable conditions to guarantee its integrity as a nation." He urged Lebanese to put aside their differences and make their country into a model of Christian-Muslim harmony. He finally emphasized his dominant theme: Lebanon's future depends on establishing forgiveness and dialogue as the guiding values in personal life and public policy.

Before he embarked on the plane, back to Rome, the Holy Father turned once again and blessed this land he held in affection, a land that was fanned by the wind of change it longed for.

One week later, as he presided over a mass in St.-Peter's square, he appealed to the international community "in order to preserve Lebanon's peace, because peace is the real mission of Lebanon, based on the cultural pluralism and the respect among its various communities." In his authorized biography of John Paul II, American author and theologian George Weigel wrote: "For some months afterward, guests in the papal apartment in the Vatican noticed a Lebanese tablecloth, decorated with embroidered cedars, on the Pope's dining room table. Like the "martyr-city" of Sarajevo, what he had termed "martyr-Lebanon" was a country he was determined the world would not forget."[15]

THE MARONITE RESPONSIBILITY

The Pope entrusted the Maronites with a new mission. Officials, media, clerics, and the average citizen noticed the special honor made to Patriarch Nasrallah Sfeir, and through him, to the Maronite Church. Sfeir accompanied the Supreme Pontiff in his Popemobile, greeted him at the overture of the gigantic mass, just as he did the night before in Harissa. (He, of course, did not fail to insist on the need for Lebanon to recover its full sovereignty, independence, and free will.) Most of all, it is to the Maronite Patriarch that the Pope personally handed over his "Apostolic Exhortation" during the mass, in front of the Eastern Patriarchs and bishops and the political leaders, in a symbolic gesture broadcast live on satellite TV throughout the Arab world. Having done that, he embraced him. Sfeir assured him that the Apostolic Exhortation "will serve as a guide on the way to a genuine civil peace."

This demonstration of the Roman Pontiff's affection was not only due to the long history of Maronites' loyalty to Rome.[16] By distinguishing the

Maronite Church, John Paul II was also ascribing it a big responsibility: the implementation of his message to the Catholics of Lebanon, and through them, to the Catholics and Christians of the Middle East. The Apostolic Exhortation was the most important document for Eastern Catholic Churches since Vatican II, it was their new Magna Carta, a modern Constitution for oriental Christians, according to both Christians and Muslims.

No issue has been neglected in the papal document. It was a subtle blend of spiritual preoccupations and political realities. Spiritual renewal was at the core of the Pope's message to the Catholics of Lebanon and the Middle East, and various passages bore his personal stamp. This renewal started from within before expanding to reach out to other communities: to non-Catholic Christians, through ecumenical dialogue, and to Muslims, through national dialogue.

"Unity in diversity" of the various churches was an important concept of the Apostolic Exhortation. The document also called for "prophetic gestures of reconciliation" among Christians, Muslims, and political leaders. The Pope recommended the Catholic churches to preserve the diversity of their liturgical and spiritual traditions, the specificity of their oriental roots, and to increase their cooperation through the Assembly of Catholic Patriarchs and Bishops in Lebanon. He also stressed on the importance of building bridges with the Greek Orthodox Church, by "rediscovering and deepening the Antiochian tradition that both Eastern Catholic Churches and Greek Orthodox have in common." He said the Middle East Council of Churches is the perfect framework for ecumenical dialogue. The Pope expressed his hope that it might lead to a common celebration of Easter and a common Arabic text of the Creed and "Our Father." When he was in Lebanon, he had also met with the heads of the Greek Orthodox and Protestant Churches in his residence in Harissa.

The immersion into one's spiritual and cultural environment was pretty much the leitmotiv of the Apostolic Exhortation. "Christianity," it said, "is an essential element of the culture of the region, and in particular, of the Lebanese land, with its many religious traditions."[17] Since "the national and political identity of Lebanon has religious roots," "the fate of the Catholics is profoundly bound to the fate of Lebanon and to its specific vocation."[18]

And the fate of Lebanon was in the hands of both Christians and Muslims. They were "partners in the reconstruction of the country" and this implied "the respect of the cultural and spiritual traditions" of each group, "true recognition of essential freedoms," "the preservation of each others' rights," "justice and equality before the law," and "the opportunity for each to share responsibility in social life." In these paragraphs, the Pope addressed the concerns of the beleaguered Christian communities, who felt they were becoming second-class citizens. He called on the Lebanese authorities to "establish a social and political system that would be fair, equitable" and that "would not disregard with impunity the rights and obligations of the persons, or of cultural and spiritual communities." He said mutual respect and dialogue were the "primordial conditions for the construction and survival of a democratic Lebanon." The papal document emphasized on the fact that equal participation for all in the nation's affairs is a fundamental right. It condemned any dominating tendency or "search for privileges, for oneself or for one's own community." In the Apostolic Exhortation, human rights, equality, and democracy were elevated above the law and the Constitution, they became the yardsticks by which a just political system is measured. "To trample on human rights is to trample on God's rights," the Pope affirmed.[19] "Common good" is "the foundation of the political and moral legitimacy of authority and laws."[20] When uttered by him, the tenets of the Catholic faith would become revolutionary principles, a force of change.

The prerequisites of "total independence, complete sovereignty and unambiguous freedom" were not forgotten. In his way, the Pope said it all. He did mention both Israeli occupation and Syrian troops without naming them. They ranked first in the list of the most important current difficulties of Lebanon: "the occupation in Southern Lebanon, the economic situation, the presence of non-Lebanese forces on the territory, the still unresolved problem of the displaced, the danger of extremism and the impression among some that their rights are thwarted." The Exhortation specified that these difficulties jeopardize the democratic traditions of the country and force the young to emigrate.

On the other hand, pluralism was replaced by the word "diversity," although it did not disappear from the text. The Apostolic Exhortation did not belie the Final Message, as the Muslim leaders had hoped, but it was more nuanced.

In exchange, the Roman Pontiff made a significant concession to the Muslims. And by doing so, he addressed Christians' soul-searching and gave a new meaning to their presence in the Orient. John Paul II explicitly asked the Christians of Lebanon to immerse into their Arab environment at all levels. He used the most stunning and unequivocal vocabulary to explain his perspective of Christians' role in the Middle East and how the church sees itself in a non-Christian environment. "I want to underscore the necessity, for the Christians of Lebanon, to maintain and strengthen their ties of solidarity with the Arab world," he said. "I invite them to consider their insertion in Arab culture, to which they have contributed so much, as a privileged place for conducting with other Christians of Arab countries, a deep and authentic dialogue with the believers in Islam." "It is indeed, a common destiny that links Christians and Muslims in Lebanon and in other countries of the region," he added. "Moreover, dialogue and collaboration between Christians and Muslims in Lebanon can lead the way in other countries."[21] The Pope considered that Christian-Muslim dialogue lies on "the promotion of social justice, moral values, peace and freedom."[22] He insisted "it should not be merely a dialogue between intellectuals," but an act of living together and knowing each other better and "accepting pluralism."

But John Paul II challenged the concept of "pluralism" as viewed by some Christian Maronites of Lebanon, that is, a source of basic differences with their Muslim counterparts. Although he acknowledged that "each specific culture is still characterized by the religious and profane contributions of different civilizations that followed each other on their soil," he adopted the view that "in all nations and cultures where they disseminated, Christians don't demarcate from other peoples, neither by their country, nor by their language or their habits. . . . They conform to local customs in clothing, food and the daily existence, even as they reveal the extraordinary and truly paradoxical laws that regulate their way of life."

The Greek Orthodox shared this view but they did not expect the Roman Pontiff to call for the "re-Arabization" of his Catholic flocks in the Orient. They were pleased. Muslims were contented too by the call for a greater solidarity with the Arab world. They were also disconcerted by the tact and the diplomacy of the Apostolic Exhortation. It was indeed a masterpiece of equilibrium between Christian and Muslim expectations. On the other hand, Maronites knew, since the Synod, that the Holy See intended to urge them to adopt a policy in harmony with their Arab environment. Yet they were startled because they did not expect the Roman Pontiff to be that categorical in the terms he used. One month later, the Papal Nuncio in Lebanon, Pablo Puente, revealed that "it was not easy for the Pope to assert the Arabity of Lebanon but when he made up his mind, he spoke it out."[23]

"Christians of Lebanon totally agree with the Vatican on the necessity to adapt and to be in harmony with their Arab and Muslim environment. But they do not agree on the content and the methods to use to achieve that goal," Bishop Rahi had declared a few days before the Pope's arrival to Beirut.[24]

But after the release of the papal document, there was no turning back. The Apostolic Exhortation, in a way, revealed and reaffirmed the centralism of Rome. In the end, the Supreme Pontiff had enunciated the real mission of the Christians of Lebanon and of the Middle East. He believed that was the only way they could persevere. For those who could read behind the lines, the "number one" objective was clearly to maintain a certain amount of equal balance with the Muslims in order to conduct with them a dialogue on equal basis, at least in Lebanon. This is why the Pope wanted "all faithful of the Catholic Church to remain attached to their land and to be an integral part of their national community, to participate in the reconstruction and to preserve their Christian specificity and their missionary sense."[25] He certainly did not view the West as a model where Christians can save their religious identity. Since "Lebanon is traditionally open to all cultures and to ideas that are developing in the modern world," he warned, "it is important that this country and the region not allow themselves to be won over by the phenomenon of secularization."[26]

A NEW MISSION IN THE ARAB WORLD

There was certainly a lot to analyze and comment on in the papal document. In the next few years, the Apostolic Exhortation stimulated a profound meditation among Christians and Muslims alike. "After the Apostolic Exhortation, nothing will be the same again," said the An-Nahar editor, Ghassan Tueni, who, as a Greek Orthodox, displayed great admiration for "the Pope of hope."[27]

"The visit of the Pope and the release of the Apostolic Exhortation have ushered Lebanon into a new era, an era marked by the final maturing of the idea of Lebanon in Muslims' minds, and the idea of an Arabic Lebanon in Christians' minds," declared Shiite cleric and scholar Sheikh Hani Fahs.[28]

The Apostolic Exhortation also paved the way for a gigantic examination of conscience and reassessment of their future by the Christians themselves. In the postwar period, Christians have been so dispirited and prostrated in their rejection of the new order and of the new political realities, that they have not been able to produce any original thought. The instinct of survival has paralyzed intellectual innovation and social and political initiatives. In that regard, the Apostolic Exhortation was the most important and groundbreaking Christian reflection in years.

The Maronites in particular have been mourning the loss of charismatic leaders they could follow blindly like they always did (only to find themselves in the abyss!). They thought that the solution to their existential crisis was either to enthrone successors to Michel Aoun, Samir Geagea, and Amin Gemayel, or to bring those back one way or another. This void at the top of their political pyramid made them turn to the Holy Father, hold on to him and welcome him as their ultimate leader.

The Pope's message, though, was that they should explore new avenues, avenues that were initially theirs before they decided to follow another course. The Pope asked the Christians of Lebanon, and specifically the Maronites, to retrieve their mission in the region while simultaneously going back to their spiritual and cultural roots. Renewal was the answer, not looking back to the past. Only then, would a new generation of leaders emerge. "Being Christian in politics rather than elaborate a Christian policy, that's the point," explained the new Papal Nuncio in Lebanon, Antonio Maria Veglio.[29]

Pablo Puente left in September 1997, a few months after the Pope's visit. His mission was completed. "It is now up to the Christians of Lebanon and especially the Maronites, to carry on the task and build a new future for themselves and for their fellow Muslim countrymen. His Holiness has showed the way. The Holy See did its utmost to help the Christians regain a sense of confidence."[30]

Historically, the Christians of Lebanon have been tugged in two opposite directions: opening up to the other or turning inward in times of crisis. This pattern of behavior is common to all minorities, and certainly to all Eastern Christian groups. The Pope saw that their identity could no longer be preserved in an attitude of rejection and in the anxiety of their numerical and political decline. He asked them to initiate "a missionary opening that is necessary and salutary, because each particular Church that retires within itself does not fulfill its mission anymore."[31] "Interior liberation" would help them overcome their narrow allegiances and experience real church communion.

He asked the Christians to reach out to the Muslims and to find out a common route to walk together side by side. They could do so by being the standard-bearers of social justice, human rights, democracy, women's rights. They could, as in the nineteenth century, be a driving force for the Arab world to propel it, once again, into modernity, but a modernity dissociated from "Westernization."

Christians insisted that it was a dual task, to be carried out with their Muslim counterparts. "Recent history has taught us that the most insurmountable walls can fall, but in order to build bridges, we ought to be two," wrote the editor in chief of *l'Orient-LE JOUR*.[32] "We should no longer speak about the Christians of Lebanon as an entity separate from the Muslims," said Maronite bishop Joseph Bechara, who animated a Christian movement of renewal within the church. "Christians and Muslims of Lebanon are bound by a common destiny. In Lebanon, they are still equal partners, and this a chance, not only for the Christians, but for the Muslims as well. Christian presence in Lebanon is also a Muslim responsibility."[33]

Christians of Lebanon had initiated their self-examination even before the release of the Apostolic Exhortation, largely under the impulse of the synodal process. In 1993, a group of Maronite intellectuals who refused to divulge their names published in France a "Reflection on the Crisis of the

Maronite Community" that unfortunately passed unnoticed in Lebanon but is certainly a pioneer work.[34] The document was a piece of bravery. It diagnosed the wrongs that afflicted the Maronite community and consequentially, the Lebanese society. "After independence," it said, "Maronites gradually abandoned their primary specificity, that is their cultural 'difference,' to the benefit of a situation of power. By so doing, they substituted a political order to the cultural foundation of the Lebanese society." This has led to a confrontation with the Muslims and later on, to internal clashes. The document states that, since the war, "the Maronite community is the victim of a crisis of values" and that "power, in all its forms, continues to goad each one, exacerbating rivalries." After the last episode that ended with the elimination of the Lebanese Forces and the eviction of General Aoun, Maronites have been haunted by the vacuum left within their community. "Unfortunately, the void to be filled in is not the one they think. It is not of political nature, it is existential," wrote the authors of the document. The crisis, they added, could only be solved by retrieving the original mission of the Church. "Religion has been 'tribalized' and reduced to a political identity. Maronites need to go back to their monastic traditions, intertwined with prayer, silence, modesty. They need to renew with the spirit of the Church of Antioch, and weave with other Eastern Christians the Church of the Arabs that will cooperate with Islam to the renovation of a Christian and Muslim Orient." The Maronites must also "redefine their message." "The Arab world, which has been largely inspired since one century, by the Western model, is witnessing a crisis. The Maronites, who were the first in that part of the world, to make the choice of the West, have lived, before the others, the collapse of that model. This is why they are better placed to understand why Western modernity has failed in the Orient and to participate to the definition of an Arab way towards modernism," prescribed the authors of that first serious introspection in postwar years.

By the same token, the Assembly of Catholic Patriarchs and Bishops in Lebanon (known by its French acronym APECL) issued a remarkable letter titled "Mystery of the Church," on Christmas 1996, in which it engaged into the same kind of self-criticism. It warned that "the Church should not reduce its role to the defense of the political interests of its community and thus become a trench or a cutting line of factionalism." The letter also called for the immersion of the Church in its "Mashreq"[35] roots.

Many resented the fact that only Christians were engaged into this programmed exercise of self-criticism. Why didn't the Muslims feel the need to do the same?

Yet people like Seoud el-Mawla acknowledged that "Muslims too must contemplate their relation with the other, examine the notion of respect and difference with the other. . . . We, Muslims, must think about ways to open the door for a Christian participation in the project of Islamic reform launched by people such as Jamaleddine Afghani and Mohammed Abdo, in order to build a balanced society based on justice and solidarity. On the Lebanese level, the Christians of Lebanon have the responsibility to recreate a model of freedom and democracy for the Arab world, and that will enhance the position of moderate Islamists."[36]

No doubt that the papal document was stirring a productive joint meditation among the Lebanese. It was a time of grand reckoning. But this thinking focused more on the political perspectives. What about the reconciliation process?

The Apostolic Exhortation explicitly called the people of Lebanon and its rulers to embark in "courageous and prophetic acts of forgiveness and of purification of the memory." This "purification of conscience" was all the more important that an amnesty law had been voted and no accountability for war crimes was envisioned. All former militia leaders (except Samir Geagea) had been associated to the exercise of power. The amnesty law favored amnesia, although "one must keep alive the memory of what happened so that it never happens again," said the papal document.[37] An amnesty law is an issue to discuss in post-conflict societies. Some view it as intended to avoid reopening old wounds and the resurgence of divergences. They put the imperative of national reconciliation before justice. Chile's Pinochet case has become a worldwide example of that theory.

But amnesty can be viewed as a fast-track exoneration of war crimes perpetrators. Cambodia also confronted that dilemma, when King Sihanouk refused to sign the amnesty for former leaders of the Khmers Rouges. An amnesty law also inhibits any attempt to reflect on the reasons of war. It is like curing an illness without looking for its origins.

South Africa's Truth and Reconciliation commission is certainly an interesting model. When it published its 3,500-page report, it was "bound to reawaken many of the difficult and troubling emotions that the hearings themselves brought," said South African president Nelson Mandela. More interesting was the comment of Archbishop Desmond Tutu, chairman of the commission. In his foreword to the report, he wrote: "The truth can be, and often is, divisive. However, it is only on the basis of truth that true reconciliation can take place. True reconciliation is not easy; it is not cheap; it is not about being cosy. Reconciliation based on falsehood, on not facing up to reality, is not true reconciliation at all."[38] In a book he published later on, he maintained that there could be "no future without forgiveness."[39]

Do people forget or do they choose to forget? And does forgetting mean forgiving? Would the act of forgetting favor the recurrence of conflict in a few generations? Or on the contrary, does keeping alive the memories of past horrors feed the rancor? Each country, each society chooses to cope with its past according to its capacities and to the solidity of its social and political consensus. Lebanese find it accommodating to forget. It is one of their strengths and has been their asset in coping with the ravages of war. Still, deep inside them, they know that something has to be done in order to move forward in the reconciliation process.

In postwar Lebanon, a "purification of conscience" is yet to come. As one Maronite politician said: "Because we failed to go through that purification of conscience in 1840, 1860 and 1958,[40] war has broken out in 1975. We must prevent this from happening again."[41]

Chapter 13

Peace without Eastern Christians?

At the heart of Christian-Muslim relations lie the future of the Middle East peace process and the thorny issue of Jerusalem. Since the Madrid conference, the peace talks have been bogged down in the swamps of extremism, ill will, and the internal politics of the Arab and Israeli parties in desperate need of support and legitimacy to justify each step toward peace. The light that dawned at the end of the tunnel in 1991 has been alternately disappearing and flickering since then. "The peace process is like running a long-distance marathon in deep desert sands," acknowledged U.S. Assistant Secretary for NEA, Martin Indyk.[1]

The rise of fundamentalism on one hand, accelerated on the other hand by the Israeli governments' policy of land confiscation, settlements building, and harsh conditions of living imposed in the West Bank, have had a double effect: they dramatically worsened the situation of Arab Christians, particularly those living in the occupied territories and in Jerusalem, but they also increased awareness that Christian-Muslim solidarity is necessary.

A SHRINKING PRESENCE

On January 1998, the heads of all fourteen Eastern Churches, Catholics and Greek Orthodox, Chalcedonians and non Chalcedonians, Protestant and Latin, held a historic gathering in Nicosia, organized by the Middle East Council of Churches, to assess the situation of their flocks all over the region. On top of their agenda were the issues of Jerusalem, Christian emigration from the Middle East and the unity of Eastern Christianity within the diversity of its branches. At the opening session, Latin Patriarch of Jerusalem Michel Sabbah insisted that the problem of

Jerusalem be incorporated in the final communiqué, "to warn all Churches as well as the international community against the dangers besetting the Holy City and subsequently, the world peace."

Patriarch Sabbah is convinced that "Jerusalem is the key to peace in the region," and that "what will be imposed to it by force will not help peace in the region, not even in the world."[2] He has been the fervent advocate of "Jerusalem as a political capital for two states: Israel and Palestine, and as a spiritual capital for the three monotheistic religions: Christianity, Islam and Judaism." But he does not hide his anxiety concerning the dramatic decline of the Christian population in the Holy Land since 1948 (in 1999, they amounted to 170,000 in Israel/Palestine and 300,000 if one adds up those living in Jordan, "out of 14 million Christians in the Middle East," specifies Patriarch Sabbah). The situation is yet more worrying in Jerusalem where the number of Christians continued to dwindle after 1993 Israeli-Palestinian accords, due largely to emigration under economic, political, and religious pressure. Christians in the Holy City represent less than to 2 percent, that is less than 4,000, according to Sabbah.[3] For the first time in history, the prospect loomed of a Holy Land without living Christian communities—which meant Christian holy places reduced to the status of museums.

The constant outflow of Eastern Christians toward the West has been an increasing source of preoccupation for all Eastern Churches and it has driven them to close ranks. Sorrow and nostalgia marked their meeting in Nicosia as they looked to the current map of the region. Armenian Catholics Karekine II called Christian emigration "the suicidal form of genocide" and Greek Orthodox patriarch Ignatius IV Hazim considered it a "dogmatic scandal that the birthplace of Christ be emptied from Christians." And he added: "Imagine Mecca without Muslims, for instance." Hazim gives the example of the Greek Orthodox community: "I can say that 75% of the faithful under the jurisdiction of the seat of Antioch are in Latin America. Entire villages are empty. We all know that this whole region was overwhelmingly Christian before the arrival of Islam. The seven churches mentioned by St John the Divine in the Gospels, in Minor Asia (Turkey today), no longer exist. If we look at North Africa, where there was once a vibrant Christian community, there are places bare of any remaining Christian trace."[4]

In their final communiqué in Nicosia, the Eastern Patriarchs stressed the importance for Christians to remain attached to their land, "a land that was the cradle of the Christian faith." They pointed out to "the danger of heavy Christian drain from South East Turkey, the tragic situation of the Iraqi people, the plight of the population under Israeli occupation in Palestine, Lebanon and Syria, and the Turkish occupation of Cyprus."

The participants at the Nicosia meeting considered it natural to deal with political issues, "since our mission in the Orient is to witness to the truth with courage, because we are part of this region and we live its ailments and so we are destined to express its hopes and despair," as they stated in the communiqué. They saw that the new missionary duty of Eastern Christianity is "to share the burdens and the destiny of our Muslim counterparts in our respective countries, and to join our efforts in a struggle for freedom, justice, respect of diversity, equality and human rights."

Among the various difficulties facing Christians in their Arab countries, the issue of Islamic fundamentalism was tackled in closed session but it was not stressed in the plenary session and the press conference. Coptic Pope Chenouda III was all the more careful not to raise sensitivity in his country, Egypt, while the U.S. Congress was studying a legislation on religious persecution introduced in both chambers by Representative Frank Wolf and Senators Arlen Specter, Don Nickles, and Connie Mack. This legislation stirred mixed feelings among Eastern Christians: on the one hand, it was good to reinforce international scrutiny of states' behavior with respect to political participation and discrimination against their minorities, but on the other hand, it could be used as a political tool by the United States to put more pressure on governments, under the pretext of defending the Christians. Rather than improving their situation, this would increase tension between Muslims and Christians, as the former will come to view the latter as the Trojan horse of the West in Arab societies. The Religious Persecution Act could undoubtedly have a backlash effect on those whom it intended to defend and protect.

This explains why the Nicosia summit was characterized by a will to avoid acting like "minorities" and emphasized on the fact that Christians are the first inhabitants of the Orient, that they are deeply rooted in their land and are citizens of their countries on equal level with their Muslim counterparts, with whom they share the same problems and challenges, and intend to build a joint future based on participation and equal rights. In that perspective, Islamic fundamentalism was perceived as the expression of a social and political crisis in the Arab world, which required that both Christians and moderate Muslims work together for the development of their societies.

It is also significant that the heads of Eastern Churches in Nicosia avoided referring to the West as a power to rely on because they believed, "the West is no longer Christian and its policy, its development and its social life are not based on Christian principles."

The emigration of Eastern Christians was not only a mere Christian problem. The Muslim intelligentsia, especially in Egypt and Lebanon, was increasingly concerned by the outcome of that social and brain drain that affected their society, its political and economic development, and its once pluralistic features. Christian emigration was somehow a yardstick of the democratic evolution of Arab society. The head of the Supreme Shiite Council in Lebanon, Sheikh Mohammad Mehdi Shamseddine, has been outright about it: "I believe that the emigration of any Christian group from an Arab country or society reflects the failure of that society or that State. In dealing with this issue, we should first start exercising self-criticism, and that means we should blame Arabs and Muslims," he said.[5] "Then, we have to look at foreign influence, and especially the role played by the Zionist movement and some Western policies, to induce Christians to emigrate out of fear from their Arab societies. I believe there is a concerted action to empty Arab societies of their Christian citizens. Finally, are the religious and cultural authorities of the Christians totally innocent from this creeping conviction among their mainstream that they should look for a better life elsewhere?"

Sheikh Shamseddine also said he "opposes the idea of Islamists in power, because Islam is not a power project, it is a cultural project." "The most dangerous challenge facing contemporary Islamic movement is the presentation of Islam as a nation project, against the will of the nation and with methods that put Islam at odds with its own societies, as is happening in various places." And Shamseddine cites Algeria and "some trends in Egypt." "This is why I advise Islamist groups to stay out of the mechanisms of power, from city councils to the higher office," he added.[6]

A MUSLIM-JEWISH DIALOGUE?

Aside from rattling the foundation of Arab societies, Christian emigration is believed to be the prelude to a greater danger looming ahead on the regional level, in regard to confrontation with Israel. A new conviction has emerged in the last couple of years that Israel wanted to breach Christian-Muslim dialogue and replace it with a Muslim-Jewish axis. For this to happen, the region would be emptied of its Christians, and Oriental Islam would hence be isolated. Patriarch Michel Sabbah and Lebanese representative of Dar el-Fatwa in inter-religious dialogue Mohammad Sammak think that scenario is already taking place. "Eastern Christians are a bridge between Arab and Western civilizations," explains Sabbah. "Their demise and exodus from the Arab countries will provide an excuse for those who are publicizing the image of an intolerant Islam that is unable to live and interact with another religion or another culture and that does not respect freedom of religion and belief."[7]

During the plenary session of the Synod on Lebanon, Mohammad Sammak had warned against exactly the same risk of exclusion of Eastern

Christianity from the making of future and peace in the Middle East. Arabic Islam would be left alone, facing Israeli hegemonic attempts in the region and cut off from any link or bridge with the West.

Patriarch Sabbah estimates that "the Jews, as a political entity as well as a religious one, are more interested by dialogue with Islam than a dialogue with us, local Christians. They'd rather establish dialogue with European Christians because of the international impact of that dialogue."

Whereas on the regional level, Islam is more numerous and more powerful. This is why it is important that our Muslim fellows preserve the unity of the Arab rank with their Christian counterpart, so that dialogue with the Jew can only be established on a tripartite basis: Islamic-Christian-Jewish, and so that the Arab presence, in its Christian and Muslim components, could be secured."[8] On another occasion, he commented: "The force of the Arab position common to Christians and Muslims depends on a measure of coordination and mutual understanding. It depends above all on the Muslim capacity to understand and accept the Christian position."[9]

THE HOLY SEE AS A THIRD PARTY

Sabbah is the first Arab to hold the Latin seat of Jerusalem since the Patriarchate was reinstated in 1847. Born in Palestine (Nazareth), he was nominated by Pope John Paul II in December 1988. In his position regarding Jerusalem, he sways between his direct attachment to Rome and the Arab nationalistic stand of other Eastern churches. Indeed, many Eastern Christian prelates, particularly non-Catholics such as Patriarch Hazim, Pope Chenouda, and Anglican bishop of Jerusalem Samir Kafity,[10] preferred to distance themselves from the Vatican's position in relation to Israel. Although their view regarding the City of Jerusalem did not differ much of the Vatican's line, they did not consider the Holy See as their "spokesperson" and as Arab Christians, refused to be under Roman tutelage. On the theological level, they also resented what they called "the Judaization of Christianity" that is occurring out of a guilty conscience born in the West in the wake of the Holocaust.[11]

When he can, Sabbah tries to build bridges of understanding between local churches and the Vatican on the issue of Jerusalem. "The Vatican supports the local Church but does not replace it. Local churches may have their own position, different from the Vatican, regarding Israel."[12]

In an address to the Middle East Council of Churches held in Beirut in June 1996, he nonetheless explained "that the position of the universal Catholic Church, defined by the Holy See of Rome, is continuous with the line of the local churches to acknowledge respect for the rights, the jurisdictions and the duties of all. That is why every Catholic initiative ought be taken only in coordination with the other churches present in Jerusalem."

Eastern Christians and Muslims like to remember the time the Holy See was adamant in its condemnation of Israel's practices and regularly supportive of Arab positions. Until 1993, the Holy See was the only Western "state" that did not recognize Israel and had not established diplomatic relations with Tel-Aviv. Thus Eastern Churches in the Holy Land felt encouraged to adopt strong nationalist stances. The melkite hierarchy in the Holy Lands did not hesitate to support overtly the Palestinians; the example of former patriarchal vicar Hilarion Capucci, arrested by the Israelis in 1974 for conveying weapons to the Palestinians, remains famous.

The Fundamental Agreement signed December 30, 1993, between Israel and the Holy See was a turning point. It established diplomatic relations between the two States and triggered some disappointment and misunderstanding in the Arab world. Yet, article 11.2 of the agreement says: "The Holy See . . . is solemnly committed to remaining stranger to all merely temporal conflicts, which principally applies specifically to disputed territories and unsettled borders." However, according to the same article, the Holy See maintains "in every case the right to exercise its moral and spiritual teaching office."[13] The 1993 agreement was followed in November 1997 by an accord in which the State of Israel recognized the legal personality of Catholic institutions in Israel. As George Weigel emphasized in his official biography of John Paul II, the November 1997 agreement illustrated, in the eyes of the Holy See officials, the continuity of their Middle East policy and "the unchanging character of their basic diplomatic interest in the region, which is to secure the Church's legal position in Christ's native land."[14]

According to an Italian journalist and author, Giancarlo Zizola, "the diplomatic recognition of the State of Israel by the Vatican has occurred on secular basis, without accepting the religious value of the link between the Jewish people and 'its' land."[15] For his part, Weigel estimates that "several objectives seem to have intersected in the unified mind of Pope John Paul II": aside from securing the Church's historic interests in the Holy Land, "there was John Paul II's intuition of Jewish pain and his theological commitment to getting the long-delayed theological dialogue (broken-off more than 1,900 years before) between Jews and Catholics under way again."[16]

The new policy of the Holy See has nevertheless been criticized by the Palestinians. Eastern Churches were reserved, although they understood that the Holy See was acting "as a State who seeks to preserve its interests, not as a Church," said Patriarch Hazim.[17] Even Holy See officials would recognize later on that their relations with the State of Israel "have hardly been helped by the failure to resolve the Palestinian problem, the lack of respect for certain UN Security Council Resolutions and duly concluded international agreements, without forgetting the annexation by force of a part of the City of Jerusalem."[18]

But the Holy See was also aware that both Israel and Islam preferred to deal with a strong Christian interlocutor who had international authority rather than with the waning Christians of the Orient. This advantage would allow the Vatican to defend its long-standing position on Jerusalem, that is, to secure international legal guarantees to preserve the special character of Jerusalem. Officials of the Holy See believed this position presented the most comprehensive outlook of the Holy City's future and that neither local churches nor Islam should oppose it since it encompassed their demands. In October 1998, after the conclusion of the Wye River accords, the Vatican took a step further and announced that it wanted to take part in upcoming Israeli-Palestinian negotiations on the future of Jerusalem, since the City has aspects which go far beyond the legitimate national interests of Israelis and Palestinians. The Holy See considered that any possible solution should have the support of the three monotheistic religions. In May 1998, the Pope had hoped international guarantees of the unique and sacred character of the Holy City would be in place by the year 2000.

To the Holy See, Jerusalem "as a sacred heritage common to the three monotheist religions" is a universal cause which therefore requires that the entire international community should act as a guarantor. Archbishop Jean-Louis Tauran explained that the Holy See strictly favors a special internationally guaranteed statute for the most sacred areas of the City, in order to preserve and protect the identity of the Holy City in its entirety and in every aspect:

- the historical, material, religious and cultural characteristics;
- the equality of rights and treatment for those belonging to the three religions, in the context of their spiritual, cultural, civic and economic activities;
- the rights of freedom of religion and worship for all, and of access to the shrines for residents and pilgrims alike, whether from the Holy Land itself or from other parts of the world.

This request of the Holy See regards, first and foremost, the most religiously significant part of the City, namely the Old City. But such a formula would have to be extended to other shrines outside the Old City and beyond Greater Jerusalem, in Israel as well as in the West Bank.[19]

The Eastern Christian patriarchs and bishops would more often insist on the natural and indissoluble link between the religious dimension of the "Jerusalem issue" and the political question. Precisely because of the city's sacred character, they required that the political solution granted Jerusalem the status of "open city."

One shared conviction between the Holy See and Christian and Muslim Arabs is that "peace and coexistence in the Holy Land and the Middle East have no future unless an answer is found to the political question of Jerusalem," as Archbishop Jean-Louis Tauran said during a Symposium on Jerusalem convened by Patriarch Sabbah in October 26, 1998. Tauran added that the Vatican does not accept "the distinction often made between the question of the Holy Places and the question of Jerusalem." One year later, he further developed that point of view, emphasizing on the unity between "the shrines themselves, which are the symbols of our faith," and "the living shrines" made up of the communities living in Jerusalem. He explained:

> For this reason, the Holy See is not only concerned with the religious aspect of the city. It also has the right and duty to concern itself with the political and territorial aspect insofar as this remains unresolved or, even more, when it becomes a cause of conflict, injustice, violation of human rights, fear or insecurity for its people. And, what is worse, the political and territorial aspect becomes an obstacle for the free expression of faith, to which every citizen is entitled and which should be guaranteed for and by all. In the final analysis, we could say that the Holy See is concerned in an immediate and concrete way with questions relating to religion, while it is concerned with the other questions—political, economic, etc.—when these have a moral dimension.[20]

Jerusalem was in the heart of the existential crisis that has been shaking the Middle East for over half a century. And "the failure to find an adequate solution to it compromises further the longed-for peaceful and just settlement" of that crisis, as Pope John Paul II wrote in his 1984 apostolic letter on Jerusalem.

So in the "Muslim-Jewish negotiations" for peace in the Middle East, the third "invisible" party has thus become the Roman Catholic Church. It has imposed itself upon the two parties, the Israelis and the Palestinians, as a spiritual force and a universal Church of one billion believers (estimates of the Vatican) but also as a state with regular diplomatic representations and cultural and material interests.

This dialogue between Western Christianity and Israel on one hand, and between Muslim Arabs and Israel on the other, sidelines the Eastern Churches. "Israel is building bridges with the Arab Islamic majority of the region. We should be wary because that sort of dialogue is casting Arab Christianity aside, and may even take place at its expenses. Israel's interests lie with the Islamic majority who can recognize the existence of the Israeli entity, not with Arab Christianity, since the Arab Churches have rejected Israel from the very beginning," wrote Mohammad Sammak.[21]

PUSHING FOR A COMMON CHRISTIAN-MUSLIM AGENDA

In the last few years, as religious intolerance grew in the Middle East and Western news reports more frequently featured embattled Christian minorities, especially Copts in Egypt, and simmering sectarian tensions in the region, the Arab Muslim intelligentsia and establishment—as well as Muslim religious leaders in Beirut and in Cairo's al Azhar—displayed a particular willingness to open up to their local Christian elites and religious authorities. This overture was driven by two imperatives: first, the need to invalidate Samuel Huntington's "Clash of Civilizations" theory, in fact a postulate on a "clash of religions" in which Islam is presented as the major threat against the West—a West viewed as embodying Christian values; second, the need to counter the new orientation in the U.S. Congress but also in the state department to monitor religious persecution and to advocate religious freedom all over the world. China and the Middle East were two particular focus points in this new "foreign policy priority" as set forth by Secretary of State Madeleine Albright.[22]

Muslims in the Middle East expected their Christian counterparts to refute any allegation of religious persecution or religious confrontation between Islam and Christianity. And Eastern Christians have indeed met these expectations. Copts living in Egypt have strongly expressed their opposition to the Freedom from Religious Persecution Act in Congress and eminent Coptic figures such as Youssef Boutros-Ghali, minister of economy and brother of former UN Secretary General Boutros Boutros-Ghali, testified on Capitol Hill against that bill. Full page ads in major American newspapers rebutted "the false claims of persecution against Copts in Egypt," affirmed that "Copts and Muslims are very friendly towards one another," and "denounced the continuous attempts of hostile dark forces against Egypt that play on the religious sentiments of foreign communities outside Egypt."[23]

At every opportunity granted to speak about their life and prospects in the Middle East, Arab Christians have carefully avoided distinguishing their pain and ordeals from those of their Muslim countrymen. In the last couple of years, Arab Christians have roused increased interest in the U.S. academic sector, and conferences have been organized by various organizations such as the Evangelicals for Middle East Understanding (EMEU), the Holy Land Christian Ecumenical Foundation (HCEF), and others, to deal with "The Future of Christianity in the Middle East," "Endangered People: Christians in the Holy Land," "Middle Eastern Christians in the Islamic Context."[24] Notwithstanding their eloquent titles, these conventions have not been used by Eastern Christians to develop a "cause" on their own. Instead, they have provided an opportunity to expound the vision of a common Arab Christian and Muslim future and to sensitize public opinion on the situation in the Middle East and the West Bank in general. The peace process, the Palestinian cause, and the yoke of the Israeli occupation in the West Bank have been on top of the agenda of those Arab Christians invited to speak in American forums. Because they can more easily appeal to the West and win over its sympathy and support, Arab Christians have deliberately put their "advantage" at the service of a common national struggle conducted with their Muslim brethren. Despite the unuttered anguish that pervades their description of every day's painful reality in the Middle East, from the West Bank under Israeli occupation to Iraq under international embargo, to Egypt, and despite frequent reports in the Western media that they are often subject to brutal persecution or discrimination in their homelands (especially in Egypt and Palestine) at the hand of the authorities or extremist groups, Middle Eastern Christians have regularly depicted the difficulties they are facing as being common to both Muslims and Christians. In one conference, Reverend Naim Ateek, director of the Sabeel Theology Center in Jerusalem, enumerated five specific Christian challenges: (1) unity among Christian churches; (2) meeting Islam and understanding Muslims ("We've been living with the Muslims for the last 1,400 years," he said, adding that the Crusades have done more harm to Eastern Christians than the Arab invasion); (3) confronting Zionism and the oppression of the Palestinians by the State of Israel, which raises the importance of working for political justice; (4) emigration; and (5) the struggle for democracy and the need for Palestinians to have their own state.[25]

In their efforts to alleviate the sufferings of their people, Eastern Christians have found support in various powerful institutions such as the National Council of Churches in the U.S.A (NCCU.S.A), World Vision, the Equestrian Order of the Holy Sepulchre of Jerusalem (linked to the Latin Patriarchate of Jerusalem), and many others in Europe and the United States.

Eastern Christians have also been advocating the cause of Jerusalem in the West and putting all their resources to defend the "common Muslim-Christian Arab position" in Western capitals. This common position was defined in a conference held in Beirut, in June 1996, under the title: "Muslims and Christians Together for Jerusalem," which gathered for the first time Muslim and Christian religious authorities from all Arab countries.

"Jerusalem is our common cause and the mother of all causes," said the final communiqué. "No authority in the world has the right to judaize Jerusalem or to internationalize it, or to erase its Arab Muslim-Christian character. No authority on earth has the right to take decisions regarding Jerusalem's Christian-Muslim identity. Any decision taken by any side, on the regional or international level, that alters this identity, is invalid and illegitimate in its origin and its effects." Condemning Israel's policy of forced exile imposed on Jerusalem residents, Christian and Muslim alike, the communiqué denounces the "confiscation of the City" and warns that "no peace can last without justice and based on persecution." Thus, "the liberation of Jerusalem," the "defense of its Arabity and of its religious pluralism," the "support of the Palestinian institutions in Jerusalem," and the "non-recognition of any diplomatic representation based in Jerusalem" are common objectives that should bind all Arab states. The conveners agreed "to work together, Christians and Muslims, so that Jerusalem be a city of reconciliation, of justice and peace for all."

On October 19, 1998, the three Jerusalem church leaders Patriarch Diodoros I (Greek Orthodox Patriarch of Jerusalem), Patriarch Michel Sabbah (Latin Catholic Patriarch of Jerusalem), and Patriarch Torkom Manoogian (Armenian Apostolic Patriarchate of Jerusalem) addressed a letter to the Israeli Minister of Interior, protesting the Israeli government policy of confiscation of identification cards from East Jerusalem Palestinians, with the consequent loss of right of residency in Jerusalem. They expressed deep concern about the 600 percent increase over two years in the number of cards being confiscated. "Hard-working and peace-seeking Christians are being forced out of the city. Many of these families or individuals face losing their access to the city of their birth through the revocation of their residency rights," they wrote. "We must remind you that what impacts Palestinians in general doubly impacts Christian Palestinians in particular." They called on the State of Israel to safeguard the rights of the Christian communities, to halt any future confiscations and to rescind recent changes in its policies.

Led by their U.S. counterparts in the Greek Orthodox, Armenian Orthodox, and Catholic hierarchies, twenty-six top American Orthodox, Protestant, and Catholic leaders wrote a strong letter of support to the Jerusalem Patriarchs and addressed their own letter of protest to the Israeli ambassador to the Unites States. In that second letter, released publicly on February 8, 1999, the church leaders wrote: "The churches in the Holy City of Jerusalem are not composed only of stones, but more importantly of faithful, worshiping believers. Any further diminution of their numbers or weakening of their vitality is a matter of great concern to the churches everywhere."[26]

THE PRECARIOUS FATE OF THE CHRISTIANS AND THE UNCERTAIN FUTURE OF THE MIDDLE EAST

Despite the endeavors of Eastern Christians and their hope that Christian-Muslim solidarity will prevail as the Arab world confronts critical political, cultural, and economic challenges, incidents like the clashes that occurred between Palestinian Christians and Islamists in Nazareth in spring 1999 for a small plot of land below Nazareth's Basilica of the Annunciation, and the subsequent Israeli ruling to allow the building of a mosque on portions of the disputed land, remind us of the precarious fate of those living on the fault line separating two worlds.[27] Eastern Christians were once again wedged between a rock and a hard place, between Israel's cynical politics and the rise of Islamist claims. And once again, the secret to survival was carved in keywords such as compromise and concession. Latin Patriarch Sabbah came with a conciliating proposal: the building of a Center for religious dialogue associating the three monotheistic faiths. The proposition was ignored by both sides.

In a world increasingly caught in the mayhem of renewed particularism and intolerance, where fifty-six conflicts were believed to be linked to religion,[28] the situation of some groups and minorities in the Middle East could only become more uncertain as the conflicts simmering in various parts of the globe were likely to have direct repercussions on them. Somehow, the geopolitical concept of the Middle East at the turn of the twenty-first century has expanded: a new Middle East is shaping, stretching from the Gulf to the Mediterranean Levant, from North Africa to Turkey and even Central Asia. Religious and ethnic strife in any of these places could, like an epicenter, send shock waves all around its peripheries in that highly volatile region.

Thus a long-standing "Arab Church" like the Greek Orthodox Church has looked with great alarm at the atrocities committed in Bosnia and in Kosovo by the Serbs, and has cautiously dissociated itself from their behavior. (Yet the Greek Orthodox community was destabilized by the NATO bombings on Yugoslavia. As to Arab Muslims, they had mixed feelings about these strikes that accelerated the exodus of Albanians from Kosovo and confirmed once more in their eyes, after Iraq, the double-standard policy of the United States when it comes to the rights of self-determination for the peoples. Israel and the Palestinians are naturally the parallel referred to).

In Huntington's theory, Greek Orthodox Christianity stands on the geographical line (the "fault line") separating East from West, or rather Islam from the West. Therefore it could become the wrestling arm of Western

Christianity with the Muslim civilization. The Russian war against Islamists in Daghestan and Chechnya disturbingly fit within that scenario.

However it is certainly not this way that the Greek Orthodox in the Arabic world, Western world, or Russia view themselves. Mohammad Sammak tells his experience as a Muslim delegate to the October 1995 summit in Tachkent (Ouzbekistan), where "for the first time in Central Asia's history," he recounts, "Muslim and Christian Greek Orthodox have convened to assess their relations and draw from other experiences, such as the Lebanese experience. I was asked to talk about Lebanon's experiment in coexistence." The Russian Greek Orthodox Church had sought indeed to ease the tensions that arose in the aftermath of the (first) Chechnyan war, to adjust the relationship between Russian Greek Orthodox and the Islamic states of Central Asia and to strip potential conflicts in that part of the world from any religious connotation.[29]

For a century now, Christians in the Middle East have chosen to hew to the ideological lines of the Arab world and to espouse Arab destiny in a "joint national struggle." For those among the Maronites of Lebanon who were restive and sought a separate—or at least a differentiated—destiny, the Holy See has reminded them of that imperative. But the Arab world itself does not have joint objectives anymore, nor is there an "Arab ideology" or an "Arab cause." The crisis the whole region is going through is precisely due to the failure of Arab nationalism and its replacement by an Islamic revival, called fundamentalism. So where do Arab Christians stand? Between non-democratic regimes and Islamist opposition groups, the "choice" is not really a choice.

Many think they should stand by their moderate Muslim counterparts, who, according to Egyptian lawyer and writer Mohammad Selim el-Awwa, are the silent majority.[30] The Holy See's vision of their role, according to the 1995 Apostolic Exhortation, is that of the "locomotive" of democratic transformation in their respective countries. Lebanon is the place where they can assert this role and extend the model to the rest of the region where Christian minorities live side by side with Muslims. This joint Christian-Muslim struggle for democracy, social justice, and freedom of religion is indeed the only logical and promising perspective for Eastern Christianity and for the Middle East as well. Provided that Christians resist the luring temptation of the West. And provided their Muslim countrymen show their readiness for building a shared future together. In many ways, Christians' perpetuation in the birthplace of Christianity is a Muslim's responsibility, and Muslim religious leaders in Lebanon have publicly acknowledged that.

There is a widespread conviction in the West that only peace could improve the situation of Christians in the Middle East. In the Middle East, this hope is tinged with fatalism, since people are increasingly skeptical about the outcome of the so-called peace process. They believe the vicious cycle of violence is not likely to break soon and that "time does not help peace," as Patriarch Sabbah of Jerusalem put it.[31] In a situation of "no peace, no war" or *status quo,* neither culture nor economy, and certainly not democracy, can prosper. The mission of the Christians of the Orient has traditionally been framed into their cultural and economic contribution. By essence, it is a mission of peace.

Eastern Churches have lately increased the pace of their meetings, to reflect on Christian presence in the Middle East in the third millennium. The Middle East Council of Churches has purposely chosen Lebanon to host all the heads of Eastern Churches for the year 2000.

Meanwhile, the first Convention of the Catholic Patriarchs and Bishops in the Orient was held in May 1999, also in Lebanon, with the participation of Roman cardinals, observers from various countries of emigration (Europe, Canada, the United States, Australia), representatives of the Catholic Church in North Africa, fraternal delegates of Greek Orthodox and Protestant Churches, the general secretary of the Middle East Council of Churches, experts, and lay people. In all, over 210 participants from 27 countries gathered to assess the future of Christianity in the Middle East; the relations between Catholic, Orthodox, and Protestant Churches; relations with the Muslims and with the Jews; the issue of Jerusalem; peace prospects in the region; human rights; Christian emigration; and the rights of freedom, equality, and self-determination.

The working document of the Convention stated that "the foundation of dialogue with our Muslim brothers as we have practiced it for centuries, is a 'living together' that is an irreversible experience.... It is a daily dialogue, away from formalities. We share with them the same cultural heritage in which each of us contributed its own specific genius. And so it created between us, in the Orient, a civilization kinship." The accent was put on "our shared responsibility in building a free country and an adult citizen, in mutual respect and understanding of common values and a joint vision of man." The document also distinguished between Arab civilization and Islam. "In the Arab Orient, the Christian is embedded in his Arab and Christian identity. He has been a pioneer, before and after Islam, in the vitality of the Arab and oriental culture."

Emigration remains of course a central problem. Christians were leaving "because of difficulties that keep them away from active collaboration in public life ... and because many of them are denied their fundamental human rights." Christians and Muslims who attended these gatherings and conferences were aware that both the future of the Middle East and its cultural, social and political profile were at stake at the turn of the twenty-first century.

Would these intensified meetings be enough to retain Christians in their birthplace? Would Muslim elites as well resist the temptation of giving up the struggle for democracy in their homelands? Innovation, initiative, boldness are the qualities required to transform reality. Along with men of vision and peace. Unfortunately, "what Arabs find at home is economic lethargy and social stagnation," writes journalist and author Milton Viorst. "The energy, the daring, the entrepreneurial spirit that suddenly appeared in Pacific societies remain largely absent in the Middle East. The Arab world seems weighed down by pessimism over its future, if not outright despair."[32]

Hindering the Arab world's development instead of propelling it is its diversity and pluralism, or rather the Arab world's ability to deal with its pluralism and use it as a resource instead of seeking unity and uniformity, these code words of a vanished dream of the one *umma*. Charles Winslow phrased it well when he wrote:

> Above and beyond talk about eternal Syria, a Christian refuge, a promised land, Arab unity and the Islamic purification of territory stands the real pluralism of peoples and culture in the Middle East.... There are too many differences to sort out in each of the national cocoons that the Europeans drew up after the first World War. Unless the world is willing to provide the subsidy, none of the religious or ideological contenders can dominate the whole arena or any of its parts. People in the Middle East must not only learn to live with differences but also must institutionalize the means of doing so.... The individual needs security at the communal level, something parallel to what the old Ottoman millet system used to provide.[33]

Pluralism, recognition, security for each individual and all communities, equal rights, political participation, freedom of religion, sovereignty, justice, these are the main keys for a prosperous future in the Middle East. As long as these principles remain mere aspirations, the entire region will keep suffering from the exodus of its most talented and skilled people.

A Maronite legend told by Father Michel Hayek speaks of two twin semi-gods, Hafroun and Nafroun, born on a mountain peak near Ehmej village, north of Lebanon. Hafroun, as his name indicates (*hafar,* in Arabic), digs the soil in order to cultivate it, but he ultimately dies of hunger and cold on his unfertile rock. His brother, Nafroun, as his name suggests (*nafar,* in Arabic), goes far away, seeking fortune overseas. The ocean carries him away to unknown lands and he cannot find his way back. "All the history of the Maronites' relation with their land is condensed in this legend," says Hayek. "On the land of gods, there are the Hafrouns, those who cling to their mountain and work hard to make a living there, despite the elements and men's hostility. And there are the Nafrouns, those émigrés who ventured beyond the seas. The challenge of the Maronites is to contradict myth by reality, to break fatality so that the Hafrouns, those who stayed, don't die out of misery in their mountain villages, and the Nafrouns, those who emigrated, don't lose the memory of their fatherland in the anonymity of the world."[34] This challenge is also the same for all Christians of the Orient.

Conclusion

Lebanese like to compare their country to the Phoenix rising from its ashes, and in a certain way, they are right. Throughout their long and terrible ordeal, the Lebanese people showed a remarkable resiliency that no other people experiencing the crucibles of civil war has displayed. In less than a decade, the scars left by the war in downtown Beirut and on the facades of the buildings have disappeared. The city is booming; banks, trade, and tourism, once the hallmarks of Lebanon's economy, are prospering again. Lebanon, as a marketplace and an attraction house, is back.

And just like before the war, wealthy businessmen and emirs from the Gulf have relocated their leisure activities in Lebanon, seeking there what they did not find in their own countries: an ersatz of Westernization represented by the liberal thinking and permissive way of life that characterizes Beirut. A number of Christian and Muslim entrepreneurs are promoting this glittering and shallow facade of a certain Lebanon that slides into bewilderment amid the neon lights of the nightclubs, cabarets, and casinos stretching along the Christian coastline of Jounieh, north of Beirut. This Lebanon that is losing its soul and making a lot of profits has no other meaning than to give the rest of the Arab world a faked and artificial glimpse of what modernism could be.

But there is another Lebanon, the one that is born out of an idea, the Lebanon that carries a message, on the borderline of both worlds, the East and the West. Up the hill overlooking the Jounieh bay, Bkerké—"the Vatican of the Orient," as one priest once put it—stands up as the symbol of that original message. It is the guardian of the hinterland, where the green cliffs of Mount-Lebanon with its convents and abbeys shelter the monastic spirit of early times. Finding the meaning of Lebanon again is what John Paul II has called for Christians and Muslims to do together. It will be their "quest for the Grail" in the twenty-first century. More especially, the Christians of Lebanon are expected to redefine their geostrategical function in their Arab and Muslim environment. They are called to rebuild a country meant to be much more than an Oriental Monte-Carlo. If they don't come out with a clear and new vision of their historical role in the region, Lebanon will lose its singularity and dilute in the familiar landscape with homogenized patterns of the many Arab countries surrounding him. Then all Eastern Christians can do is to survive as fading minorities and relics of the past.

Wedged between two currents, globalization on one side and, on the other side, the resurgence of national and religious identities, including Islamic revivalism, Lebanese Christians must avoid yielding to the temptation of a sectarian behavior. Instead, they can oppose a modernist speech to the fundamentalist trends, both Islamist and Jewish, that are confronting each other in the region and setting the background for what is called the "peace process." The mission Lebanese Christians are called to fulfill in the third millennium consists of shedding the boundaries of sectarianism, overcoming the minorities approach, opening up to the Arabic and Muslim majority that is eager to enter the twenty-first century, and becoming a leading force by promoting human, cultural, and social values as well as the universal values of development, freedom, and equality. To be able to achieve that, they first have to go through an "inner conversion." War has corrupted minds and souls, and Christians, principally the Maronites, have forgotten that their primary aim is not power *per se,* but to be a vector of civilization, of modernity, of cultural openness. In order to foster an era of renewal and changes within the Arab societies, they have to initiate renewal and changes within their own communities and inspire their Muslim countrymen to do the same. Only then will a new generation emerge with the purity of intentions and the impetus of the origins.

In their endeavor, Lebanese and Eastern Christians, along with their Muslim partners in this "Operation Renewal," can only hope for the advent of new leaders in the Middle East who are able and willing to lift the shackles from the minds and implement the salutary political, economic, and cultural reforms badly needed for their societies to catch up with the rest of the world.

By and large, Lebanon is expected to lead the way. Its challenge illustrates somehow the challenge of the entire region. The failure of the Lebanese would mean the failure of a meaningful experiment in the Arab world to manage religious pluralism and cultural diversity, and to institutionalize freedom, equality, respect and participation for all. It would deprive the Arab world of a model it could relate to, reminiscent of its lost "Andalus" (twelfth-century Andalusia). And furthermore, it would deprive Eastern Christians of the only regional platform where they could find solace and refuge in moments of hardship and make their voices heard thanks to the freedom of speech Lebanon has preserved and has shared with others (all others, including the Palestinians chased from their homes by the Israelis) through its liberal political system. For Lebanon has been the only Arab place where Christians have enjoyed equal political rights and have been on equal footing with their Muslim compatriots. This explains why the million and a half Christians there have made more noise than the seven million Copts in Egypt. This fact simply means that no matter what the numbers are, at the end of the day the real issue is the nature of the political institutions and regime a country chooses for itself. Democracy (with what it entails in terms of equal rights), freedom (in its religious, cultural, and political components), and decent conditions of living and working, are the only guarantees for a prosperous future in the region, but more especially they are, for Eastern Christians, the sole incentives to keep anchored in their homeland those who did not leave yet.

For centuries, the name of Lebanon ("the Lebanon") has been associated with freedom and independence. These words have been its motto, its *raison d'être*, its mission in a region regularly crushed by invaders. Is the untamed spirit of the Lebanon still dwelling in its valleys and mountains at the dawn of the third millennium? With its independence at stake, Lebanon has been a hostage to the international process that will determine its future. Lebanese will still have to belie those who think they are not able to manage their own independence or to secure stability without the support of outsiders because there are too many differences to sort out, because "Levantine people are prone to conflict," as has been written, because for over twenty years, Lebanese have not been able to master the "inside-outside" game that pervaded their sovereignty. To prove all these allegations wrong may well be the ultimate challenge of the Lebanese together.

Many Lebanese writers have been tempted to draw a parallel between Lebanon and Jerusalem. The country and the city both stand as the symbols of a great encounter between the three monotheistic religions, Christianity, Judaism, and Islam. Jerusalem represents the spiritual capital of the world's greatest faiths and Lebanon embodies a Pact between all religious groups.

Both have been burnished by centuries of conflict in this fascinating but tormented Levant that has witnessed the ebb and flow of conquering empires and has kept traces of their civilizations.

Both are today the testing ground of the ability of peoples of different religions to live and work together in peace, respect, and understanding. Both are also going through a determinant phase for the future of Eastern Christianity and subsequently, for the future of the Arab identity of the region, forged by centuries-old Christian-Muslim interaction and conviviality.

And both Lebanon and Jerusalem are enduring in their flesh the travails of a protracted process aimed at establishing peace in the Middle East.

But will there ever be peace in that part of the world where God chose to connect with mankind, through a Covenant (for the Jews), through His Son (for the Christians), and through a revealed text—the Qur'an—(for Muslims)?

For the peoples and the rulers of a region that has not known a single era of tranquillity in the twentieth century, peace would be the most dramatic change. It would certainly represent "a moment of truth" since most of the local regimes are going through a period of transition. Would this transition be a democratic one? Would it resolve the crisis of legitimacy the ruling elites in the region have regularly faced? Would the sacrosanct stability, a cornerstone of U.S. foreign policy in that region, still hold or would the Pax Americana soon be challenged by a new emerging guard and by new regional alliances? Would social transformations and the demographic boom in Arab countries lead to turmoil or would they induce more inclusive political and economic reforms? Questions multiply as the twenty-first century unfolds. If ever there is peace between the peoples of the Middle East, what would its outline look like?

"The historical experience that we have had with Islam under the shade of Arab civilization, in which the Jews have also played an important role, is the model that can be followed to draw the outlines of the future," stated the Patriarchs of the Orient in their 1999 Convention in Lebanon. Then again, they asked this lingering question that haunts the torn land of Abraham: "Til when the children of the Abrahamic faith will persist, in the face of God and of all men, living in an enmity that contradicts their primary spiritual fraternity?"

Nothing big, nothing bold has been achieved by man without the twinkles of hope, dream, and temerity. "The Christians dream of a day when the divided nations of the Mashreq will join again and meet in the name of Abraham and when Jerusalem will become the Capital of the reconciled Orient and the City of peace for the whole world," once wrote Michel Hayek. His own personal dream is that of a United States of the Semitic Levant, stretching from the Mediterranean shores to the two rivers of Mesopotamia (the Tiger and Euphrates). The Arab-Israeli conflict, he says, is the perpetuation of the ancient rivalry between Ismael and Israel, sons of Abraham. So it is from the Orient, from Israel and Ismael, that salvation or damnation will come.

Notes

* All French and Arabic text and source materials that appear in this book have been translated in full by the author.

CHAPTER 1

1. Teaching Christian theology to future imams and Islamic civilization to University students is part of the USJ activities. Since 1977, father Augustin Dupré La Tour established at the St. Joseph University the Institute for Muslim-Christian Studies, to counter the effects of the war and provide for a renewed approach to the teachings of Islam and Christianity. In 1996, the Institute signed a cooperation agreement with Hisham Nashabé's Institute of Islamic Studies of the prestigious Sunni Maqassed foundation in Beirut.
2. See Jean-Pierre Valognes, *Vie et Mort des Chrétiens d'Orient,* Fayard, 1994; and Yoakim Moubarac, *Pentalogie Antiochienne/Domaine Maronite* (7 vol.), Beirut, Cénacle Libanais, 1984.
3. George Antonius, *The Arab Awakening: The Story of the Arab National Movement,* Philadelphia, J. B. Lippincott, 1938, pp. 32, 37–39.
4. Conversation with author, summer 1994.
5. Valognes, ibid., p. 223.
6. Michel Hayek, "Arabism is the Problem of the Arabs," *An-Nahar al-Arabi wal Douali,* no. 131, November 5–11, 1979).
7. Conversation with author, winter 1999.
8. Amin Maalouf, *Les Identités Meurtrières,* Grasset, 1998, p. 26.
9. This Western malaise has been blatant during the Lebanese civil war, when Western countries (especially France, Italy, and the United States) did not "logically" stand by Christian militias fighting the Palestinians and their allied Muslim militias. The West's rejection or abandonment of the Christians has been analyzed by Valognes (in *Vie et Mort des Chrétiens d'Orient,* p. 191) as the expression of a certain remorse the West feels towards the Palestinian cause, a new interest in Islam and a willingness to expiate its colonial past. All of this at the expense of their "brothers in religion in the Orient." The West actually feels more comfortable in welcoming those of them who are willing to emigrate and who might enrich Western societies with their great potential. As for those who choose to

stay, they'd better keep a low-profile in their societies, lest they should disturb the "monolithic" feature of the Islamic world and the politics that goes with that perception.

10. Anthony Wessels, *Arab and Christians?* Kampen, Kok Pharos, 1995; Kenneth Cragg, *The Arab Christian: A History in the Middle East,* London, Mowbray, 1992; El Hassan Bin Talal, *Christianity in the Arab World,* Amman, Royal Institute for Inter-Faith Studies, 1995.
11. Ibid.
12. Jean Corbon, *L'Eglise des Arabes,* Paris, Editions du Cerf, 1977.
13. Maalouf, op. cit.
14. Hayek, op. cit.
15. Paul Tabar, in *The Beirut Review,* Spring 1994, p. 95.
16. Interview with author.
17. This sentence was pronounced years ago by Syrian president Hafez Assad.
18. Waddah Sharara's social analysis of Lebanon, in *ShuFiMaFi,* "a free weekly news report on Lebanon and the Lebanese," interview published by Idrel.com.lb, August 27, 1999.
19. Quoted by Selim Abou, in his March 19, 1999, speech: "The Inputs of the University," p. 7.
20. Interview in *An-Nahar,* January 1996.
21. Interview of Ambassador Daniel Jouanneau with author in *As-Safir* daily, May 28, 1998.
22. Selim Abou, Choghig Kasparian, and Katia Haddad, *Anatomie de la Francophonie Libanaise,* Université St. Joseph et AUPELF-UREF, June 1996.
23. Those were Père Allard, P. Dumart, P. de Jerpagnion, P. Finnegan, P. André Masse, and P. Kleuters.
24. Interview with the author, November 1995, at the Vatican Synod.
25. Ibid.
26. Ibid.
27. Conversation with author.
28. The fathers of Syriac-Maronite spirituality, and the founders of the Syriac-Maronite doctrine and liturgy.
29. Yoakim Moubarac, "Introduction for an Aggiornamnto of the Maronite Church," (unpublished) p. 263.
30. Televised message of Pope John Paul II to the Catholics of Lebanon, June 21, 1991, and message to the Catholic patriarchs, archbishops and bishops of Lebanon, June 20, 1992.
31. "Coexistence and Identity," December 11–12, 1998 at the seminar, "The Identity in the Constitution and the Apostolic Exhortation" organized by the movement A Church for Our World.
32. Iliya Hariq, *Politics and Change in a Traditional Society, Lebanon 1711–1845,* Princeton: Princeton University Press, 1968; Tannus al-Shidyaq, *A Chronicle of Notables in Mount-Lebanon,* (2 vol.), Beirut, 1970; and Yoakim Moubarac, *Pentalogie Antiochienne/Domaine Maronite* (7 vol.), Beirut, Cénacle Libanais, 1984.

33. Hamid Mourani, "Maronite Identity Between Distress and Renewal," December 12, 1998 at the seminar, "The Identity in the Constitution and the Apostolic Exhortation," op. cit.
34. The first postwar president Elias Hrawi (1989–1998) was the only one to be "chosen" from the "periphery," that is his hometown of Zahlé (an overwhelmingly Greek Catholic city), in the Biqaa Valley.
35. Sawda's main works are: *For Lebanon* (in Arabic), Beirut, 1924; *For Independence* (in Arabic), Beirut, 1967; and *The History of Lebanese Civilization* (in Arabic), Beirut, 1972.
36. Between the Christian militia of the "Lebanese Forces" and the Christian wing of the army led by General Michel Aoun.
37. Mourani, op. cit.
38. Article published in *An-Nahar*, March 19, 1998.

CHAPTER 2

1. Although there were a good number of Shi'a in Mount-Lebanon, fair enough to be represented in the Mount-Lebanon assembly established under the Moutassarrifiya regime (1861–1914).
2. Commemorating the martyrdom of Ali's son, Hussein, in Karbala (Irak) in 680. Ali, whom the Shi'a community follows, was the brother-in-law of the Prophet.
3. Father Maurice Borrmans, *Orientations for a Dialogue between Christians and Muslims* (in French), Secrétariat for Non-Christians, Cerf, 1987.
4. Gerard Figuié, *Le Point sur le Liban*, Beyrouth, Anthologie, 1994.
5. The precise number is 3,111,828. Census carried out by the Ministry of Social Affairs, in cooperation with the United Nations Fund for the Population (UNFP), and published in October 1996. The census does not include, however, the number of Palestinian refugees in Lebanon, estimated to be over 360,000.
6. Some observers would see it as echoing a broader Sunni-Shi'a confrontation at a regional scale: from Bahrein to Pakistan to Iran, Iraq, and Afghanistan.
7. Interview of author with Sayyed Hani Fahs. Also see Fahs's article, "Shi'a Priorities in Lebanon," *As-Safir*, 1997.
8. Interview with the author, *Ces Hommes qui Font la Paix* (Those Men Who Make Peace), edited in Paris, L'Harmattan, 1995.
9. Fouad Ajami, *The Vanished Imam: Musa al Sadr and the Shia of Lebanon*, Ithaca, Cornell University Press, 1986.
10. Interview with the author.
11. Interview with the author, *As-Safir*, June 20, 1995.
12. Interview with the author.
13. Jean-Pierre Valognes, *Vie et Mort des Chrétiens d'Orient*, Fayard, 1994, p. 221.
14. Mohammad Sammak, *Introduction to the Muslim-Christian Dialogue*, Dar An-Nafaes, Beirut, 1998.

15. Ibid., p. 108.
16. Journalist and writer Elias Khoury, *An-Nahar* special, May 10, 1997, p. 19.
17. Sammak, op. cit., p. 85.
18. Ibid., p. 112.
19. Interview with the author, *As-Safir,* June 20, 1995.
20. Hassan Nasrallah, interview in *Al-Wasat,* March 15, 1999.
21. John J. Donohue, S.J., "Muslim-Christian Relations: Dialogue in Lebanon," Center for Muslim-Christian Understanding, Georgetown University, 1996.
22. Radwan al-Sayyed, cited in ibid., p. 9
23. Sammak, op. cit.,p.101
24. Mohammad Sammak, article in *Asharq al-Awsat,* May 21, 1997.
25. The "Hojair conference" held by the Shi'ites of Jabal 'Amel in April 24, 1920, vowed for unity with Syria under King Faysal, the son of Sherif Hussein of Mecca, before he was defeated by the French in Maysalun (1920). The "Sahel conference" presided over by Sunni leader Selim Ali Salam in 1936 seemingly opposed the adjunction of the four cazas (representing the North, the South, Beirut, and the Biqaa) to Mount-Lebanon. According to former president Amin Gemayel, "that conference was aimed against the French and President Emile Eddé, who had signed a cooperation treaty with them. But once the Christians fought for independence, Muslims withdrew their separatist claims" (interview with author).
26. These principles are developed by Mohammad Sammak in op. cit., p. 173.
27. Sayyed Hani Fahs, "The Shi'a Priorities in Lebanon," *As-Safir,* 1997.
28. Speech delivered in Baalbeck on August 31, 1985, the seventh anniversary of Musa al-Sadr's disappearance.
29. The Mufti of Baalbeck, Sheikh Khalil Shoucair, quoted in *As-Safir,* March 1997.
30. Augustus Richard Norton, *Amal and the Shi'a: Struggle for the Soul of Lebanon,* Austin, University of Texas Press, 1987, p. 42.
31. Norton quoting Karim Pakradouni, *La Paix Manquée,* Beirut: Editions FMA, 1989, p. 106.
32. Nizar Hamzeh and R. Hrair Dekmejian, "The Islamic Spectrum of Lebanese Politics," *The Beirut Review,* Spring 1994.
33. Interview with the author, *As-Safir,* June 21,1995.
34. Waddah Sharara's social analysis of Lebanon, in *ShuFiMaFi,* "a free weekly news report on Lebanon and the Lebanese," interview published by Idrel.com.lb, August 27, 1999.
35. Sammak, op. cit., p. 104.
36. Stunning examples corroborate the deep impact of living together on a daily basis. A former president of the Bar Association tells the story of a Shi'a wedding he attended, in which the man leading the procession was handling a censer like a priest would, and was censing people around him.
37. Sharara, op. cit.
38. Hans Putman, *L'Eglise et l'Islam sous Timothée 1er (780–823)* Beyrouth, Dar el-Machreq-Librairie Orientale, 1977.

39. Amin Maalouf, *Les Identités Meurtrières,* Grasset, 1998, p. 86.
40. Interview in *As-Safir,* May 4, 1998.
41. Borrmans, op. cit., p. 20.
42. Wajih Kawtharani, article in *As-Safir,* April 29, 1998.
43. Radwan as-Sayyed, article in *As-Safir,* April 29, 1998.
44. *L'Orient-LE JOUR,* December 6, 1997.
45. Sharara, op. cit.
46. Quoted by Charles M. Sennot, "Christians Are a Dwindling Force in War-Ravaged Lebanon," *Boston Globe,* January 19, 1999.
47. Sammak, op. cit., p. 96.
48. as-Sayyed, op. cit.

CHAPTER 3

1. This idea is defended by one of the most liberal Shi'a ulema, Sayyed Mohammed Hassan el-Amine, who calls for an earnest dialogue "that would free both sides from narrow sectarianism." See conference published in *An-Nahar,* December 8, 1992.
2. Respectively signed by Jerome Chahine, Sleiman Takieddine, Sami Makarem, Father Jean Corbon, Father Mouchir Basil Aoun, Bishop Gregoire Haddad, and Hassan Kobeyssi.
3. Quoted in *Al-Hayat,* October 11, 1993.
4. Ghassan Tuéni, *Une Guerre pour les Autres* (A War for the Others), édition Jean-Claude Lattès, 1985.
5. The Ta'if meeting of all Lebanese MPs convened in September 1990 under the impulse of the tripartite Arab committee (including Algeria, Morocco, and Saudi Arabia), the direct sponsorship of Saudi Arabia, the behind-the-scenes Syrian interest, and the U.S. blessing, to put an end to the war.
6. Ahmed Beydoun, *The Trends in the Lebanese War* (in Arabic), Beirut, The Arabic Cultural Center, 1990, p. 163.
7. *An-Nahar,* May 10, 1997.
8. On February 20, 1975, Imam Sadr held a conference in a church in downtown Beirut and the next day his picture appeared on the front pages of newspapers, Sadr sitting under a big cross stretching on the wall behind him.
9. A first attempt had taken place earlier, in 1954, in Bhamdoun (Lebanon), under the impulse of an American organization, but it produced no tangible result.
10. In *An-Nahar,* op. cit.
11. See Cardinal Francis Arinze, "Christian-Muslim Relations in the Twenty-first Century," Center for Muslim-Christian Understanding, Georgetown University, 1998.
12. The committee included Mohammad Sammak (Sunni), Hareth Chehab (Maronite), Seoud el-Mawla (Shiite), Gabriel Habib (Greek Orthodox),

Camille Menassa (Greek Catholic), Abbas Halabi (Druze), and Jean Salmanian (Armenian Orthodox).
13. The Mufti of the Republic Sheikh Hassan Khaled was killed in 1988 in a car explosion, and Maronite Patriarch Nasrallah Sfeir was assaulted in Bkerké by Christian extremists in 1990.
14. Mohammad Sammak, *Introduction to Christian-Muslim Dialogue,* Beirut, Dar An-Nafaes, 1998, p. 80
15. In John J. Donohue, "Muslim-Christian Relations: Dialogue in Lebanon," Center for Muslim-Christian Understanding, Georgetown University, 1998, p. 9.
16. "Christianity and Islam: Reflecting Mirrors," Center of Christian-Muslim Studies, University of Balamand, Lebanon, 1997; Review in *An-Nahar,* May 10, 1997.
17. Gregoire Haddad, "What to do?" *An-Nahar,* May 10, 1997.
18. Jean Corbon, article in *An-Nahar,* May 10, 1997.
19. Ibid.
20. Ibid.
21. Sammak, op. cit., p. 81.
22. Ibid., p. 104.
23. Jean-Pierre Valognes, *Vie et Mort des Chrétiens d'Orient,* Fayard, 1994, p. 206.
24. Father Mouchir Basil Aoun, article in *An-Nahar,* May 10, 1997.
25. Sammak, op. cit., pp. 20 and 74.
26. Maurice Borrmans, *Orientations pour un Dialogue entre Chrétiens et Musulmans,* Cerf, 1987, p. 40.
27. See Corbon, op. cit.
28. *An-Nahar,* May 10, 1997.
29. "The Christianity and the Islam of Lebanese People: Reflections on an Orphan Dialogue" (in Arabic), in *The Trends in the Lebanese War,* Beirut, The Arabic Cultural Center, 1990.
30. *An-Nahar,* May 10, 1997.
31. Presentation at the Synod on Lebanon, November 28, 1995.
32. Sheikh Mohammed Mehdi Shamseddine, *The Umma, the State and the Islamic Movement,* Al-Ghadir, 1994, p. 106.
33. *An-Nahar,* special issue, May 10, 1997.
34. Interview in *An-Nahar,* January 1996.
35. *Time Magazine,* special issue, Winter 1998–99.
36. Joseph and Laure Moghaizel Foundation. The Moghaizels have been the standard bearers of human rights and women's rights in Lebanon for decades. A good number of modern laws were voted in Parliament under their impulse.
37. Antoine Messarra, Democratic Culture and Regional Role, press conference, October 23, 1997.
38. Charles Winslow, *Lebanon: War and Politics in a Fragmented Society,* New York, Routledge, 1996, pp. 290–4.
39. A position all too evident but given the past cooperation of Christian militias with Israel in wartime (a cooperation that did not necessarily reflect

the Christian mainstream's convictions), some estimated that the Christians' political stands in postwar era had to be clearly defined.
40. Seoud el-Mawla, article in *As-Safir,* April 3–4, 1997.
41. Ibid.
42. The Greek Orthodox Patriarch had even been supportive of Faysal of Syria against the French. Those decided to transfer his seat to Damascus.
43. Interview with author, *As-Safir,* January 29, 1998.
44. "Maronite priests who wear the emblem of the Cedars on their stole cause us a spiritual problem," confided a Greek Orthodox bishop to the author. "The Maronites are clearly the Church of a land, we are rather a Church of citizens of the State."
45. *L'Orient-LE JOUR,* June 9, 1998, p. 3.
46. Interview with author, *As-Safir,* January 29, 1998.
47. Conference, "Cultural Diversity and Political Unity," May 18, 1993.
48. Roundtable organized by the French-speaking daily *L'Orient-LE JOUR,* June 3, 1997.
49. Interview with author, July 1998.
50. Shamseddine, The Umma, the State and the Islamic movement, Al-Ghadir, 1994, p. 105.
51. Edgar Morin, "Penser la Méditerranée" (To Think the Mediterranean), *Confluences,* éditions L'Harmattan, Hiver 1998–99, p. 42.
52. Conversation with author.

CHAPTER 4

1. "Christians of the Orient" is the literal transcription of the French expression "Chrétiens d'Orient." It has a broader meaning than the English version of "Eastern Christians" and a more historical and cultural outlook. This is why I tend to use this expression more often when I refer to them.
2. Jean-Pierre Valognes, *Vie et Mort des Chrétiens d'Orient,* Fayard, 1995, p. 838; and Tarek Mitri, "Qui sont les Chrétiens du Monde Arabe?" in *Version Originale,* no. 7, April 1998.
3. Study conducted by researcher Ralph Ghodbane, published in *An-Nahar,* special issue, January 1998.
4. Valognes, op. cit.; and Ghodbane, ibid.
5. Ghodbane, op. cit.
6. Ghodbane, op. cit., p. 5.
7. The Holy Land Christian Ecumenical Foundation organizing the first National Conference for Christians and their Churches, October 2, 1999, Washington, D.C.
8. Census conducted by the "Office of the Cereals" during World War II, under supervision of the Allied Forces, for the purpose of food supplies.
9. Ghodbane, op. cit.
10. Assaad Haidar, article in *Al-Mustaqbal,* February 18, 1984.
11. According to a private research group, MASS, 1987.

12. Sample survey conducted by Reach Consulting Institute-Beirut.
13. Ghodbane article, op. cit.
14. *The World Fact Book,* 1995.
15. *The World Fact Book,* 1997–98.
16. Cited in Ghodbane, op. cit.
17. Boutros Labaki, "Emigration Since the End of Wars in Lebanon (1990–98)," *Travaux et Jours,* St. Joseph University, no. 61, Spring 1998.
18. Sample survey conducted by Anis Abi-Farah, "The Lebanese emigrants, 1975–96," in *al-Shou'oun al-Iktisadiya,* November 1997, no. 34, p. 30.
19. A study by Nabil Harfouche, former president of the World Lebanese Cultural Union: "Statistics of Lebanese emigration" (in Arabic), *al-'Amal,* April 13, 1978.
20. Houda Zreik, "The Decision Making for Provisional or Permanent Emigration from Lebanon," *Al-Moustaqbal al Arabi,* May 1981, pp. 89–91.
21. Michael Humphrey, "Muslim Lebanese," in *The Australian People: An Encyclopedia of the Nation, its People and its Origins,* Angus and Robertson, 1988, p. 677.
22. *Al-Hayat,* June 17–18, 1989.
23. Francoise Chipeaux, "One Million Refugees on the Roads," *Le Monde,* August 24, 1989, p. 6.
24. Boutros Labaki, op. cit.
25. Interview in *Al-Anwar,* November 5, 1995.
26. Frank Geseman and Helga Auschiitz, *Lebanese refugees of the civil war in the Federal Republic of Germany* (in German), Berlin, Berlin Institute of Compared Social Studies, 1995, pp. 8–9.
27. According to *The World Fact Book* of 1997–98, the average rate is 3.24 children born per woman and the population growth rate is 2.16 percent (1996 est.) for a population of 3.7 million. According to Professor Ibrahim Maroun (at a conference organized by the Lebanese Foundation for Permanent Civil Peace, May 1997), who referred to the *Association of Banks in Lebanon: Economic Letter,* October 1997, and also *L'Hebdomadaire Francais, Problèmes économiques, La Documentation Francaise,* July 1, 1992, birthrate is 1.6 percent, and the average family size is 4.7 members / family. There are 660,000 families in Lebanon, for a population of 3.1 million. Figures in Lebanon are really a tricky issue!
28. David Yaukey: *Fertility Differences in a Modernising Country: A Survey of Lebanese Couples,* Washington, NY, Kennikat Press Port, 1972, p. 29; Joseph Chamié, *Religion and Fertility: Arab Christian-Muslim Differentials,* Cambridge, Cambridge University Press, 1981, p. 44; Theodor Hanf, study conducted in summer 1988 and reproduced by a private Lebanese firm.
29. Sample survey conducted by Marie-Thérèse Salhab in 1985 on the comparative demographic growth of the Maronites and the Shiites. Cited by Professor Ibrahim Maroun in his research paper "The Demographic, Economic and Institutional Power of Maronites in Lebanon," 1989, as part of the preparatory documents for the Maronite synod (private source).
30. Interview of Walid Joumblatt in *al-Dyar,* February 20, 1998.

31. Zouheir Berro, article in *As-Safir*, February 2, 1998.
32. Mohammed Sayyed Ahmad, article in *An-Nahar*, January 10, 1998.
33. Fadlallah "This Is What Islam needs," *An-Nahar*, January 10, 1998.
34. Boutros Labaki, op. cit., p. 132.
35. Jaber Ragheb, article in *As-Safir*, November 13, 1993.
36. *Association of Banks: Economic Letter*, no. 10, October 97, pp. 3 and 14.
37. Research study conducted by expert Iskandar Chalfoun in 1985/86, published by author in *As-Safir*, January 19, 1993. The study did not include non-registered enterprises, which flourished during the war.
38. Charles M. Sennot, "Christians Are a Dwindling Force in War-Ravaged Lebanon," *Boston Globe*, January 19, 1999.
39. Michel Chiha, *Lebanon at Home and Abroad, Propos d'Economie Libanaise, Politique Intérieure*, Beirut, Editions du Trident, 1964, 1965, 1966. Also see Paul Tabar, "The Image of Power in Maronite Historical and Political Discourse," *The Beirut Review*, Spring 1994.
40. Boutros Labaki's study based on Anis Abi-Farah research on the Lebanese emigrants, op. cit.
41. Study conducted in cooperation with the United Nations Fund for Population Activities, (FNUAP), 1994–1996, Beirut.
42. Interview with author, *As-Safir*, December 14, 1995.

CHAPTER 5

1. Official sources estimated at 350,000 the number of Lebanese emigrants in Africa (1993), but this number has decreased in the last couple of years as troubles broke out in various African countries. In places such as Liberia, Zaire, Sierra Leone, and Nigeria, Lebanese colonies were aggressed, forcing dozens of thousands of them to flee back to Lebanon.
2. His visit was followed by the inauguration of the first direct Beirut-Sao Paolo flight on the wings of the national Middle East Airlines.
3. *Le Monde, Bilan du monde, L'année économique et sociale, 1996–97*, p. 66.
4. Study conducted by author and published in a set of three articles in *As-Safir*, May 1993.
5. Yoakim Moubarac, "Introduction for an Aggiornamento in the Maronite Church," (unpublished).
6. Interview in *Famille Chrétienne*, no. 1008, May 8, 1997.
7. Moubarac, op. cit., p. 183.
8. Boutros Labaki and Khalil Abou-Rjeily, *An Assessment of Lebanon's Wars 1975–1990*, (in French), Beirut, 1993; Robert Kasparian, André Beaudoin, and Sélim Abou, *The Population Displaced by War in Lebanon* (in French), a study conducted jointly by the St. Joseph University, Beirut, and Laval University, Québec, Editions L'Harmattan, 1995.
9. Mobarac, op. cit., p. 176.
10. Kasparian, Beaudoin, and Abou, "Introduction," op. cit.
11. Before the SLA finally withdrew from that region in Spring 1999.

12. The "Damascus road" crosses the Lebanese capital, splitting it into two sectors (known during wartime as East Beirut and West Beirut), and then continues through the Aley, Bhamdoun resorts in the Shouf mountain to the Biqaa Valley and from there reaches the Syrian capital.
13. Doctorate thesis in political science submitted at the University of Grenoble, France 1976, cited in the preparation works for a Synod of the Maronite Church, Father Yoakim Moubarac's archives.
14. Official statement, November 30, 1992.
15. Damour's population was massacred by the Palestinians and their Lebanese allies during the first years of the war, as a reprisal for the siege and the fall of the Palestinian camp of Karantina in the Eastern suburbs of Beirut at the hands of the Phalangist party.
16. Some analysts say that Joumblatt also fears a Shiite "overflow" on his Western flank.
17. Beiteddine reverted to state control in February 1999, under current President Emile Lahoud, who made it his summer residence.
18. Pierre Helou is a leading Maronite figure who has been deputy of Aley and Baabda for years, while Fouad el-Saad (a former deputy too) is the grandson of the former president of the republic under French mandate, Habib Bacha el-Saad. His family's origins and vast domain are in the Shouf.
19. Deir el-Kamar, whose walls encompass the palace of the Grand Emir of Lebanon, Fakhreddine II, is also the birthplace and hometown of the late president of the republic, Camille Chamoun, whose son Dany was assassinated with his wife and children in 1990. After Dany's death, his brother Dory became the leader of the National Liberal Party, founded by his father Camille. The Chamouns and the Joumblatts share historical bonds, due to the friendship of Camille Chamoun and Kamal Joumblatt, Walid's father. This friendship is the main reason why Walid Joumblatt directly intervened to preserve and protect Deir el-Kamar from the massacres of 1983.
20. Labaki and Abou-Rjeily, op. cit.; Khalil Abou-Rjeily, "L'émigration forcée des populations à l'intérieur du Liban," *Monde Arabe,* Maghreb-Machreq, no. 125, 1989, pp. 53–68.
21. Report issued by the Ministry of the Displaced, July 1997.
22. Report issued by the Ministry of the Displaced, in *An-Nahar,* July 22, 1997, p. 7.
23. Private group study presented to the Maronite episcopate of Mount-Lebanon, August 1997.
24. *An-Nahar,* September 2, 1995, September 14, 1996, and October 31, 1996.
25. *L'Orient LE-JOUR,* July 6, 1998.
26. Kasparian, Beaudoin, and Abou, op. cit., p. 138.
27. Quoted in Kasparian, Beaudoin, and Abou, op. cit.

CHAPTER 6

1. Conversation with author.

2. The Holy Father used a rhymed sentence in French: "J'étais affectivement Libanais, je suis devenu effectivement Libanais."
3. Carl Bernstein and Marco Politi, *His Holiness Pope John Paul II and the Hidden History of Our Time,* Bantam Books, 1996, p. 208 and p. 303.
4. Conference held in December 1998 at the Center for Muslim-Christian Understanding, Georgetown University.
5. Archbishop Tauran's lecture, "The Holy See and the Middle East," given at the Catholic University of America, Washington, D.C., March 10, 1999.
6. Ibid.
7. Message from His Holiness to the Catholic patriarchs, archbishops and bishops of Lebanon, June 20, 1992.
8. Interview with author, December 12, 1995, during the Synod in Rome.
9. See Albert Mansour, *The Coup d'Etat against Ta'if* (in Arabic: Al-Inqilab 'ala Ta'if), 1993, Dar el-Jedid, Beirut.
10. Video taped message of the Holy Father to the Catholics of Lebanon, July 1991.
11. Interview with author.
12. Interview with author, December 1995.
13. Mohammad Sammak, interview with author.
14. Bishop Beshara Rahi was very much popular precisely because he spoke out eloquently, denouncing "the occupation of Lebanon by foreign forces" and the corruption of its rulers.
15. The main Eastern Catholic Churches are the Maronite, the Greek Catholic, the Syrian Catholic, the Armenian Catholic, the Coptic Catholic, and the Chaldean. Except for the Maronite Church, they all derive from the Orthodox trunk (Greek Orthodox, Syrian Orthodox, Armenian Orthodox, Coptic Orthodox, and Assyrian). The Latin Church which seat is in Jerusalem is hardly viewed as a historically Eastern Church, but it is definitely bound to the fate of Eastern Christianity and was part of the Synod.
16. Video taped message of the Holy Father to the Catholics of Lebanon, July 1991.
17. Televised address of Cardinal Lustiger in Notre-Dame of Harissa, October 1995.

CHAPTER 7

1. Interview with author, December 1995.
2. Conversation with author.
3. Interview with author, *As-Safir,* December 7, 1995.
4. Interview with author, *As-Safir,* May 10, 1993.
5. *Agence France-Presse,* December 1995
6. Interview with author, *As-Safir,* December 7, 1995.
7. Conversation with author, December 1995, at the Vatican.
8. Archbishop Jean-Louis Tauran, "The Holy See and the Middle East," lecture at the Catholic University of America, Washington, D.C., March 10, 1999.

9. Interview with author, December 1995.
10. Interview with author, *As-Safir*, December 6, 1995.
11. Interview with author.
12. Ibid.
13. Ibid.
14. *La Croix*, November 11, 1995, p. 14.
15. John Donohue, S.J., "Religion between Violence and Reconciliation," Conference at the Orient-Institute, Beirut, September 1998.
16. Charfé is the seat of the Syrian Catholic patriarchate (Lebanon).
17. Radwan Sayyed, "Discussing the Final Message," *As-Safir*, December 23–24, 1995.
18. Ibid.

CHAPTER 8

1. Interview with author.
2. Interview in *Famille Chrétienne*, May 8, 1997.
3. Quoted in *L'Orient-Express*, May 1997, p. 45.
4. Ibid.
5. Ibid.
6. Exclusive interview with author, December 1995, in Rome.
7. *L'Orient-Express*, May 1997, p. 44.
8. Ibid.
9. Interview with author, *As-Safir*, December 14, 1995.
10. Quoted in *Famille Chrétienne*, May 8, 1997, p. 6.
11. Quoted in *As-Safir*, June 12, 1996, p. 9.
12. "Writing the History of Lebanon: Where Do We Go from Here?" a seminar organized by the Association of the Makassed alumni, April 20, 1993.
13. "Writing the History Book," *As-Safir*, June 12, 1996.
14. Ibid.
15. The palace reverted to state control only in 1999.
16. Ahmad Beydoun, *Identité confessionnelle et temps social chez les historiens libanais contemporains,* Beyrouth, Université Libanaise, Distribution Librairie Orientale, 1984.
17. The Shiites.
18. Cited by Ahmad Beydoun, op. cit., p. 558.
19. "The Young Don't Know," *As-Safir*, September 24, 1992.
20. Conclusions of a seminar organized by the Moghayzel Foundation, "Democracy in the Universities," March 1998.
21. Antoine Messarra's presentation of the "Observatory for Democracy" project at the forty-ninth anniversary of the Human Rights Declaration, press conference organized by the Lebanese Human Rights Association and the Moghayzel Foundation, December 10, 1997.
22. The Lebanese media reported that Syrian workers were beaten in the southern suburbs of Beirut by Shiite youngsters frustrated by the defeat of

the Lebanese soccer team at the PanArab Games organized in Beirut, Summer 1997.
23. *L'Orient-LE JOUR,* March 7, 1998.

CHAPTER 9

1. Geagea has been sentenced to life imprisonment for the 1990 assassination of Dany Chamoun, leader of the National Liberal Party and a rival for the leadership of the Maronite community. He has been acquitted for the blasting of a church in 1994, but he is still accused of being involved in the civil wartime assassination of a Christian lawyer and of then Prime Minister Rashid Karame.
2. The 1992 electoral law was discriminatory in that it imposed double standards in the carving of electoral districts: the big *mohafazat* in mixed regions, to weaken Christians' vote and undercut their ability to send opposition representatives to Parliament, and to ensure the success of pro-regime candidates; and the smaller *caza* in the Shouf, to allow Druze leader Walid Joumblatt to send his electoral list to the Parliament. As a minority group, the Druze could only have a significant representation in Parliament on a small electoral district basis (the *caza*).
3. The Maronite League, which was linked to the Maronite Patriarchate, had a pending appeal against the decree of naturalization, before the Council of State, the highest jurisdiction dealing with administrative issues. This appeal did not prevent the newly naturalized from voting in the 1996 elections. TV reports of LBCI showed trucks bringing loads of naturalized Syrians from their Syrian hometowns across the border for the sole purpose of casting their ballot in some Biqaa villages so that they would tip the balance in favor of pro-regime candidates.
4. This number has been registered by the United Nations Relief and Works Agency (UNRWA) in 1998.
5. Communiqué of the APECL issued by its information committee, *Jal el-Dib,* May 15, 1998.
6. Volker Perthes, "Myths and Money: Four Years of Hariri and Lebanon's Preparation for a New Middle East," *Middle East Report,* Spring 1997.
7. Until the election of current President Emile Lahoud, who lifted the ban.
8. The decree was abolished when President Lahoud was elected.
9. Human rights lawyer Ghassan Mokheiber says one tactic employed by officials is a refusal to "receive" documents from newly-formed NGOs, as required by the constitution (this provision is referred to as "'ilm wa khabar"), thereby putting the organizations in danger of being classified as illegal "secret societies" (*Daily Star,* March 22, 1999).
10. The Lebanese Constitution expressly forbids the renewal of the six-year presidential term and even prohibits the president from running for office again before another six years elapse.
11. In *L'Orient-LE JOUR,* June 3, 1997.

12. Albert Mansour, "Al-Inqilab 'ala Ta'if," Beirut, *Dar al-Jadid,* 1993.
13. Ibid., pp. 225, 226, 227.
14. Even the militia of the "Lebanese Forces," which is initially an offshoot of the Phalangists, chose a "pragmatic approach," under its leader Samir Geagea, who accepted Ta'if (this would be the direct cause of the fight against General Aoun, who rejected the accord). Ultimately, Geagea ended up on trial and in prison on various war crimes charges, with the death penalty sought for him by the public prosecutor.
15. Georges Saadeh, *My Story with Ta'if—Ambiguities and Ordeal, Mismanagement and Deception* (in Arabic), Beirut, 1998. The book is prefaced by Algerian diplomat Lakhdar Ibrahimi, who was the mediator of the Arab tripartite committee during the Lebanese crisis and the "war of liberation" against Syria.
16. Review of Hezbollah's press releases and communiqués in Lebanese newspapers, September 1986, August 1987, and September 1989.
17. Interview with author, in *As-Safir,* December 8, 1992.
18. Ibid.
19. Sheikh Naim Kassem, ibid.
20. In an interview to the daily As-Safir, April 30, 1996.
21. The committee for support of the Islamic Resistance, ad published in As-Safir and other papers, March 1996
22. Even Iranian President Mohammad Khatami recognized that "Lebanon is the victim of his defense of the Arabs and the Muslims," in *An-Nahar,* October 30, 1999.
23. Hilal Khashan, "Partner or Pariah? Attitudes toward Israel in Syria, Lebanon and Jordan," *The Washington Institute Policy Papers,* No. 41, 1996, p. 13.
24. Al Mustaqbal television, March 2, 1995.
25. *L'Orient-LE JOUR,* March 7, 1998.
26. In a letter issued September 22, 1999, Samuel Berger, National Security adviser to President Clinton, reassured the American Task Force for Lebanon that "I believe that Lebanon must be treated as an equal partner in the peace process." He confirmed a previous statement of his that "Lebanon is an indispensable part of the equation," and stressed that "Secretary Albright's visit to Lebanon (early September 1999) was a strong signal of our commitment to the Lebanese people."
27. Faysal Selman, *As-Safir,* July 1999.
28. Interview in *Al-Wasat* weekly magazine, March 15, 1999.
29. Hezbollah obtained its own reconstruction project of Beirut's southern suburbs, Elyssar, as the Shiite counter-plan to Hariri's downtown site of Solidere.
30. Paul Khalifeh in *L'Orient-LE JOUR:* "Hezbollah impervious to the wind of change that blows in Iran," August 15, 1998 (in French).
31. Elias Hrawi's speech at the Islamic Conference Summit in Teheran, December 10, 1997.

32. *Association of Banks in Lebanon: Economic Letter,* issue no.10, October 1997, pp.3 and 14. Cited by Ibrahim Maroun during a conference organized by the Lebanese Foundation for Permanent Civil Peace, May 17, 1997.
33. Hrawi and Syrian president Hafez Assad signed a "Fraternity, Cooperation and Coordination" agreement in 1991 that provided a substratum for the successive economic, water, and military treaties between the two countries.
34. Interview with author, in *As-Safir,* May 28, 1998.
35. *The Lebanon Report,* published by the Lebanese Center for Policy Studies, Spring 1997, p. 8.
36. Interview in *Famille Chrétienne,* May 8, 1997.

CHAPTER 10

1. But unlike countries such as Turkey and Morocco, who were also compelled to fight drug cultivation and drug dealing, Lebanese farmers did not receive any compensation or international aid to support a substitute agriculture. Consequently, poverty and unemployment have increased in that region.
2. General Jamil Sayyed, "The Integration in the Lebanese Armed Forces: A Transitory Experience or a Permanent Policy?" 1997. A study intended for military officers and chiefs of staff.
3. Ibid., p. 32.
4. Ibid., p. 12.
5. Ibid., p. 13.
6. Ibid.
7. Ibid.

CHAPTER 11

1. Kamal Salibi, *A House of Many Mansions: The History of Lebanon Reconsidered,* London, I. B. Taurus, 1988.
2. See Michael Hudson, *The Precarious Republic: Political Modernization in Lebanon.* New York, Random House, 1968.
3. Constitution expert and historian Edmond Rabbath has extensively written about that subject. See especially *La formation historique du Liban politique et constitutionnel: Essai de synthèse,* Beyrouth, Université Libanaise, Distribution Librairie Orientale, 1986.
4. Rabbath, ibid.
5. Ibid.
6. Nawaf Salam, "The Individual and the Citizen in Contemporary Lebanon" (in French), Paris, *Le Liban d'Aujourd'hui,* CNRS, 1993.
7. Michael Hudson, "Trying Again: Power-Sharing in Post–Civil War Lebanon" *International Negotiation,* Netherlands, 1997.

8. Rabbath, ibid.
9. One of the main advocates of that thesis was nationalist writer Yusif Sawda, who played a major role in the fight for independence under French mandate. Paul Tabar has developed some of Sawda's political discourse in "The Image of Power in Maronite Historical and Political Discourse," *The Beirut Review,* Spring 1994.
10. See Hudson, ibid.
11. Interview with author, July 1998.
12. Hassan Saab, *Islam and the Challenges of Modern Life* (in Arabic), Beirut, 1965.
13. George Corm was appointed Minister of Finance in the first government under President Emile Lahoud's tenure.
14. Farid el-Khazen, "Changing Political Arabism and the Reality of Arabism in Lebanon," conference held at a private symposium, Beirut, December 11–12, 1998.
15. Michael Hudson, "Interventions in Lebanon: the Domestic Context and Perspectives," in Milton J. Esman and Shibley Telhami, eds., *International Organizations and Ethnic Conflict,* Ithaca, NY, Cornell University Press, 1995, pp. 126–47.
16. Jamil Sayyed, *The Integration in the Lebanese Armed Forces: A Transitory Experience or a Permanent Policy?* Beirut, 1997 (see Chapter 10).
17. Interview with author, December 1995, at the Vatican.
18. Mohammad Sammak, *Introduction to the Muslim-Christian Dialogue,* Beirut, Dar an-Nafaes, 1998, p. 146.
19. Ibid., p. 176.
20. In "Les Cahiers de l'Orient," first trimester of 1994, p. 221.
21. Quoted in *L'Orient-LE JOUR,* December 18, 1998, p. 2.
22. In *L'Orient-LE JOUR,* June 3, 1997.
23. Charles Winslow, *Lebanon: War and Politics in a Fragmented Society,* New York, Routledge, 1996, p. 294.
24. "The Observatory of Democracy," press conference in Lebanon, October 23, 1997.
25. "Principles of Peace: Northern Ireland and the Middle East," remarks by Senator George Mitchell, Fares Lecture, Tufts University, November 4, 1998. Also see George Mitchell, *Making Peace,* New York, Alfred A. Knopf, 1999.
26. Antoine Messarra, *The Lebanese Pact: The Message of Universality and its Constraints* (in French), Beirut, Distribution Librairie Orientale, 1997, p. 154.
27. Michel Hayek, interview in *Le Réveil,* January 15, 1979.
28. Nicolas Murad, *Notice historique sur l'origine de la nation maronite,* Paris, 1844. Reproduced in 1988 by Cariscript, Paris.
29. In *l'Orient LE-JOUR,* June 3, 1997.
30. Yoakim Moubarac, *Introduction to A Conciliar Reform Within the Maronite Church,* p. 143–144, unpublished.

31. Antoine Messarra, "The Head of State, Guardian of the Principle of Legality," in *L'Orient-LE JOUR*, October 19, 1998.
32. Carole Dagher, *Ces Hommes qui Font la Paix* (Those Men Who Make Peace), Paris, Editions L'Harmattan, 1995, p. 289.
33. Inauguration of the meeting of the Assembly of Catholic Patriarchs and Bishops, in *L'Orient-LE JOUR*, November 30, 1992.

CHAPTER 12

1. Since then, Geagea has been acquitted in that particular case since no evidence proved his direct involvement in the blasting of the Church. But he is still charged with other war crimes.
2. Interview in *L'Orient-LE JOUR*, May 1, 1997.
3. Catholic Almanach, 1997–98; Annuario Pontificio, Città del Vaticano, 1996, 1997, and 1998.
4. Interview in *L'Orient-LE JOUR*, May 9, 1997.
5. Interview in *L'Orient-LE JOUR*, May 6, 1997.
6. Ibid.
7. According to Druze leader Walid Joumblatt, the meeting in Damascus was "a direct response to the Pope's journey and to the orientations of the Lebanese Church." Interview in *As-Safir*, May 9, 1997.
8. Interview in *As-Safir*, May 3, 1997.
9. Cited in *Le Figaro*, May 12, 1997, and *Libération*, May 12, 1997.
10. Quoted in *L'Orient-LE JOUR*, May 12, 1997.
11. According to the Vatican's estimates.
12. Gebran Tuéni, director of *An-Nahar*, quoted in *Libération*, May 12, 1997.
13. "Peace be with you," in Arabic.
14. That was in 1979.
15. George Weigel, *Witness to Hope: The Biography of Pope John Paul II*, Cliff Street Books (Harper Collins Publishers), 1999, p. 818.
16. In the early sixteenth century, Pope Leo X had described the Maronites of Lebanon as "a rose among the thorns."
17. The Apostolic Exhortation, rendered public on May 10, 1997, Libreria Editrice Vaticana, CITE DU VATICAN, Introduction, first paragraph (p.4 in the original French version).
18. Ibid., paragraph 6 (p. 10).
19. Ibid., paragraph 115 (p. 182).
20. Ibid., paragraph 95 (p. 152).
21. Ibid., paragraph 93 (titled: "Solidarity with the Arab world"), (p. 148).
22. Ibid., paragraph 89 (p. 144).
23. Quoted in *As-Safir*, June 21, 1997.
24. Interview in *L'Orient-LE JOUR*, May 1, 1997.
25. Apostolic Exhortation, paragraph 121 (p. 189).
26. Ibid., paragraph 15 (p. 24).

27. Conference on the Apostolic Exhortation, in *L'Orient-LE JOUR,* June 19, 1997.
28. In *L'Orient-LE JOUR,* June 19, 1997.
29. Conversation with author, Spring 1998.
30. Conversation with author, Summer 1997.
31. Apostolic Exhortation, paragraph 78 (p. 125).
32. Issa Goraieb, article in *L'Orient-LE JOUR,* May 11, 1997.
33. Interview with author, winter 1998.
34. In *Les Cahiers de l'Orient,* first trimester 1994, Paris.
35. The original Arabic name of the Levant.
36. In *L'Orient-LE JOUR,* June 3, 1997.
37. Apostolic Exhortation, paragraph 114 (p. 179).
38. In *The Washington Post,* October 30, 1998.
39. Desmond Tutu, *No Future Without Forgiveness,* Doubleday, 1999.
40. In 1840 and 1860, large-scale massacres of Christians by the Druzes occurred in Mount-Lebanon; 1958 marks the first Christian-Muslim outburst in post-independence Lebanon and was a prelude to the 1975 civil war.
41. Samir Frangié, article in *L'Orient-LE JOUR,* June 7, 1997.

CHAPTER 13

1. Conference organized by the Middle East Policy Council on Capitol Hill, September 1998.
2. Speech at a banquet organized by The Holy Land Christian Ecumenical Foundation on October 2, 1999, Washington D.C., closing a conference entitled: "Endangered People: Christians in the Holy Land—Can They Survive the Millenium?"
3. In Jerusalem in 1922, the Christian population was 51 percent. By 1990 it had dropped to 4 percent; now it is less than 2 percent. Figures given by The Holy Land Christian Ecumenical Foundation.
4. Interview with author, in *As-Safir,* January 29, 1998.
5. Interview in *As-Safir,* January 23, 1997.
6. Ibid.
7. Interview with author, in *As-Safir,* January 27, 1998.
8. Ibid.
9. Address to the Middle East Council of Churches, in Beirut, June 16, 1996, on the question of Jerusalem.
10. Kafity has been a honorary co-president of the Middle East Council of Churches.
11. Greek Orthodox Patriarch Hazim, interview with author, January 29, 1998.
12. Interview with author, in *As-Safir,* December 6, 1995.
13. May 1996 note by the Vatican Secretariat of State titled: "Jerusalem: Considerations of the Secretariat of State."

14. George Weigel, *Witness to Hope: The Biography of Pope John Paul II,* Cliff Street Books (Harper Collins Publishers), 1999, p. 697.
15. Giancarlo Zizola, "The New Arms of the Vatican," (in French)*Le Monde Diplomatique,* January 1998.
16. Weigel, op. cit., p. 713.
17. Greek Orthodox Patriarch Hazim, interview with author, January 29, 1998.
18. Archbishop Jean-Louis Tauran's conference, "The Holy See and the Middle East," at the Catholic University, Washington, D.C., March 10, 1999.
19. Ibid.
20. Lecture of Archbishop Jean-Louis Tauran at Cathedral High School Auditorium, New York City, October 23, 1999, during his visit to the permanent observer mission of the Holy See to the United Nations.
21. Mohammad Sammak, *Introduction to a Muslim-Christian Dialogue,* Beirut, Dar an-Nafaes, 1998, p. 164.
22. Secretary Albright's remarks at the Columbus School of Law, the Catholic University, Washington, D.C., "American Foreign Policy and the Search for Religious Freedom," October 23, 1997, in U.S. Department of State's Dispatch, November 1997.
23. "A Message from the Christians of Egypt," published in *The Washington Post,* November 5, 1998, p. A47, and signed "by more than 2000 from the most prominent writers, journalists, businessmen, lawyers, physicians, entertainers of the Christians of Egypt."
24. Evangelicals for Middle East Understanding (EMEU) national convention, November 5–7 1998, National Presbyterian Church, Washington D.C., "Religious Freedom and the Future of Christianity in the Middle East;" the HCEF's conference on October 2, 1999, Washington, D.C.; EMEU's conference on November 4–6, 1999, San Francisco.
25. Reverend Ateek at the EMEU National Conference, November 5, 1998.
26. National Council of Churches News, February 8, 1999.
27. The Palestinians have always been known as the most "secularized" of the Arab people, and sectarian polarization was not a common feature of their society. Was the rise of fundamentalism changing that? Were the Israelis activating the cleavages, as Arab news media and various analysts hinted?
28. In its *News Highlights,* October 26, 1999, the Ecumenical News International (ENI) reported that officials of the major faiths and heads of international organizations signed in Geneva, on October 24, 1999, a one-page document called the Geneva Spiritual Appeal, asking all political and religious leaders and organizations to ensure that religions are no longer used to justify violence and conflict. The group launching the appeal believe that fifty-six conflicts around the world are linked to religion.
29. Sammak, op. cit., p. 84.
30. Interview with author, *As-Safir,* August 1998.
31. In his speech at the banquet of the HCEF, Washington, D.C., October 2, 1999.

32. Milton Viorst, *In the Shadow of the Prophet: The Struggle for the Soul of Islam*, Anchor Books/Doubleday, 1998, p. 5.
33. Charles Winslow, *Lebanon: War and Politics in a Fragmented Society*, New York, Routledge, 1996, p. 297.
34. Michel Hayek, "The Maronite Church and the Land," (in French) paper presented at the Maronite Congress in New York City, 1980.

Bibliography

Abou, Selim, Choghig Kasparian, Katia Haddad, Anatomie de la Francophonie Libanaise. Université St. Joseph et AUPELF-UREF, Juin 1996.

Abou, Selim, Robert Kasparian, André Beaudouin. "The Population Displaced by War in Lebanon (in French: La population déplacée par la guerre au Liban), a study conducted by St. Joseph University, Beirut, and Laval University, Québec, 1995. Editions L'Harmattan.

Ajami, Fouad. The Vanished Imam: Musa al Sadr and the Shia of Lebanon. Ithaca: Cornell University Press, 1986.

al-Shidyaq, Tannus. A chronicle of Notables in Mount-Lebanon. 2 vols Beirut, 1970.

Antonius, George. The Arab Awakening: The Story of the Arab National Movement. Philadelphia: J. B. Lippincott, 1939.

Arinze, Cardinal Francis. "Christian-Muslim Relations in the Twenty-first Century," Center for Muslim-Christian Understanding, Georgetown University, 1998.

Armstrong, Arthur Hilary. Re-discovering Eastern Christendom; essays in commemoration of Don Bede Winslow, edited by A. H. Armstrong & E. J. B. Fry. London: Darton Longman & Todd (1963)

Armstrong, Karen. Jerusalem: One City, Three Faiths. London: Harper Collins, 1996.

———. A History of God: the 4000-year quest of Judaism, Christianity, and Islam. New York: Alfred A. Knopf; distributed by Random House, 1993.

———. Muhammad: a Western Attempt to Understand Islam. London: Victor Gollancz, 1991.

Bernstein, Carl and Marco Politi. His Holiness Pope John Paul II and the Hidden History of our Time. New York: Bantam Books, 1996.

Beydoun, Ahmad. Identité confessionnelle et temps social chez les historiens libanais contemporains. Beyrouth: Université Libanaise-Distribution Librairie Orientale, 1984.

bin Talal, El-Hassan. "Christianity in the Arab world," Amman: Royal Institute for Inter-Faith Studies, 1995.

Boisset, Louis. Foi Chrétienne et inculturation au Proche-Orient. Beyrouth, ISSR, 1992.

Borrmans, Maurice. "Orientations pour un dialogue entre Chrétiens et Musulmans." Secrétariat pour les non-Chrétiens, Cerf, 1987. Nouvelle édition revue et corrigée.

Chamié, Joseph. Religion and Fertility: Arab Christian-Muslim differentials. Cambridge: Cambridge University Press, 1981.

Cheikho Louis, Les Savants Arabes Chrétiens en Islam (622–1300). St. Paul, Liban, 1983.

Chiha, Michel. Propos d'Economie Libanaise and Politique Intérieure. Beyrouth: Editions du Trident, 1964, 1965, 1966.

Corbon, Jean. L'Eglise des Arabes, Paris: Editions du Cerf, 1977.

Corm, George. Contribution à l'étude des sociétés multiconfessionnelles, Effets socio-juridiques et politiques du pluralisme religieux. Paris: 1993.

Cragg, Kenneth. The Arab Christian: a History in the Middle East. London: Mowbray, 1992.

Dalrymple, William. From the Holy Mountain: A Journey Among the Christians of the Middle East. An Owl Books. New York: Henry Holt & Company, 1997. First Owl Books Edition 1999.

David, Yaukey. Fertility Differences in a Modernising Country: a Survey of Lebanese Couples. Second Edition. Port Washington, N.Y: Kennikat Press, 1972

Donohue, S.J., John. "Muslim-Christian Relations: Dialogue in Lebanon." Center for Muslim-Christian Understanding, Georgetown University, 1996.

Esposito, John L. Islam and politics, 4th Edition. Syracuse: Syracuse University Press, 1998

Esposito, John L. and John O. Voll. Islam and democracy. New York: Oxford University Press, 1996.

Fawaz, Leila Tarazi. Understanding Lebanon. Princeton, N. J.: Program in Near Eastern Studies, Princeton University, 1986.

Figuié, Gérard. Le point sur le Liban, Beyrouth: Anthologie, 1994.

Geseman, Frank and Helga Auschiitz, "Lebanese refugees of the civil war in the Federal Republic of Germany," Berlin Institute of Compared Social Studies. Berlin, 1995.

Haddad, Yvonne Yazbeck, John Obert Voll, and John L. Esposito; with Kathleen Moore and David Sawan. The Contemporary Islamic Revival: A Critical Survey and bibliography. New York: Greenwood Press, 1991.

Hanf, Theodor. Coexistence in Wartime Lebanon: Decline of a State and Rise of a Nation. London: I. B. Taurus, 1993.

Hariq, Iliya. Politics and Change in a Traditional Society, Lebanon 1711–1845. Princeton: Princeton University Press, 1968.

Hayek, Michel. Le Baptême des Larmes. Paris: Gallimard, 1972.

Hayek, Michel. Le Mystère d'Ismael. Paris: Editions Mame, 1964.

Hourani, Albert Habib.-Arabic Thought in the Liberal Age, 1798–1939. Cambridge; New York: Cambridge University Press, 1983.

———. The Emergence of the Modern Middle East. Berkeley: University of California Press, 1981.

———. A History of the Arab Peoples. Cambridge, Mass.: Harvard University Press, 1991.

Hudson, Michael. The Precarious Republic: Political modernization in Lebanon. New York: Random House, 1968.

Huntington, Samuel. The Clash of Civilization and the Remaking of World Order. New York: Simon & Schuster, 1996.

Khalaf, Samir. Lebanon's Predicament. Columbia University Press, 1987.

Khashan, Hilal. "Partner or Pariah? Attitudes Toward Israel in Syria, Lebanon and Jordan," The Washington Institute Policy Papers, n. 41, 1996.

Labaki, Boutros & Khalil Abou-Rjeily. An Assessment of Lebanon's War 1975–1990" (in French), Beirut:1993.

Labaki, Boutros. "Emigration Since the End of the Wars in Lebanon (1990–98) (in French), Travaux et Jours, St. Joseph University, Beirut, Spring 1998, n.61

Maalouf, Amin. Les Identités Meurtrières. Grasset, 1998.

Malik, Habib C. *Between Damascus and Jerusalem: Lebanon and Middle East Peace.* The Washington Institute for Near East Affairs. August 1997.

Mansour, Albert. "The Coup against Ta'if" (in Arabic: al-Inqilab 'ala Ta'if), Dar el-Jedid, Beirut, 1993.

Messarra, Antoine. "The Challenge of Coexistence." Oxford: Centre for Lebanese Studies, 1988.

Messarra, Antoine. "The Lebanese Pact: the Message of Universality and Its Constraints" (in French). Beirut: Distribution Librairie Orientale, 1997.

Miller, Judith. God has ninety-nine names: reporting from a militant Middle East. New York: Simon and Schuster, 1996.

Mitchell, Senator George. Making Peace. New York: Alfred A. Knopf, 1999.

Moubarac, Yoakim. Pentalogie Antiochienne/domaine maronite (7 vols.), Beyrouth: Cénacle Libanais, 1984.

Norton, Augustus R. Amal and the Shia: Struggle for the Soul of Lebanon. Austin: University of Texas Press, 1987.

Pakradouni, Karim. La Paix Manquée. Beirut: Editions FMA, 1989.

Phares, Walid. Lebanese Christian Nationalism: The Rise and Fall of an Ethnic Resistance. Lynne Rienner, 1995.

Picard, Elizabeth. Lebanon,-A Shattered Country: Myths and realities of the Wars in Lebanon. Translated from the French by Franklin Philip. New York: Holms and Meier, 1996.

———. Liban, état de discorde: des fondations aux guerres fratricides. Paris: Flammarion, 1988.

Putman, Hans. L'Eglise et l'Islam sous Timothée 1er (780–823). Beyrouth, Dar el-Machreq, Librairie Orientale, 1977.

Rabbath, Edmond. La formation historique du Liban politique et constitutionnel: Essai de synthèse. Beyrouth: Université Libanaise: distribution Librairie Orientale, 1986.

Saadeh, Georges. My Story with Ta'if: Ambiguities and Ordeal, Mismanagement and Deception (in Arabic), Beirut, 1998.

Salibi, Kamal. "A House of Many Mansions: The History of Lebanon Reconsidered." London: I.B. Taurus, 1988.

Salibi, Kamal. "East Side Story, West Side Story: Contrasting Lebanese Views of the Civil War." CCAS, Georgetown, 1985.

Sammak, Mohammad. Introduction to the Muslim-Christian Dialogue (in Arabic), Beirut: Dar an-Nafaes, 1998.

Sawda, Yusif. For Lebanon (in Arabic), Beirut 1924.

———. For Independence (in Arabic), Beirut, 1967.

———. The history of Lebanese Civilization (in Arabic), Beirut, 1972.

Shamseddine, Sheikh Mohammad Mehdi. The Umma, the State and the Islamic Movement (in Arabic). Al-Ghadir publications, Beirut, 1994.

Shararah, Waddah. Al-Ummah al-qalaqah : al-Amiliyun wa-al-asabiyah al-Amiliyah alá atabat al-dawlah al-Lubnaniyah. Beirut : Dar al-Nahar, 1996.

Szulc, Tad. Pope John Paul II: the biography. New York: Scribner, 1995.

Tuéni, Ghassan. Une Guerre pour les Autres. Paris: Edition Jean-Claude Lattès, 1985.

Tutu, Desmond. No Future Without Forgiveness. New York: Doubleday, 1999.

Valognes, Jean-Pierre. Vie et Mort des Chrétiens d'Orient. Fayard, 1994.

Viorst, Milton. In the Shadow of the Prophet: The Struggle for the Soul of Islam. New York: Anchor Books/Doubleday, 1998.

Weigel, George. Witness to Hope: the Biography of Pope John Paul II. Cliff Street Books, Harper Collins Publishers, 1999.

Wessels, Anthony. Arab and Christians? Kampen: Kok Pharos, 1995.

Index

'Achoura, 33, 36
Abdel-Nasser, Gamal, 19
Abdo, Mohammed, 198
Abou, Selim, 22–4
Afghani, Jamaleddine, 198
Aflak, Michel, 17, 19
Al-Jama'a al-Islamiya, 37, 56
Amal, 35–6, 37, 42, 80, 87, 143
Amchiti, Jeremie, 97
American University of Beirut (AUB), 16, 127–8, 134, 148
Amin, Sayyed Mohsen, 33
Angeloni, Luciano, 91, 99
An-Nahar, 49, 61, 67, 70
Aoun, Michel, 70, 72, 91–3, 100, 103, 134, 138, 143, 144, 154, 189, 195, 197
Apostolic Exhortation (1997), 49, 52, 56, 192–8
Arabity, 9, 19–24, 28, 31, 46, 47, 61, 143, 194, 211
Arinze, Francis, 98, 114, 120
Assad, Bachar, 155–6
Assad, Hafez, 99, 155–6, 180
As-Safir, 58, 76, 131–2
Audeh, Elias, 56, 61, 62, 104, 140

Bacha, Habib, 123, 126
Baker, James, 180, 181
Balfour Declaration, 40, 69
Bechara, Joseph, 22, 117, 126, 196
Berri, Nabih, 36, 42, 58, 73, 80, 139, 142, 144, 152, 156
Beydoun, Ahmed, 35, 50, 55, 132, 135

Bkerké, 24, 51, 136, 139, 140, 145–8, 153, 155–6, 217
Borrmans, Maurice, 55, 100, 107–8, 117
Boulos, Jawad, 132
Boustany, Boutros, 17
Boutros, Fouad, 61, 184
Boutros-Ghali, Youssef, 209
Buhigas, Celestino, 96–7
Bustros, Cyrille, 116

Capucci, Hilarion, 206
Carlos, Juan, 95
Casaroli, Agostino, 92, 96
Cayla, Leon, 170
Chalfoun, Khalil, 118
Chamoun, Camille, 35
Chamoun, Dory, 151
Charafeddine, Abdel-Hussein, 33
Chehab, Fouad, 157, 174
Chiha, Michel, 77
Chirac, Jacques, 26, 154
Confessionalism, abolition of, 9, 176–7
Consensual democracy, 9, 119, 177–9
Corbon, Jean, 54, 107

Debs, Youssef, 30, 132
Dhimmi, 18, 62, 169
Dialogue, Christian-Muslim, 8–10, 49–64
Displaced, 83–90. See also émigrés
Djerejian, Edward, 34, 180, 181
Donohue, John, 40, 109, 120
Druze, 26, 70, 72, 80, 83, 85, 86–8, 112–3, 131, 150–1, 170

Ducruet, Jean, 109, 117

Ebeid, William Makram, 18
Eddé, Raymond, 35, 151
Émigrés, 79–83. *See also* Displaced
Etchegaray, Roger, 96, 101, 120

Fadlallah, Sayyed Mohammad Hussein, 25, 36–8, 40, 43, 44, 46, 52, 55, 57, 75, 93, 108, 126, 146, 184, 185
Fahs, Sayyed Hani, 34, 38, 64, 195
Ferzli, Elie, 155
Francophony, 24–6
Frangié, Samir, 56, 155

Gannagé, Emma, 110
Gatti, Liugi, 84, 87, 96, 99, 115
Geagea, Samir, 8, 138, 174, 183, 189, 195, 198
Gemayel, Amin, 92, 138, 144, 195
Ghali, Wassef Boutros, 18
Greater Lebanon, establishment of, 30, 41, 83
Greek Orthodox, 19, 26, 39, 59, 60–2, 70–3, 117–8, 212–3

Haddad, Gregoire, 53, 128
Halaby, Abbas, 102, 108, 112–3
Hamadé, Marwan, 25, 176
Hamas, 38
Hariri, Rafik, 9, 26, 35, 39, 44, 58, 73, 82, 87, 89, 108–9, 118, 120, 129, 135, 136, 141, 148–52, 156, 184
Harissa, 91, 98, 105, 124, 185–6
Hayek, Michel, 19, 21, 63, 119, 179, 180, 215, 220
Hazim, Ignatius IV, 18, 60–1, 76, 140, 202, 206
Helou, Pierre, 87, 151
Hezbollah, 10, 34, 36–8, 40, 43, 56, 58, 62, 73, 97, 108, 124, 134, 139, 140, 145, 150, 154, 185
Holy See, the, 91, 93–4, 97–9, 100, 103, 109–10, 113, 116, 152–3, 184, 188, 194, 196, 206–8, 213
Hoss, Selim, 42, 45, 57

Hrawi, Elias, 46, 50, 81, 92, 100, 137, 139, 141, 142, 152, 156, 177
Hudson, Michael, 171, 174
Huntington, Samuel, 2, 7, 40, 45, 209, 212
Husseini, Hussein el-, 42, 143, 144, 184

Ibrahimi, Lakhdar, 92
Ihbat al Masihi, al, 137–8, 147
Instrumentum Laboris, 107–8, 119
Islamic Jihad, 38, 40
Israel, 4, 38, 69, 86, 150, 185, 205–206, 211

Jabal 'Amel, 33, 45, 132
Jamhour, Notre-Dame of, 15, 28, 67
Jerusalem, 69, 98, 185, 201–2, 205–7, 210–11, 214, 219, 220
Jesuits, the, 15–16–17, 27–8, 52, 109, 117
Jezzine, 86, 96–7, 116, 147
John Paul II, Pope, 3, 7, 8, 10, 27, 31, 49, 50, 52–3, 54, 59, 92, 94–101, 104–5, 109–12, 116, 120, 124–5, 138, 154, 179, 183–99, 205, 206, 208, 217
Jouanneau, Daniel, 25, 154
Joumblatt, Walid, 9, 25, 58, 72, 74, 86, 87–9, 96, 108, 131, 139, 141, 144, 150, 151, 167
Judaism, 204–9. *See also* Israel

Kabbani, Mufti, 120
Kamar, Deir el-, 88
Kan'an, Ghazi, 155
Kanaan, Mohammed, 125
Karam, Simon, 155
Kaslik, the Order of, 112, 127, 133
Kassem, Naim, 146
Kataeb, party the, 88, 143, 155
Kawtharani, Wajih, 56
Khaddam, Abdel-Halim, 99, 156, 180–1
Khairallah, Khairallah, 17
Khaled, Hassan, 42
Khashan, Hilal, 148

Khatami, Mohammed, 2, 40, 98
Khodr, George, 51, 54, 61, 101, 117, 120
Khoury, Elias, 39
Klat, Hector, 21
Kobeyssi, Hassan, 55
Kolvenbach, Peter-Hans, 5, 27, 55, 56, 102, 109, 175
Koueyter, George, 90

Labaki, Boutros, 71, 72, 76, 109, 110–1, 118
Lafon, Jean-Pierre, 25
Laghi, Pio, 78, 114, 128, 130
Lahoud, Emile, 155, 156, 157, 159–60, 163–4
Lammens, Henri, 132
Lebanese Armed Forces, 160, 163, 185
Linneamenta, 53, 101, 103–4, 107, 108, 113
Lumen Gentium, 39
Lustiger, Jean-Marie, 82, 105–6, 119, 132

Maalouf, Amin, 19, 20–1, 45
Manoogian, Torkom, 211
Maronites, 10, 16–7, 20–1, 25–31, 42, 60–2, 72–3, 77, 79–80, 82–3, 85, 93–4, 104, 112, 115–6, 123, 138–43, 151–6, 167, 168, 171–2, 180–1, 191–9
Massignon, Louis, 51
Mawla, Seoud el-, 52, 59, 62, 102, 108, 112, 113, 121, 143, 176, 179, 197
Meouchy, Boulos, 30
Messarra, Antoine, 57–8, 119, 133, 177–8, 180
Meyendorff, John, 121
Middle East Council of Churches, 107, 121, 192, 201, 205–8
Millet, regime the, 68, 169, 215
Mitri, Tarek, 76
Moubarac, Yoakim, 17, 24, 28, 31, 51, 82, 83, 179–80

Mount-Lebanon, 16, 29, 30, 34, 43, 51, 61, 68–9, 73–4, 83–5, 88–9, 161, 69, 170–2
Mourani, Antoine Hamid, 29, 31
Movement of the deprived, the, 34

Naccache, Alfred, 21
Naccache, Georges, 59
Nahda, 17, 28, 33, 46, 113
Najm, Pierre, 188
Najmeh, Elias, 184
Nasrallah, Sayyed Hassan, 36, 40, 146, 150, 185
National Pact, 3, 6, 11, 34, 41, 50, 59, 167–81
Norton, Augustus Richard, 42
Nostra Aetate, 39

Opus Dei, 124–5
Ottoman Empire, 1, 16, 25, 45, 68, 169

Pakradouni, Karim, 42
Paul VI, Pope, 97–8
Pironio, Eduardo, 114
Pluralism, 9, 11, 23–5, 29, 47, 56–7, 63–4, 75–6, 113, 119, 161, 174, 193–4, 211
Puente, Pablo, 62, 84, 91–4, 98, 108, 109, 110, 111, 116, 183, 194, 196

Qabalan, Abdel-Amir, 37
Qannubin, 30, 105

Rabbath, Edmond, 169, 170–2
Rafd, 34
Rahi, Bechara, 101, 113, 123, 140, 155, 183, 194
Ratzinger, Joseph, 114
Renan, Ernest, 5
Rida, Ahmed, 33

Saab, Hassan, 173
Saad, Fouad el-, 87, 88
Saadé, Antoun, 17
Saadeh, Georges, 143–4, 155

Sabbah, Michel, 116, 201–2, 204–5, 211, 212, 214
Sadr, Musa, 34, 35, 36, 42, 51, 57
Safavid, the, 33
Salam, Nawaf, 67, 110, 171
Salibi, Kamal, 47
Samaha, Michel, 155
Sammak, Mohammad, 39, 40, 41, 44–7, 52–5, 101, 102, 108, 112, 113, 119–21, 175, 204, 213
Samné, Georges, 17
Sarkis, Elias, 31
Sawda, Yusif, 30, 132
Sayegh, Daoud, 109, 118
Sayyed, Jamil, 160–4, 174
Sayyed, Radwan el-, 47, 53, 56, 121
Schotte, Jan, 101, 103–4, 107, 111–2, 118–20
Selman, Faysal, 149
Selman, Talal, 58, 127
Sfeir, Nasrallah Boutros, 24, 29, 30, 56, 61, 62, 82, 92, 93, 101, 104, 115, 123, 138–40, 145–7, 152–6, 188–91
Shamseddine, Mohammed Mehdi, 36–7, 42–3, 52, 56, 58, 63, 113, 120, 124, 173, 176, 184, 204
Sharara, Waddah, 24, 43, 44–5, 47, 56
Shari'ah, 62, 170
Shiites, 26, 33–7, 41–3, 70, 72–3, 77, 80, 82, 85, 108, 124, 129, 144, 156, 167, 170, 176
Siking, Tom, 67, 110
Silvestrini, Achille, 84, 96, 99, 103–5, 114, 120
Sodano, Angelo, 92, 109, 114–5, 118, 153
St. Joseph University, 15, 22, 25, 67, 90, 109, 127, 133–4, 150
Sunnis, 25, 34–7, 70, 72, 77, 82, 84, 108, 124, 129, 156, 168, 170
Synod for Lebanon, 5, 7, 10, 27, 29, 49, 52, 53, 94, 100, 101–4, 107–21, 123, 124, 126, 130, 138, 184, 193
Syria, 9–10, 23, 37, 99, 108, 132, 134–5, 143, 154–6, 162–3, 184

Ta'if accords, 3, 6, 7, 21–2, 50, 59, 70–1, 83, 92, 100, 102–3, 108, 115, 130, 135, 137, 139, 142–4, 151–2, 162, 173–5
Takieddine, Halim, 42
Takla, Saliman Bechara, 17
Tantawi, Mohammad, 98
Tauran, Jean-Louis, 84, 87, 92, 96, 98, 99, 100, 109, 115–6, 153, 154, 183, 184, 207–8
Toufayli, Sobhi, 146
Tueni, Ghassan, 50, 61, 67, 195
Turk, Fouad, 71
Tyan, Elie, 21

Umma, 46, 169
United States, 7, 38, 147

Valognes, Jean-Pierre, 18
Vandrisse, Joseph, 116
Vatican II, 39, 104, 110, 115, 117
Vatican, the, 52, 73, 78, 84, 87, 92, 95–9, 103, 108–9, 116, 118, 120–1, 153, 156, 184, 191, 206–8
Veglio, Antonio Maria, 110, 196
Viorst, Milton, 215

Weigel, George, 191, 206
Wilayat al-faqih, 33, 149
Winslow, Charles, 59, 177, 215
Wojtyla, Karol, 100, 184. *See also* John Paul II, Pope
Wolf, Frank, 203

Yazegi, Nasif, 17

Zakhem, Sam, 72
Zeidan, Camille, 130
Zein, Ahmed 'Aref-, 31, 33
Zizola, Giancarlo, 206
Zoghbi, Phares, 24